Perfect Being Theology

Other titles in the Reason and Religion series:

Peter Byrne: *The Moral Interpretation of Religion*
ISBN 0 7486 0784 6

Stephen T. Davis: *God, Reason and Theistic Proofs*
ISBN 0 7486 0799 4

C. Stephen Evans: *Faith Beyond Reason*
ISBN 0 7486 0794 3

Paul Helm: *Faith and Understanding*
ISBN 0 7486 0922 9

Perfect Being Theology

Katherin A. Rogers

Edinburgh University Press

Edinburgh University Press Ltd
22 George Square, Edinburgh

Typeset in 11 on 13 pt Sabon
by Hewer Text Ltd, Edinburgh, and
printed and bound in Great Britain by
MPG Books Ltd, Bodmin

A CIP record for this book is
available from the British Library

ISBN 0 7486 1012 X (paperback)

Contents

Introduction

'Should I believe in God?' is perhaps the most practical question one can ask. But there is a question which must precede it: 'What does "God" mean?' Before one can reasonably judge *that* something exists, one needs to have some idea of *what* it is. Perfect being theology represents one method for answering the question, What is God? The starting assumption, shared by the vast majority of Westerners past and present, whether theist or atheist, is that a being who is the source of all and a worthy object of worship must be the most perfect being possible. A second assumption, confined to a considerably narrower segment of humanity, is the view that human reason can and should apply the tools of philosophy to unpacking the concept of a most perfect being possible.

A philosophically adequate analysis of the nature of God is the optimistic aim of this work. Our questions will include: What are the attributes of a perfect being? For example, must God be absolutely simple? Are these attributes inherently coherent? Does timelessness, for instance, make sense conceptually? Are these attributes consistent with one another? For example, if God exists outside of time, can He be omniscient and know what time it is *now*? Can a perfect being possess any limitations? Do the logically impossible? Sin? What would be the relationship between this perfect being and the world which it produces? What role does human freedom play in the system authored by this being? Why would a perfect being allow evil? These are just a few of the issues to be addressed in this attempt at perfect being theology.

I contend that this enterprise is not as wildly foolhardy as it might appear at first. True, the diminutive philosopher faces the task of exploring a subject infinite by definition . . . and we are not talking about some abstract mathematical infinity, but an infinite *person*, a person possessing power and knowledge and goodness without limit. A daunting object of inquiry! But fortunately we can follow a path that has already been carved out . . . and by giants. In this work I shall take the Middle Ages to be the Golden Age of perfect being theology, and Augustine of Hippo (354–430), Anselm of Canterbury (1033–1109), and Thomas Aquinas (1225–74) as the most successful proponents of the method.

This is not an exercise in intellectual history, though. My approach will be to bring the medievals into the present debate, arguing that their work provides the most adequate answers to the puzzles of perfect being theology. Many contemporary philosophers of religion will find this conclusion woefully wrongheaded. (If we were all in agreement there wouldn't be any point in making the case, would there?) I have consistently ended by defending the medieval position, but with respect to each of the issues in question I have tried to present the main arguments for the various opposing sides so that the reader can appreciate what the debate is about. And I have tried to cite the most important contemporary sources to provide the reader with a starting point for further investigation. Sometimes (only rarely!) I have felt forced to conclude that the medieval system has left some problems outstanding. This conclusion, though, may more often be a result of lapses in my own scholarship and analysis than of some lacuna in the thought of Augustine or Anselm or Aquinas.

I am very grateful to Paul Helm for asking me to write this book for his series, Reason and Religion, and especially thankful for his willingness to permit me to defend my own (medieval) approach. I thank him, too, for his painstaking, thoughtful and extremely helpful editorial advice. There are views in the book which he thinks are wrong, or at best extremely implausible, but thanks to his help I hope I have at least managed to express them more clearly. And thanks, too, to my colleagues Jeff Jordan and Michael Rea, whose work on my behalf far exceeded the call of collegial duty. Their analytic expertise in reading and commenting on the entire first draft of the manuscript has saved me from numerous philosophical gaffes. If blunders and unclarity remain the fault is mine. My gratitude also goes to Mary Imperatore and Gail Ross who have helped in innumerable ways with the preparation of the manuscript. Finally, thanks to the editors at Edinburgh University Press for their understanding in extending my deadline when illness and death in the family prevented me from following my original work schedule.

1

Why Perfect Being Theology?

Nine hundred years ago St. Anselm of Canterbury, then a monk in the monastery at Bec, prayed for a single, short argument by which to prove almost everything about God. He became so wrapped up in his search that he began to lose sleep and have trouble paying attention at divine services. He had just about resolved to give up the search, fearing it might be a temptation of the devil when, 'suddenly one night during matins the grace of God illuminated his heart, the whole matter became clear to his mind, and a great joy and exultation filled his inmost being'.[1] What he had received was the 'ontological' proof which he records in the second chapter of his *Proslogion*, and which is arguably the single most discussed argument in the history of the philosophy of the last thousand years. Anselm begins by defining God as 'that than which a greater cannot be conceived,' proceeds to prove that such a being must exist in reality, and then goes on, in the rest of the *Proslogion,* to a lucid and systematic analysis of the concept 'that than which a greater cannot be conceived'. Thus he began the method which today is called perfect being theology. In this first chapter I shall address the questions of why and how one might engage in continuing Anselm's work.

If one were not convinced of the divine sanction for this way of going about things, one might wonder if the analytic unpacking of a definition is really a fruitful way to approach and address the living God of the Judeo-Christian worldview. (I will be working within the Christian tradition, though as much of the discussion of the divine nature will be sufficiently general it could apply to Judaism and Islam.) Even if worship involves some intellectual grasp of the being worshipped, why start with the concept of 'that than which a greater cannot be conceived' rather than with a table of attributes listed in Scripture or gleaned from accounts of immediate experience of the divine? There is value in both alternatives, but without interpretation Scripture and accounts of immediate experience present a variety of images of God, sometimes jumbled or even contradictory. Neither can render the consistent and complete account which an adequate philosophy of God requires. It is the aim of this book to show that beginning with Anselm's concept of God will allow us to discover such an account.

Can we be sure that we have the right definition of God? Thomas V. Morris argues that it is intuitively obvious that God must be a perfect or best possible being.[2] (I take it that 'perfect' and 'best possible' are interchangeable for 'that than which a greater cannot be conceived' though 'greatest conceivable being' may not be, as we will see.) To my knowledge it is the case that in all the debates between various conceptions of the nature of God, none of the participants argues for a God whom they judge to be *less* than the best. For example, the process theologians who argue against the traditional view that God is eternal and immutable hold that it is neither possible nor desirable that God should be so transcendent. God is best in virtue of being engaged with the created universe and capable of becoming better than He is. *That* God is the best seems taken for granted. What that means is the subject of debate.

Further, if we are actively religious, then we not only think about God, we also worship Him. We judge God to be *worthy* of worship, and to be absolutely unique in this respect. We feel required to adopt an attitude towards God which would be entirely inappropriate if directed towards other things. God is superior to us in a radical way unparalled by anything else. But, as Anselm points out in Chapter 3 of the *Proslogion*, if we limited creatures could actually conceive of a being superior to God, some extra-divine standard to which we could judge that God had failed to measure up, 'then the creature would rise above the creator and be the judge of the creator, which is plainly absurd'.[3] A being than which *we* can conceive a greater could not be worthy of worship. Anselm goes on in *Proslogion* 15 to make the stronger case that even a being whose nature was limited to the best that we imperfect creatures can imagine would not be worthy of worship. We can certainly conceive that there is a being whose nature exceeds our mental capacities, and that being would be greater than the greatest we can imagine. The chapter is entitled, 'That [it] is greater than can be conceived'. We must define God as the best possible, otherwise we are imagining a finite being woefully limited by our own imperfections and hence undeserving of our worship. How we can possibly talk or think properly about a being whose nature transcends our capacities is another question, to be addressed in the next chapter.

Another reason for beginning with the assumption that God must be a perfect being is that it is this conception of God which (at least some of) the most adequate arguments for the existence of God prove. It has been popular in anglophone thought for the last two or three centuries, at least outside of Roman Catholic circles, to hold that the traditional proofs for the existence of God are unsound, invalid, or at best don't convince people. For a very long time we were told that the very language we used to talk about God was meaningless. However, as the history of philosophy has been told through most of the twentieth century, the death knell of a philosophically viable natural theology came with the work of Hume and Kant and their confreres. As the century ends, philosophy of religion is making a roaring comeback and Hume and Kant seem to be in retreat. Perhaps it is time to reexamine the pre-modern dictum that the existence of God can be proven. In any case, the standard proofs argue for the God of Anselm's definition. So if one is willing to allow that the standard proofs for the existence of God are, if not conclusive, at least plausible, it will follow that, if there is any God at all, it is most likely to be the best possible being of perfect being theology. I think this becomes clearer if one imagines, by way of contrast, trying to prove a lesser god.

Suppose we are wondering whether or not to commit ourselves to belief in Zeus or Odin. The most effective way to prove the existence of these lesser deities would be to come into contact with them, and even then one might have doubts. Speaking for myself it would not be enough to see Odin walking down the street, or even riding through the sky on his eight-legged steed, for me to commit to belief in him as that very Odin of Norse mythology. I am not sure what it would take, and, luckily, I do not expect it to be an issue. But suppose you did come into contact with Zeus or Odin in a way sufficient to convince you of their existence. If you then went on to investigate their natures, the only appropriate evidence to hand would be your experiences of these beings. You could not start with a concept or definition, entailed by your proof, and then unpack it to derive a philosophically adequate understanding of Odin or Zeus.

Things are different with Anselm's God. Consider some of the standard proofs for His existence. The various versions of the 'ontological' argument, beginning as they do with the definition of God as a perfect or maximally great or best possible being, obviously lead to the existence of a perfect being whose nature can be deduced from our concept. And a number of the causal arguments, depending on how they are cast, lead to a God who must be 'that than which a greater cannot be conceived'.

Aquinas' fourth way, for example, and myriad earlier Platonic proofs, appealing to some variant of the doctrine of participation, argue that all limited goods must have their source in a being which is the maximum possible of each. Even the standard proofs for a first cause of the existence of the things (cosmological arguments) and proofs arguing that design requires a designer (teleological arguments) which can proceed without any underlying nod to participation lead to a source of all which must transcend the limitations of the created universe. In my view these latter sorts of argument alone do not necessarily render a perfect being, but (depending on the version) they can point to the creator's having most of the attributes of Anselm's God. If contingent beings require a different sort of explanation then there must be an independent and necessary being. If the physical universe must be made and sustained by a transcendent source, it is unlikely that this source would be bound by the categories of the universe like time and space. If all that exists is kept in being by this source, then the source must be extremely powerful. If everything is related in an orderly fashion, this points to both unity and omniscience. All of these connections can be questioned, of course, and all of these attributes are the subject of energetic debate. Nonetheless, as will emerge throughout the course of this work, the reasons for believing that God must be a best possible or perfect being are closely related to the reasons for believing that there is a God at all.

If it is the case that many proofs for God prove a perfect being, that religious practice suggests a perfect being as the only object worthy of worship, and that the vast majority of philosophers who attempt to describe God take their own version of the divinity, whatever it may be, to be the best possible, then, it could be argued that in a sense almost any philosopher who is talking about God is doing perfect being theology. We will reserve the title of perfect being theologian for those who attempt a systematic analysis of the divine attributes beginning with the concept of God as limitless perfection. I will argue throughout the course of this book that some who attempt such analyses fall short of success. Whether these thinkers are doing perfect being theology inadequately, or have ceased doing it altogether, can be left an open question.

I should mention here that I am using 'God' as a descriptive name, a title such that anything than which a greater *can* be thought is just not God. William Alston has recently argued that it is better to view 'God' as a proper name which refers to the divine being of immediate experience and religious tradition. The practical advantages of such an approach, according to Alston, are

First, the primacy of direct reference provides a reassurance that God can be successfully referred to by the weak and foolish as well as by the wise and the proud . . . Second, the prospects for taking radically different religious traditions to all be referring to and worshiping the same God are greatly increased.[4]

I do not find these consequences advantageous. None of us can comprehend the intrinsic being of God, and there will be debate about what perfection involves, but if we are so 'weak and foolish' as to use the term 'God' of a being whom we judge to be imperfect and than whom we can conceive a better, I would say we are not really thinking of God at all. And is it really a positive consequence of Alston's proposal that worshippers of the petty, cruel and adulterous Zeus are really worshipping the same being as those who worship Anselm's God and vice versa?

In any case, it will not be necessary to canvas the debate since the arguments in this book can proceed on either understanding of how the term 'God' is used. If one party to the discussion of a particular attribute holds that the views of the other party are demeaning to God, then the one who takes 'God' to be a description may say that what the opposition has called 'God' is not really God at all, whereas the one who takes 'God' to be a proper name may say that the opposition has offered a picture of God which is entirely at odds with the reality. If one were a believer in the Judeo-Christian God who suddenly learned that it is in fact Odin who made and governs the universe, this would be equally horrifying, whether one described one's catastrophic discovery as finding out that there is no God, or as learning that God is completely different from what one had supposed.[5]

From the standpoint of both religious worship and philosophical consistency the method of perfect being theology seems a reasonable way to attempt to know God better. How, then, should we begin to unpack the concept of 'that than which a greater cannot be conceived'? Fortunately we can appeal to the work of the intellectual giants in the long and distinguished tradition of Western philosophy of religion. Though Anselm's is the first example of a clear and systematic attempt at perfect being theology, questions about the nature of the perfect source of our world pre-date Socrates and receive powerful and sophisticated analyses in the work of Plato and Aristotle. Plotinus, embracing both Platonic and Aristotelian doctrines, constructed a unified philosophical/religious system which would exercise a double impact on the medieval synthesis of reason and revelation; first through the work of Augustine, undoubtedly the most influential thinker in Western Christendom, and in a second reincarnation when his work, mistakenly attributed to Aristotle, was rediscovered by the great Islamic philosophers who had such a profound impact on European thought in the later Middle Ages. Plotinus' work is largely a philosophic/ mystical meditation on the nature of the transcendent source of all, the One, with the corollary issues of how we can think of and relate to such a being. When Augustine and later thinkers who were committed to the God of biblical revelation came to approach their faith in the light of Greek thought the result was what we can call the 'classical God of the Philosophers'. In this medieval tradition most philosophers agreed that certain attributes must be applied to 'that than which a greater cannot be conceived'. He is perfect unity, immutable and eternal. He is absolutely independent and necessarily existent. He is the omnipotent, omniscient and ubiquitous source of all. He is Being Itself and Goodness Itself. And He is a rational creator who does what He does as a matter of free choice out of love. It is adherence to this set of divine properties which distinguishes what I shall term 'traditional' perfect being theology.

In the Middle Ages and ever since, philosophers have raised serious questions about this analysis of the nature of God. Are the divine attributes internally incoherent or mutually inconsistent? Can the God of the Philosophers be the same as the God revealed in the Bible? Can we speak meaningfully about God at all? These issues are hotly argued among contemporary philosophers of religion, and I hope to advance the current debate by bringing to it the insights of the great medieval syntheses of reason and revelation.

But why should the contemporary philosopher, unmoved by antiquarian interests, bother with the work of these long-dead men? In my view, the medieval approach to philosophy of religion was more successful than the contemporary has yet proved to be. I see at least two reasons for this. First, the medievals were consciously systematic. They did not attempt to solve one philosophical puzzle in isolation and then move on to another as so often seems to be the *modus operandi* among contemporary analytic philosophers of religion. It is not surprising that present thinkers often find the traditional attributes confusing and inconsistent. Their focus on the trees makes it hard for them to see the forest, which in turn skews their understanding of the nature, role and relationship of the trees.

Second, the medievals had the backing of powerful epistemic and metaphysical systems. Both the Neoplatonism of Augustine and Anselm and the (Neoplatonic?) Aristotelianism of Aquinas provide all-encompassing frameworks within which to make sense of God and creation. Modern philosophy, the legacy of Hume and Kant, has told us we can't make sense out of much of anything. There were, of course, empiricially inspired sceptics in the Middle Ages. Algazali and Ockham, both fideists with empiricist leanings, present profound critiques of the enterprise of natural theology. However, their approach did not become dominant until much later. It is an approach which is antithetical to the attempt to offer a philosophical analysis of God and His relation to creation. Throughout the present work this point will be strengthened when it is seen how useful the medieval approach is for answering current questions. And perhaps this can serve as an inspiration to reexamine the pre-modern epistemology and metaphysics which may have a lot to offer the post-modern philosophical community.

Augustine, Anselm and Aquinas will be the medievals most frequently cited in this treatment of perfect being theology, though others will be mentioned throughout. For example, on the issues of divine foreknowledge and freedom William of Ockham's work is extremely important and very much at odds with the thought of his predecessors. I will argue that Ockham's views cannot support an adequate perfect being theology, but, assuming my criticisms are cogent, whether this brands Ockham a bad perfect being theologian or places him quite outside the fold is a matter of definition. In any case, my paradigm will be the approach taken by Augustine, Anselm and Aquinas.

Clearly for the European intellectual tradition (I do not say 'Western' since that includes the great medieval Islamic and Jewish thinkers of North Africa and the Middle East) Augustine and Aquinas are the most influential philosophers of the Middle Ages. The philosophies of both are firmly rooted in orthodox Christianity, and often we can treat their views on God as almost identical. They do, however, represent different epistemic and metaphysical approaches, which will be discussed when the differences bear on the issues at hand. Anselm, as even his most ardent fans must admit, does not have the breadth or the depth of Augustine or Aquinas. With respect to epistemology and metaphysics, though he does introduce a lucidly analytic method, in terms of content he follows squarely in the Augustinian Neoplatonic tradition.[6] But Anselm does have something which Augustine and Aquinas do not, and that is a very clearly spelled-out libertarian doctrine of human freedom. Augustine is certainly a *compatibilist*, and Aquinas is probably one. Both insist on the freedom of the human creature, but hold that the creature chooses what it most desires so that, given all the facts about a certain person in a certain situation, a particular choice may be free, but is nonetheless inevitable . Thus Augustine can say, for example, that the redeemed human being accepts God's grace freely, yet saving grace is absolutely irresistible. On the compatibilist analysis a host of puzzles with respect to the concept of a perfect being can be avoided. Free (in the compatibilist sense) creatures do not seem to interfere with divine omnipotence. Omniscience can encompass the future since God can know how He will manage everything including human motivations. But the problem of evil becomes acute. If God could have prevented all the moral evil in our world by controlling everyone's choices without infringing on anyone's freedom, why does He not do so? Augustine's answer is, 'God only knows'.[7] Anselm solves the problem of moral evil by appealing to the value of indeterminist freedom. Real human freedom, morally significant freedom, means open options. Though one chooses one way one really could have chosen otherwise. Thus the ultimate responsibility for a free choice rests with the creature. God literally *cannot* control a free choice. And then the problems with omnipotence and omniscience arise. Thus, while Anselm has neither the stature nor the influence of Augustine or Aquinas, he does represent a different and important perspective within the classic tradition, so his work is useful to the project of applying the medieval approach to contemporary problems in the philosophy of religion. My own view is that in the final analysis Anselm's version of perfect being theology is the most likely to allow for a satisfactory picture of God and creation.

A final methodological point; throughout this work I shall take the Bible seriously as the inerrant word of God. In the medieval tradition to which I am appealing this would have gone without saying, but in a contemporary philosophical discussion, it may need a word or two of justification. In anglophone philosophical circles the vast majority of theists are believers in the God of biblical revelation. There are a myriad answers to the questions of how and why a philosopher might come to this belief, but in any case the fact is that the God whom most of us *care* about is the one we associate with biblical revelation. So it is important to take the Bible seriously.

Clearly the Bible is not a philosophical document. Nonetheless the often asked question of whether the God of Abraham, Isaac and Jacob can be the God of the Philosophers, is a philosophical question and one which will pervade this work. What is this perceived tension between the God of the Bible and Anselm's Perfect Being? It is often said that the God of Augustine, Anselm and Aquinas, the immutable, eternal, transcendent source of all, cannot be the personal, loving God who acts as an agent in the world and takes an interest in individuals. Process theologians, prefering the latter image of the divine to the former, take this position to its extreme, thoroughly repudiating traditional perfect being theology. Charles Hartshorne writes, 'Classical theism is for me false a priori, a tragic error'.[8] Hartshorne holds that creatures have real power and produce real effects, even upon God. And this, in Hartshorne's view, classical theism takes to be impossible. Hartshorne's God is not separate from the world, but is rather the Soul of the world. His God is in time, acting and reacting through creation. God is always the best being that there is, but is constantly changing and becoming better. Process theology does not claim to adhere to a biblical conception of God and has moved far outside the fold of orthodoxy.

The scope of the present work does not permit an investigation of this challenge to classical Anselmianism, but the fundamental criticism is echoed by many philosophers of religion who do see themselves as participants in the orthodox tradition. The perfect being Anselm describes, beyond time and space and quite unlike us, seems too distant to hear us or to care.

William Alston notes a

> pervasive tension in Christian thought between 'the God of the philosophers and the God of the Bible', between God as 'wholly other' and God as a partner in interpersonal relationships, between God as the absolute, ultimate source of all being and God as the dominant actor on the stage of history.[9]

Thinkers in the classic tradition would be surprised to learn of this 'pervasive tension'. As philosophers and as believers they are unwaveringly committed to a God who is both the eternal source of all and the one who answers prayers. Both Anselm and Augustine frequently address God personally in the course of their philosophical writings, asking for help in their work, thanking Him when they have received it, or just praising God now that they have a clearer vision of His greatness. The first chapter of Anselm's *Proslogion* is an extended prayer, and the first premise of the argument in Chapter 2 is addressed to God. ' For we believe that *You* are that than which a greater cannot be conceived [my italics].' Chapter 4 concludes, 'Thank you, good Lord, thank you, because what before I believed through your gift, now I understand through your illumination, so that even if I did not want to believe that you exist, I could not fail to understand.' There is no doubt that Anselm saw himself as engaged in an immediate and personal relationship with God.

Had Anselm simply failed to see a tension between his philosophical life and his religious life? No. To believe that God is too transcendent, too infinite, to know or care about us here on planet Earth is to limit God. An omniscient God *must* have numbered the hairs on our heads! And perhaps it is a comment on our own times that so many contemporary philosophers see a tension between transcendent perfection and concern for creation.

The medievals take it for granted that love is a real power. Love is a virtue. God is Love. As Aquinas says, 'God loves all existing things . . . the love of God infuses and creates goodness in things'.[10]

Since we are used to spatial, temporal and limited manifestations of love and its corollaries such as mercy and forgiveness, it may be hard to envision how an eternal and infinite person exhibits these qualities. It will be an especially vexed question whether or how creatures can affect an omnipotent, absolutely independent creator. I will deal with these issues throughout this work. But God's loving concern is as non-negotiable a perfection as omnipotence or omniscience in the classic tradition. In fact Anselm himself goes about as far in this direction as a philosopher can go. In *Why God Became Man* he argues that, given the goodness of God and the state of human affairs, it was necessary that God become Christ and die for our salvation. The 'God of the Philosophers' would not be 'that than which a greater cannot be conceived' were He not also the God of biblical revelation. In the next chapter I will offer a quick sketch of this perfect being and introduce the difficulties we can expect to encounter as we work through the analysis of His nature.

NOTES

1. Eadmer, *Life of Saint Anselm Archbishop of Canterbury*, p. 30.
2. Thomas V. Morris, 'Perfect Being Theology', pp. 19–30.
3. Translations are my own unless otherwise noted.
4. William Alston, *Divine Nature and Human Language*, p. 115.
5. Michael Durrant offers a defense of the descriptivist approach in 'The Meaning of "God" – I'.
6. See my *The Neoplatonic Metaphysics and Epistemology of Anselm of Canterbury*.
7. *On the Literal Meaning of Genesis* XI, X, 13.
8. Charles Hartshorne, 'Grounds for believing in God's existence', p. 17.
9. Alston, *Divine Nature and Human Language*, p. 147.
10. Thomas Aquinas, *Summa Theologiae* (henceforth ST) I, Q.20, art.2 (I will be using the translation in *Basic Writings of Saint Thomas Aquinas*, trans. Anton C. Pegis).

2

Perfection and Its Problems

Suppose we allow that God is 'that than which a greater cannot be conceived'. Can we unpack this concept to come to a coherent view of the divine? According to Anselm this definition entails that God must actually be *greater* than we can conceive. Doesn't this mean that our attempt is doomed at the outset? In this chapter, after a quick sketch of how to begin the project of perfect being theology, I will discuss how it is possible for the limited creature to speak and think of the limitless creator, and then outline the list of attributes traditionally applied to 'that than which a greater cannot be conceived' with a quick explanation of why these attributes are seen as necessary to God. I shall conclude with a preview of the various problems that are raised against this picture of a perfect being in contemporary philosophy of religion.

How, then, to describe a perfect being? We can begin with two principles, which, according to the tradition, at least as developed by Aquinas, boil down to the same thing. First, as the source of all, God is *unlimited*. Any quality that would entail a limitation is to be denied of Him. Thus, for example, medieval and (most) contemporary philosophers of religion agree that God is incorporeal since being embodied is a limitation. The scope of the activity of those of us with bodies is confined to the capacities of those bodies. For example, even a body which encompassed the entire universe could not be *wholly* present everywhere at once. Any quality which is inherently limiting will be denied of God, and any perfection attributed to God will be attributed in an unlimited degree.

Interestingly, the earlier medievals seem to steer clear of using the term 'infinite' of God. Perhaps this is a holdover from the ancient association of 'infinite' with 'incomplete', 'unfinished' and hence imperfect. Anselm, writing at the end of the eleventh and beginning of the twelfth centuries uses variations on *infinitus* rarely, and does not describe the divine nature as 'infinite' in his philosophical works.[1] By the time of Aquinas in the mid-thirteenth century it is commonplace to speak of God as infinite in his very Being.[2] I shall use the term 'infinite' in connection with the traditional view of God, and I think it is safe to hold that, though the earlier philosophers do not use the term, this is not evidence of a fundamental shift with regard to basic beliefs about the divine nature. In *Proslogion* 20 Anselm says that God is 'before and beyond everything' and 'by no means has an end'. Here he is talking mainly about God and time, but I think it is fair to say that he would agree that there is 'no end' to God's wisdom, power, and so on.

A second principle, enunciated by Anselm in Chapter 5 of the *Proslogion*, is that 'God is whatever it is better to be than not to be'. In the contemporary idiom, God must possess every 'great-making' property. The problem lies in deciding which properties are 'great-making'. Both in the past, and today, the enumeration of great-making properties has proceeded largely on the basis of intuition. For example, you 'just see' that something possessing reason is superior to something which does not. True, the medieval philosophers in the tradition which we are drawing upon could have added that, since existence is good, the more there is to you, the better. The ability to reason adds a new dimension to the manner of one's existing, and so rationality is a great-making property because the being with life *and* rationality has more to it than the being which is merely alive. (The notion of degrees of existence will be defended in Chapter 3.) I find this plausible and hope that our analysis of the nature of the perfect being will make this view more persuasive to the contemporary reader than it may seem at first glance, but I fear that we can never quite escape the need for intuition. This may just be the nature of things when it comes to values. If you do not see that it is better to be able to do things and to think than not, that a cat is better than a rock, and a human better than a pig, it may be difficult to convince you.[3]

Fortunately there is a core of agreement among the majority of philosophers of religion, medieval and contemporary. Everybody seems willing to allow that God is knowledgeable, powerful, good and a free agent. With respect to these attributes the questions that will arise will concern their scope and nature. But there are other attributes where the issue will be whether or not they should be considered 'great-making' properties at all. There are those who do not see any value to the traditional attributes of divine unity, eternity and immutability. Some, most notably process theologians like Charles Hartshorne, see multiplicity, temporality and changeableness as virtues, inextricably bound up with the concept of a God who is really related to His creatures. How can such a conflict of intuitions be resolved? I shall argue for the tradition by presenting the motivation for seeing the debatable attributes as great-making properties and trying to show that, properly understood, they do not conflict with seeing God as the loving, personal being to whom we pray. I shall try to show that, while the critic of the classic tradition is right to insist that a distant and impersonal deity could not be all that our living God must be, he is wrong in failing to recognize that the classic tradition insists upon this point, as well. Throughout this discussion I will be, of necessity, working from a core of beliefs grounded in intuition, but there will still be plenty to argue about.

A perfect being, then, must have all the great-making properties and He must have them to an unlimited extent. Recently these core principles of perfect being theology have been challenged. Some contemporary philosophers of religion suggest that it is just impossible that God possess all the great-making properties in the highest possible degree. For example, there is the puzzle of whether or not God can make a being with a secret unknown even to Him. If not, He is not omnipotent. If so, He is not omniscient. We could solve the paradox by abandoning the tradition, choosing which trait is more important for a greatest possible being, knowledge or power, and just allow that God is limited with regard to the less important trait.[4]

Even setting aside the practical difficulty in deciding what degrees of which attributes are necessary to perfection, there are a number of serious problems with this approach. First, is this God adequate as the object of religious worship? Defenders of this position seem to allow, for example, that since a perfect being must be virtuous, and a virtuous being would not do bad things, God is less powerful than a being who can do both good and bad things. Surely from the religious point of view it is shocking to suggest that there could be a being more powerful than God.[5]

It could be insisted that we must accept a God who is so radically limited since this is the only way to resolve the various puzzles raised by the concept of a perfect being. I shall argue, however, that it is possible to resolve the paradoxes and leave God's infinite perfection and absolute sovereignty intact. This is important because the view that God possesses great-making properties, but to only a limited extent, entails consequences which are fundamentally at odds with the traditional understanding which insists that God is the perfectly unified and absolutely independent source of all. The tradition holds that creatures possess being and power and wisdom and justice and every other perfection because they receive them from God. The perfections in creatures are a limited participation of the ultimate source. Though it is sometimes necessary for us to use the language of 'having' or 'possessing', God does not 'possess' these perfections. It is not that there is God and then, added on, various 'perfect-making' properties. As the absolute source and standard He just *is* all those perfections which flow forth to be reflected more or less in creatures. God is Being and Power and Wisdom and Justice, and so on. The first chapter of Anselm's *Monologion* begins with the classic Platonic proof for God which moves from the existence of things possessing varying degrees of goodness to the existence of a source which must be maximally good, and succeeding chapters argue similarly for other perfections. In Chapter 5 of the *Proslogion*, after he has shown that 'that than which a greater cannot be conceived' must exist, he asks rhetorically, 'Therefore what good could be lacking from this highest good, through which all goods exist?' The Being which *is* Goodness and the source of all goodness could not 'have' goodness (note that in Anselm's terms all perfections are 'goods') to a greater or lesser degree.

This understanding of God and His relationship to His 'great-making' properties and to His creation, which we will be unpacking throughout this book, is the standard medieval view of the Augustinian Neoplatonists and the more Aristotelian thinkers as well. Aquinas is adamant that God, as the first efficient cause, is pure actuality which equals absolute perfection, no lack in anything. All perfections pre-exist in God, since 'nothing of the perfection of being can be wanting to Him Who is subsisting being itself'.[6] He writes, quoting the Pseudo-Dionysius with approval, 'God does not exist in a certain way; he possesses, and this before all others, all being within Himself absolutely and limitlessly'.[7]

The contemporary philosopher, of course, is free to reject the medieval approach, but one should not reject it without having at least considered it. And if one ends up deciding that Augustine and Anselm and Aquinas are fundamentally mistaken, then, in the interests of clarity, one should note that the God one has in mind is not the traditional God of the medieval philosophers. More importantly, *if* a coherent analysis of Anselm's God, the one who just is all the 'great-making' properties to the highest degree, can be offered, then surely the proposed limited divinity will have to yield pride of place to it.

Throughout this book I will argue that it is the medieval approach, with its metaphysical views on the nature of the source of all, that best solves the various paradoxes raised by the notion of a perfect being. For example, on Anselm's analysis it is immediately obvious that God, though omnipotent, cannot make someone who possesses a secret unknown to Him. Anselm's solution to the puzzle lies in an understanding of divine simplicity, so I will save consideration of it until the next chapter. Suffice it to say here that this divine 'inability' does not limit God's omnipotence in the least.

'That than which a greater cannot be conceived' is limitless, and possesses all the great-making properties to the highest degree or infinitely. In the traditional view, God, as source, actually *is* the perfections in question, and is all of them in a perfectly unified way. But now we are confronted with a perennial problem in the philosophy of religion. God is a very different sort of being from those with which we are usually concerned. How do our words apply to God? The medievals devoted a great deal of thought to this question and suggested a variety of sophisticated answers which form the foundation of the discussion to the present day.[8] To my knowledge the solutions they offered have not been superseded by any new and improved versions, so a quick canvas of the most viable of the medieval analyses of religious language should provide us with enough background to proceed.

Plotinus calls the source of all the One, and sees it as so transcendent that it is beyond all positive terms, even Being. In answer to the question of how we can speak of or describe such a thing, he responds, 'We can't.' We can seek union with the One in a mystical vision beyond reason, but we cannot talk about it. The philosophers of the Book could not go this route. The Bible speaks of God and insists that we do so in our forms of worship. We must apply our language to God. The question is, what do our terms *mean*.

Maimonides, the great twelfth-century Jewish philosopher, agrees that we must use the words employed in our sacred writing, but we do not use them to describe God positively as He is in Himself. God is absolute unity and completely unrelated to His creation. Maimonides explains in Chapter 52 of Book I of his *Guide for the Perplexed* that the tradition legitimates the application of certain terms to God, but the meaning of these terms must be negative or causal. Thus when we say that, 'God is good', we may mean, negatively, that He is not bad. It is not that God is like the goodness that we know, only much more so. 'Good' simply means not bad. It does not tell us anything positive at all about what God is like. On Maimonides' causal analysis, terms applied to God mean to indicate what He has caused. That is, to say that 'God is good' is to say that He is the cause of good things, but Maimonides insists that we cannot move from the effect to saying anything at all about the nature of the cause. Maimonides' analysis of biblical language leaves us unable to talk about God as He is.

This seems a very difficult position for the believer who is commanded to love and worship the Lord. How can we love something if we have no idea at all of what it is? As Aquinas notes, these purely negative or causal meanings are certainly not what we ordinarily intend when we speak of God. And if all attributes had a merely negative or causal meaning then any term would be as appropriate as any other. The term 'body' would be as apt as the term 'good' with respect to God since all we could mean by 'God is body' is 'He is not pure potentiality' or 'He is the cause of bodies'. Both of these statements are as correct as the purely negative or causal meanings of 'God is good', that is, 'God is not bad' and 'God is the cause of good things'.[9]

Fortunately for the future of perfect being theology, there do seem to be adequate ways of bridging the gulf between creature and creator and solving the problem of religious language. Here we can look only very briefly at three suggestions, rooted in the three different epistemologies of Anselm, Aquinas and Duns Scotus. (Scotus was a fourteenth-century philosopher who, though he sometimes used the thought of Aristotle, defended certain theses central to the Augustinian tradition, like extreme realism, the self-evidence of God and the possibility of univocal predication. We will see in Chapter 7 that he departs from both the Augustinians and the Aristotelians in his acceptance of voluntarism.) Anselm argues that we can speak of God univocally, that is, the words we use of God have the same meaning as when we use them of creatures. True, God and creatures are very different, but if a term is properly applicable to both then its significance must be sufficiently general to span the gap. An elephant is very different from a gnat, but the term 'animal' is applied univocally to both.[10] And this position follows directly from his metaphysics and epistemology. Anselm's thought falls squarely in the tradition of Augustinian Neoplatonism in which the basic relationship of creation to Creator is one of participation, and the most fundamental epistemic fact is divine illumination.

Participation means that every good quality which is possessed by a creature is possessed through some sort of 'reflecting' or 'sharing in' the nature of the divine. The relationship is closer than that of copies to the original blueprint or mirror images to the object reflected but stops short, *well* short, of identity. The divine transcends its created image even as it pervades it. If this all sounds too vague and metaphorical, the Platonist can respond that it is just very difficult to describe a causal relationship which is *sui generis* and in which the cause is God. For the purposes of the analysis of religious language, the important feature is that it is in fact the same perfection which creatures reflect and which God just *is*.

Although the perfections in question are not sensible qualities, they have no color or smell, and so on, we can recognize them in creatures because we have received knowledge directly from the source of all through divine illumination. We recognize wisdom and justice and goodness in things because we already have the idea of them in our minds, 'implanted' by God. Because of this inner knowledge we can appreciate goodness *per se* and hence apply the term 'good' to the creature in which it exists as limited and reflected and to the Creator in which it exists as identical with His nature. Anselm is adamant that the terms we use of the perfections in God and creatures are sufficiently general to cover both the unlimited cause and the created effects.[11]

Aquinas has a more difficult task when it comes to defending the view that we can speak positively, not just causally or negatively, of God's nature, 'substantially' in Thomas's terms. He insists that, barring a miracle, all our knowledge, beliefs, concepts and so on begin with experience. We have no immediate experience of God. Our understanding of the terms we use for God is drawn from our observation of creatures. But if God is infinite and perfectly unified, how could our concept of an attribute, derived from the limited creature, be properly applied to God? It cannot be applied univocally, Aquinas holds, but nonetheless we can speak properly and substantially of God so long as we recognize that our language applies analogically.

In analyzing the signification of an attributive term there are two things to be considered. There is the *res significata*, the very attribute signified, and there is the *modus significandi*, the way in which the term can be applied to the particular kind of thing in question. According to Aquinas when we use a term of very different kinds of things, the *modus significandi* changes, and so the meaning cannot be exactly the same. Thus when we say, 'The dog is good' and 'God is good' the *res significata* of the term 'good' is the same, it is goodness. We are justified in ascribing the same attribute to God and the creature because of the causal relationship between the two.[12] However, because God is infinite and unified the *modus significandi* of a term applied to God and creatures is different. We cannot possibly comprehend just *how* God is good, and so although we do have an understanding of goodness, there is inevitably a vagueness and inadequacy when we use the term of the perfect being. Contemporary philosophers of religion can exploit this insistence upon the inadequacy of our concepts when applied to God to explain why it may be impossible to express certain difficult positions with perfect clarity. Care must be taken, though, to retain the notion that there is some sameness of significance when we apply our empirically grounded terms to God. Just how Thomas himself balanced the sameness and the difference, and how they ought to be balanced, are the subject of debate among contemporary students of Aquinas.[13]

Scotus, writing in the fourteenth century, offers an interesting reconciliation between Anselm's doctrine of univocity and Aquinas' epistemology. Scotus agrees with the Aristotelians that we learn through abstraction from sense data. The question is, what exactly is the content of our abstracted concept? Aquinas held that our understanding of the meaning of the term 'good' must inevitably involve goodness as it exists in creatures. Hence we can speak of God only analogically. Scotus disagrees. He argues that in order for us to speak properly of God, there must be some underlying sameness, genuinely applicable to the creature and God, which we are capable of grasping. For example, God is not good as a dog is good. If we cannot move beyond understanding 'good' except insofar as it applies to the dog and other good creatures, then we cannot properly use the term of God. Fortunately, though our concepts are produced by abstraction from sense data, we are capable of abstracting concepts of sufficient generality that they can apply univocally to God and creatures. We get our concept of wisdom, for example, from observing creatures. In creatures wisdom is limited. Wisdom *per se*, however, is neither limited nor unlimited. Wisdom is just wisdom. When we abstract the concept we can strip it, *in intellectu*, of all the imperfections which accompany wisdom in the creature but which are not part of the definition of 'wisdom'. Thus we come to a concept of perfect and unlimited wisdom, the wisdom of God. This is not to say that the limited knower can fully comprehend what it is to be perfectly wise. We cannot imagine or somehow 'picture' perfect wisdom, what it is like to be perfectly wise, but we can grasp the concept 'perfect wisdom' enough to apply it properly to God.[14] To borrow an analogous example from Anselm, though by definition we cannot comprehend an ineffable being, we nonetheless understand the term 'ineffable'.[15] Among contemporary philosophers of religion William Alston argues for this Scotist approach.[16] The practice of religion demands that we be able to speak and think about God, and there are systematic philosophical analyses which suggest ways in which this can be done. Anselm and Scotus are perhaps a bit more optimistic than Aquinas, but even the analogical approach insists that we can speak literally and positively about God. From this point on I shall take it that when we apply attributes to God we are speaking of God Himself and we know (albeit in a limited or perhaps analogical way) what we are talking about.

It will be useful now to sketch the great-making properties which 'that than which a greater cannot be conceived' must possess. (I do not claim that this list is exhaustive.) There is an important reason for this. We limited and temporal creatures must examine these attributes piecemeal. In God they are one and identical to His nature. If one tries to analyze one attribute in isolation from the rest one inevitably fails to comprehend it properly. Too often contemporary analytic philosophy of religion works to solve this or that puzzle concerning some attribute of God but fails to take into account the relationship (that is, identity) of the attributes to one another and to God. I hope to minimize the problem by offering an outline of the key great-making properties which the reader can keep in mind as we work through the individual properties in detail in the rest of this book. This should enable us to approach perfect being theology more as a systematic whole, than as a series of isolated problems. I will conclude the chapter by noting a number of problems that will be raised against this Anselmian conception of God.

A great-making property which the classic tradition viewed as perhaps the most important, certainly non-negotiable, and which many contemporary analytic philosophers of religion seem content to jettison is simplicity. (The more detailed analysis of divine simplicity will entail that terms like 'property', 'attribute' and their synonyms are not accurate without serious qualification. Let them stand for now, in the interests of expediency.) God is perfect unity. This is the attribute to which Aquinas, in the *Summa Theologiae,* moves immediately upon having proved the existence of God. And, contrary to Peter Geach's interpretation, when Aquinas says that God is 'one' he certainly does not mean just that there are not several Gods.[17] In that case one might as well say that Peter Geach possesses simplicity just as God does, since there are not many Peter Geaches. What Aquinas means is that there is absolutely no multiplicity or composition in God. All the qualities which we attribute to God are identical to one another and to God Himself.

Why say this? Anselm's argument is simple. It is a weakness to be corruptible. Anything that can be taken apart is corruptible. Anything made of parts can be taken apart, if not in reality at least *in intellectu*. So if God were thought to be composite, we could think of His destruction. But then we could think of something greater, an absolutely indestructible being. QED.[18] Aquinas goes down the list of the various ways in which something could be composite, and shows that each of them involves the composite being in some sort of limitation or dependence on something else. So the perfect being must transcend all multiplicity, even that of a duality between essence and existence. God just *is* His very act of existing.[19] I will defend this difficult doctrine in the next chapter. Once the doctrine of divine simplicity can be appreciated and embraced, many of the apparent paradoxes raised against the Anselmian conception of God can be resolved.

God's essence (nature) is to exist, which is to say that He is a necessary

being. If He exists then He *must* exist. Whether or not this entails that His
non-existence is unthinkable, as Anselm argues, has been the subject of
debate for the past 900 years. Another way of arguing for divine necessity is
from God's absolute independence. In the classic tradition individual
things are either necessary or contingent (with various possible qualifications in either case), and to be contingent is to be caused and dependent,
since for anything that might or might not exist, an explanation is required
for its being there at all. Whether or not contingent things require causal
explanations is one of those perennial debates in modern philosophy, but
contemporary philosophers of religion seem to accept the judgement of
their predecessors that God must be uncaused and that it is greater to exist
necessarily (one current way to put it is, 'God must exist in all possible
worlds') than contingently.

Contemporary philosophers have been less willing to accept the tradition's insistence that God be immutable. According to Augustine and
Anselm and Aquinas God does not change. This does not mean just that
God's basic nature remains the same while His knowledge and activities
can differ over time. Anselm's God is perfectly simple. His knowledge and
activities are one with His nature. For God to come to know something or
to do this and then that would be for Him to change in His very being. And
that is quite impossible. God is the absolute best. He 'possesses' all the
great-making properties to the highest degree. If He were to change He
could only become a lesser being. In this traditional view of perfection
there is no room for lateral motion. But if He *could* become a lesser being,
He is corruptible. And if He is corruptible He is not 'that than which a
greater cannot be conceived'. The God of the classic tradition does not and
'could not' change.

Not only is God immutable, He is also impassive. He does not suffer
pain or sorrow. Augustine and Aquinas even seem to hold that God is not
at all affected by human activities. Augustine argues from God's omnipotence that nothing happens in the world which is not entirely under
God's control. Aquinas defends divine impassivity by pointing out that if
God, as the best, is pure actuality, there can be no unrealized potential in
Him. For us to act upon God would be for us to produce in Him some
motion from potential to actual, which is absurd. Obviously there are
difficulties here for the believer in a loving God. It may be possible, within
Thomas's metaphysics, to reconcile God as a pure act of being with the
loving Father who answers prayers. In any case the tradition does offer
another approach in the work of Anselm who insists not only that God
does but also that there is a sense in which He *must* respond to the actions
of His creatures.

Another divine attribute which most of the medievals accepted and which many contemporary philosophers reject is eternity. It is not enough to say that God is everlasting, that is that He has always existed in the past and will always exist in the future. God is eternal. He is outside of time. All of time is immediately present to God but He is not temporal. There are a number of reasons for saying this. For one thing, to be temporal is to change. A genuinely immutable being does not change even with respect to temporal location. God is unlimited. To be temporal is to exist only in this present instant, this extentionless point where the yet-to-exist future becomes the gone-forever past. The only bit of our lives to which we temporal beings have access or which we have power over is this almost non-existent present slice. God, in contrast, possesses all of Himself at once and has access to and power over everything, everywhere, always. As absolute source of all, God must transcend the limitations of His creation. The medieval philosophers and the contemporary physicists tell us that time and space are categories of the physical universe, ways of describing the relationships between physical beings. God, as creator, cannot be bound by the categories He has made. (That God is non-physical has not been questioned by the orthodox, medieval or modern, and so we will spend almost no time in defending what no one disputes.) Seeing God as eternal solves a number of apparent paradoxes. How could an immutable being also be a creator? By doing all He does immutably in His eternal 'now'. How could God know future free choices? By 'seeing' them from His eternal 'present' as they are being made.

The attributes of omnipotence, omniscience and omnibenevolence have been less controversial than the ones listed above. Almost everyone agrees that it is best for God to be as knowledgeable as possible and as powerful as possible. And no one doubts that 'that than which a greater cannot be conceived' must be *very* good in some sense of 'good' related to moral goodness. This last attribute raises the very difficult problem of why a good God permits evil, but no one doubts that goodness must be among the qualities of God. The problems with the knowledge, power and goodness of God arise as a result of the paradoxes generated when we try to analyze just what they entail and especially when we ascribe them all to the same being. Finally, everyone engaged in the project of perfect being theology agrees that God is the Creator of our world. Almost everyone holds that He is a person who creates through a free act of will. Again the questions revolve around just what this entails, and how to view God's creative activity in the light of all the other attributes ascribed to Him.

The objections raised against this conception of God are legion. Here let me offer a quick preview of the sort of problems to expect. It is common nowadays to hold that some of the great-making properties are inherently incoherent. Swinburne, for example, dismisses the idea that God is eternal, saying that he 'cannot make much sense of this suggestion'. (And he is content with the corollary 'refinement' of God's omniscience which involves denying divine foreknowledge, since a temporal God can't know future free choices.)[20] The doctrine of divine simplicity has been widely repudiated since it is taken to mean that, if God just *is* His goodness, knowledge and so on then He is a property. And it makes no sense to hold that a person is a property.

A second sort of criticism involves the view that attributes ascribed to God are mutually inconsistent. Here are a few examples. A simple being cannot know and do many things, as required by omniscience, omnipotence and creativity. An eternal being cannot know what time it is now, and hence cannot be omniscient. A necessarily good being could not do evil, and hence could not be omnipotent. No being could be both omniscient and omnipotent since an omnipotent being could make a creature who had a secret unknown to anyone but itself, while an omniscient being must know every secret. We can defend God's goodness only by holding that He could not prevent the evil choices of His free creatures, but if our choices are outside of God's control then He is not omnipotent. If God is morally good, then He must choose freely, but if He is necessarily the best then He cannot do other than the best, so God is not morally good. And what sense does it make to speak of 'choice' at all, in the case of an eternal and immutable being?

A third difficulty was noted at the end of the last chapter. Even supposing we can make sense of the great-making properties and show them to be mutually consistent, won't the concept of God at which we arrive be so distant from religious experience as to be . . . useless? What relevance could this eternal, immutable, impassive being have to us? This transcendent stranger can hardly be supposed to listen to our prayers. For us, what difference does it make whether or not such a being exists? This is a criticism that is often raised against the Anselmian approach, and I shall attempt to answer it throughout this work. Here suffice it to say that God's love, to be treated under the headings of 'Goodness' and 'Creation', is as necessary a property as any other. God cares about you and me, He listens to our prayers . . . and He does it impassively, immutably and eternally.

NOTES

1. See Gillian Evans (ed.), *A Concordance to the Works of St. Anselm*.
2. For a discussion of this change in attitude towards *infinitus* see Leo Sweeney, *Divine Infinity in Greek and Medieval Thought*, pp. 319–36.
3. I do make some attempt in 'The medieval approach to aardvarks, escalators and God'.

4. This is the approach taken by George Schlesinger in *New Perspectives on Old-Time Religion*. He presents the 'unknown secret' example in 'Divine Perfection'.
5. See, for example, Melissa Franklin, 'The indispensability of the single-divine-attribute doctrine', p. 434.
6. ST I, Q.IV, art.2.
7. Thomas Aquinas, *Summa Contra Gentiles* (henceforth SCG) Book I, Chapter 28, 9 (I am following the translation of Anton C. Pegis, University of Notre Dame edition).
8. Much of the modern discussion is carried on among Thomists (followers of Thomas Aquinas) and those conversant with the Thomistic approach like James Ross, *Portraying Analogy*. Among other contemporary philosophers of religion, it is probably William Alston who offers the most sustained discussion of religious language. In his *Divine Nature and Human Language* he argues for speaking about God literally, as opposed to metaphorically (pp. 17–63) and suggests how to go about doing so (pp. 64–102).
9. ST I, Q.XIII, art.2.
10. Anselm makes this case in discussing 'freedom' in *On the Freedom of the Will* 1 and 'justice' in *On Truth* 12.
11. See Chapter 5 of my *Neoplatonic Metaphysics and Epistemology of Anselm of Canterbury*.
12. See John Wippel, 'Thomas Aquinas and participation'.
13. See W. Norris Clarke, 'Analogy and the meaningfulness of language about God'; Ralph McInerny, *Studies in Analogy*; James Ross, 'Analogy as a rule of meaning for religious language'; John F. Wippel, 'Thomas Aquinas on what philosophers can know about God'.
14. Duns Scotus, *Oxford Commentary on the Four Books of the Sentences*, Book I, Distinction III, Questions 1 and 2.
15. Anselm, *Response to Gaunilo* IX.
16. William Alston, 'Aquinas on theological predication', p. 175.
17. Peter Geach, 'The meaning of "God" – II', p. 87.
18. Anselm, *Proslogion* 18.
19. ST I, Q.3, art.7.
20. Richard Swinburne, *Is There a God?*, pp. 8–9.

3

Divine Simplicity

Thomas Aquinas, in his *Summa Theologiae*, having proved the existence of God, moves at once to proving His simplicity.[1] For the first two thousand years of Western philosophy, just about everybody, from Parmenides on, who argues that there is a perfect source of all, argues that that source is absolutely unified. To be composite or complex in any way at all is to be limited. And the unity in question is more than just a lack of parts, corporeal or incorporeal. The perfect being of the Western tradition is so simple that He cannot be said even to 'have' a number of individual qualities. The classic tradition identifies God with His attributes and identifies each attribute with the rest. Thus Augustine in *The City of God* XI, 10 says that whatever a simple being has it just *is*. Anselm entitles Chapter 16 of the *Monologion*,

> That it is the same for [the Supreme Being] to be just, as it is for it to be justice; and the same for those other things that can similarly be said of it; and that none of these show how it is or how much it is (*qualis . . . vel quanta*), but what it is.

And Aquinas writes (ST I, Q.3, art.3), 'He must be His own Godhead, His own Life, and whatever else is so predicated of Him.' Strictly speaking, God is not (for example) wise, and powerful and good. He is Wisdom and Power and Goodness, and the three are identical.

Many contemporary analytic philosophers of religion have found this view of God's nature radically implausible.[2] This may be due in part to the fact that the traditional concept has been almost universally misunderstood in the present debate. Even those who defend a doctrine of divine simplicity almost always fail to present it in the powerful version expressed best by Aquinas, but found very clearly in earlier thinkers like Anselm.[3] The mistake is in failing to see that God is not a property but an act. In this chapter I will present some motivations for accepting the doctrine of divine simplicity, look at some contemporary criticisms, and show how the traditional doctrine does not fall prey to them. I shall try to mitigate the doctrine's *prima facie* bizarreness through analogies with human experience. Even if I succeed in making the traditional view seem plausible, there are difficult corollaries. It will prove worthwhile to explore ways in which the difficulties can be minimized because the doctrine of simplicity plays a vital role in perfect being theology and should not be abandoned except at the greatest need.

Why adopt the doctrine of divine simplicity? A perfect being must be unlimited, but to be composite or complex is to be limited. There are some sorts of composition where this is easily seen, and no one debates about it. One of the reasons to deny corporeality to God is that to be a body is to be composed of extended material parts, and so to be divisible and hence destructible.[4] No one, classical or contemporary, argues that God is a corporeal being. The classic position, though, goes far beyond a mere denial of divine corporeality and insists that there is no multiplicity of any kind in God. Why say this?

In Chapter 2 I mentioned Anselm's short argument from *Proslogion* 18 that if God can be thought to have any sort of parts at all then He can be thought to be corruptible, at least *in intellectu*. Thus we can think of a better being, one who cannot be dismantled even in the mind, and hence that than which a greater cannot be conceived must be completely simple. This probably strikes the modern reader as far too quick, especially as a 'proof' for a view which many find so counterintuitive.

An argument which seems to resonate much more powerfully today is the one drawn from divine aseity. In order to be perfect God must not depend for His existence on anything else. He must exist absolutely *a se*, from Himself. But if we posit that God *has* the properties of (for example) wisdom, power and goodness, and indeed *must* have them in order to exist as God, but we hold that these are not identical with Him, then are we not forced to the conclusion that God's existence is dependent upon things other than Himself? Anselm, in the *Monologion*, casts this argument in the Platonic mold.[5] Aquinas makes roughly the same argument in the *Summa Theologiae* (I Q.3, art.7) and Brian Leftow presents a very persuasive contemporary version.[6] Even those who reject the doctrine of divine simplicity feel the force of the argument. Plantinga writes,

Now I think the intuition – call it the sovereignty-aseity intuition – underlying the doctrine of divine simplicity must be taken with real seriousness. Suppose God has essentially the property of being omnipotent and suppose that property is an object distinct from him, is uncreated by him and exists necessarily. Then in some sense he does depend on that property. For in the first place he could not have existed if it had not; its existence is a necessary condition of his existence. And secondly he couldn't have the character he does have, couldn't be the way he is, if omnipotence didn't exist or weren't the way *it* is.[7]

Plantinga finds what he calls the 'Thomist' doctrine of divine simplicity unacceptable, and concludes that God does not exist absolutely *a se*.[8]

Aseity and simplicity are important, not only intrinsically, but also because they can help solve other puzzles. For example, consider the problem Plato raises in the *Euthyphro*. Is the good whatever God wills, or does God will what He wills because it is good? If the former, ethics seems to be a matter of arbitrary, if divine, fiat. But if the latter there is an ethical code external to God to which He must conform to be good. (He does not exist *a se* with respect to his goodness.) The doctrine of simplicity solves the problem. God neither obeys the moral order, nor does He invent it. He is Goodness Itself, and all else that is good is good in imitation of God's nature.

A parallel argument can be made for the logician's version of the *Euthyphro* dilemma. God neither invented nor is He bound by modal truths. What must be, what can be, and what cannot be all reflect God's nature which is Perfect Being Itself. If the realm of possibilities is not somehow dependent on God, and this seems to be Plantinga's conclusion, then the existence of the Judeo-Christian God as the creator *ex nihilo* is called into question.[9] This argument goes back at least to Ockham who opted for nominalism, denying that realm of possibilities rather than denying creation *ex nihilo*.[10] If one feels committed to the doctrine of creation *ex nihilo*, and if one finds nominalism metaphysically unappealing, one had better reconsider the traditional doctrine of simplicity.

There are, as we shall see, a number of other puzzles which this classic view of the nature of God solves. Moreover it plays an important role in a number of theological arguments. A case can be made that in the work of Aquinas it is the doctrine of simplicity which drives the arguments for God's various (ultimately identical) attributes in the subsequent articles of the *Summa Theologiae*.[11] The doctrine plays an important role in Aquinas' cosmological arguments.[12] And contemporary philosophers of religion have used it in cosmological and ontological arguments.[13] But if the doctrine of divine simplicity is intrinsically incoherent or inconsistent with other things we must say about a perfect being then we will have to abandon it.

There are a number of problems which contemporary philosophers of religion raise against the doctrine of divine simplicity. Alvin Plantinga offers a succinct and vivid critique of the doctrine of simplicity in *Does God Have a Nature?*

> There are two difficulties, one substantial and the other truly monumental. In the first place if God is identical with each of his properties, then each of his properties is identical with each of his properties, so that God has but one property. This seems flatly incompatible with the obvious fact that God has several properties; he has both power and mercifulness, say, neither of which is identical with the other. In the second place, if God is identical with each of his properties, then, since each of his properties is a property, he is a property – a self-exemplifying property. Accordingly God has just one property: himself. This view is subject to a difficulty both obvious and overwhelming. No property could have created the world; no property could be omniscient, or indeed, know anything at all. If God is a property, then he isn't a person but a mere abstract object; he has no knowledge, awareness, power, love or life. So taken, the simplicity doctrine seems an utter mistake.[14]

Most of the contemporary debate has centered around the questions of whether or not God could be a property, and whether or not all His properties could be identical.[15] For example, it has been argued that God is not identical with wisdom or justice *per se*, but with *his own* instance of these properties. In creatures wisdom and justice are not identical, but it does not follow that *God's* wisdom might not be identical with *God's* justice.[16] This cannot be the position of the perfect being theologian since if God's justice is held to be merely one (albeit perfect and infinite) instance of justice, then God does not exist absolutely *a se*. His existence depends in some way on there being justice for Him to exemplify. The classic tradition holds that as absolute source God is indeed Wisdom and Justice and Goodness *per se*, and other things possess these qualities through participation in the divine.

The major problem with the contemporary debate is that almost all participants misunderstand the classic doctrine of simplicity.[17] The medieval view, spelled out most clearly by Aquinas, but certainly there in Anselm, is that, strictly speaking God neither *has* properties nor *is* He a property . . . however unified and exalted. God is simply act.[18] As Aquinas sees it, striving for perfection is the same as actualizing potentials, so something which is absolutely perfect is something which is fully actualized, wholly in act.[19] This is what it means to say that God's essence just is His existence, and that His very nature is Perfect Being. Existence is not an inert property. It is an act, the act of being. Unhampered by any limitation, God is Pure Act. I fear that the modern reader is inclined to find this concept quite opaque. If we describe God as simply His act of existing, then is not this the most limited, 'thinnest' possible conception of divinity?[20] Isn't existence an on/off property shared by everything that is, and not possessed in varying degrees?[21]

The mistake here is a confusion between being-in-general with perfect being. Being-in-general is the being, the bare existence, that any existent has in order to exist. And conceptually it is exceedingly 'thin'. Aquinas himself raises a similar point as an objection against his view that God is Pure Being. Aquinas, in fact, carries the criticism several steps further and submits that if we identify God with being-in-general we end with pantheism and attributing radical imperfection to God.[22] What 'Pure Being' meant for Aquinas was not 'bare existence', but rather 'existence in the most perfect way possible'. (In the present discussion it makes no difference whether or not we call God 'Pure Being' or '*the* Pure Being'. However the latter is permissable only with the qualifications that [1] God exists 'more fully' than other beings precisely because He is the perfect existence which they reflect and [2] God, as I shall argue below, is a being who is an *act*.) Pure Being is being freed from all limitations, that is, possessing all perfections. It is act without any hindrance of potential. Is corporeality an imperfection? Then Pure Being is incorporeal. And this is not a 'limitative' or negative attribute since it is embodiment which places a limitation on being. Is it better absolutely to be animate than inanimate? Then God is alive. Is, as the Philosopher says, thinking the best activity? Then God is rational. Is it better to be a person, than not?

> Now the nature which *person* includes in its definition is of all natures the most exalted, to wit that nature which is intellectual in regard to its genus. Likewise the mode of existence signified by the word *person* is most exalted, namely that a thing exists by itself. Since then whatsoever is most excellent in creatures should be attributed to God, it is becoming that the word *person* should be attributed to God, even as other terms which are said of God properly.[23]

If it is argued that we add to the notion of being when we say that it is incorporeal, living, rational and the rest, this is true of being-in-general, the on/off property which can be attributed to all existent things finite and infinite. In the same way we add to the notion of being-in-general when we describe an existent thing as material, canine or white. When Aquinas identifies God with Being He is speaking of Infinite Being, Perfect Act with no limitations.

An analogy may help. (It is intended only to give an impression of the difference between a superior and an inferior version of the same nature, where the superior version is simply fulfilling its nature while the inferior version is made inferior through the addition of limitations. It fails to capture the crucially important causal relationship between Pure Being and the being-in-general of creatures.) Imagine a healthy oak tree growing under ideal circumstances, trunk as tall as an oak's can be, roots and branches spreading far and wide. Call this the Pure Oak. Now imagine a bonsai oak, its roots in a small pot, its trunk wrapped, its branches held down by wires. It has achieved its full growth and is eleven inches tall. Both trees possess oakness-in-general, but the Pure Oak has fully actualized its nature. It is not suffering under the limitations imposed on the bonsai oak. We might say that it possesses the perfections of not-pottedness, not-trunk-wrappedness and not-branches-wiredness, but these are not really additions to the oakness. The Pure Oak has oakness as it exists in an ideal situation and sans limitations. It is the bonsai oak which has all the additional properties and it is made smaller by them. Both trees have oakness-in-general, but it makes sense to distinguish between the oakness of any oak, and the Pure Oakness possessed only by the fully actualized specimen. Similarly it is legitimate to distinguish being-in-general from Pure Being.[24]

The doctrine of simplicity is not subject to the criticism that God is some sort of inert property, with all the difficulties that entails. Nor does the point about the 'thinness' of Aquinas' concept of Being Itself hit the mark, since Aquinas explicitly distinguishes being-in-general from God's perfect mode of existing. So when Aquinas (or, I take it, Anselm or Augustine) says that God is His omnipotence, omniscience, omnibenevolence and so on and that all of these are identical with God, what He means is that God is His act of knowing and doing and being perfectly good and these are all one act. At this point even someone inclined to give Aquinas every benefit of the doubt may feel that we have not really made much progress. We are still confronted with extremely difficult questions, of which the first is: How can God, Who is a person, possibly be an act?

It seems obvious that a person cannot be an action. But perhaps this point becomes less apparent if we look carefully at human experience. Odd as it seems to call David Hume as a witness for the defense here, the radical empiricists seem to be correct when they point out that all we can experience of ourselves, apart from our perceptions of our bodies, is our own acting and experiencing.[25] We do not experience ourselves as having properties underlying the activities. I do not, for example, have any perception of my own rationality as a property, except in that I experience myself thinking. I do not perceive my *ability* to write except in that I experience or remember the activity of writing. All we perceive is our acting, our thinking, our feeling, our perceiving. And all of these are basically actions. Or, if this seems to be too broad a use of the term 'action', at least these are much more like things we do than like properties we have. Those of us who reject radical empiricism hypothesize some one thing which does our acting and thinking and so on, a unifying self underlying our various experiences, because we see that if there is no unity somehow 'beneath' the diverse many then we as individuals do not really exist. But in terms of what we can know of ourselves through introspection, we are really rather more like actions than not. We do not hypothesize any unity underlying the diversity in God because there is no diversity. There is just the one, perfect act which is God. In order to make the traditional doctrine of simplicity somewhat more comprehensible, it is only necessary to show that in human experience there is some analogue for a person who is an act. Since what we perceive of ourselves is act, or at least active, the analogy is not hard to find.[26]

It might be argued that even if we can make some sense of the notion that God is act, this does not solve the problem of multiplicity since clearly God knows and does all sorts of different things. The classic tradition responds that both God and the solution to this problem are simple. God knows all He knows in a single act. Aquinas systematizes this view nicely when he explains that God knows all things in knowing Himself, because in knowing Himself He knows the myriad ways in which He could be imitated.[27] And He does all He does in a single act. Again the analogy with human experience is not hard to find. Suppose *you* know that Anselm was born in 1033. This single piece of knowledge incorporates various bits of information; who Anselm was, what it is to be born, what '1033' means. Suppose *you* are writing about Anselm. This single act incorporates looking at the screen, pressing the keys, and thinking. The limited human being is able to incorporate a lot of information in a single piece of knowledge and to accomplish various things in a single act. So is God, only much more so.[28] If it is insisted that this still ascribes to God a sort of complexity or multiplicity, if knowing everything and doing everything in one, single act is insufficiently simple, then the only alternative seems to be Plotinus' approach in which God is *so* unified that He doesn't exactly know or do anything. This move is not open to Christian orthodoxy, and the Thomistic version of the doctrine will prove adequate to the demands of God's perfect aseity.[29]

The question remains: How could all of the attributes we must ascribe to God possibly be identical? I take it that if a plausible case can be made that God's omniscience, omnipotence and omnibenevolence are the same act, this entails the likelihood that anything we want to say about God can be identified with this act. And in fact, in the classic tradition, the identification of God's knowledge with His power went without saying. How would an incorporeal person act *except* through thinking? When the medievals read in Genesis that in the beginning God said, 'Let there be light', they took God's 'speaking' to be thinking. And when they read at the beginning of John's Gospel that it was through the Word that all things were made, they again understood the Word, the Second Person of the Trinity, to be *logos, ratio*, the thinking of God.[30] And on the human level there is at the very least a close correlation between power and knowledge, in that in the vast majority of cases being able to do something requires, on some level, knowing *how* to do it.

We will analyze omniscience and omnipotence in Chapters 6 and 7 respectively. Here I will just point out that the doctrine of simplicity can solve a paradox raised in the contemporary debate over the nature of God. Could God make a creature which has a secret unknown even to Him? If not, He is not omnipotent. If so, He is not omniscient. But given the doctrine of divine simplicity the paradox cannot arise. In the classic tradition, God's omnipotence entails that everything that has any sort of being at all, besides God, is kept in existence from moment to moment by God's causal power. Since God's power is His knowledge, whatever is *is* because it is being thought right now by God. To hypothesize something which exists on its own not immediately caused by God's thought is to deny God's omnipotence. However we define a secret, it is some sort of a 'thing' either physical or mental. Neither the knower nor the secret could exist if it were unknown to God. So if there were a secret unknown to God, not only would He not be omniscient, He would not be omnipotent either. For God to make someone with a secret unknown even to Him would be to shed both His omniscience and His omnipotence, which is impossible. As we shall see in Chapter 7, omnipotence does not entail an ability to do the impossible. And, according to the classic tradition, a contingent existent unknown and hence uncaused by God is quite impossible. God is omniscient and omnipotent . . . and from Him no secrets are hid.

But could the power and wisdom of God be the same as God's goodness? In human experience power and goodness seem to be quite different phenomena. Stalin or Mao, in engineering the deaths of innocent millions, seem to express the epitome of earthly power. Mother Theresa, tending the poorest of the poor, is surely good. And there does not seem to be much common ground between them. In the final analysis, though, it is Mother

Theresa who better exemplifies the sort of power God has. I will have much more to say on the nature of divine power later, but here suffice it to say that in the classic tradition God's omnipotence does not mean the ability to do anything logically possible. God does not do evil. All that *is* is good and is kept in being by God. Evil is the corruption and negation and destruction of the good . . . what Stalin and Mao were so adept at.[31] But this is the opposite of the creative and productive power of God. The human analogue for divine power is the ability to behave productively and beneficially. And in the classic tradition which we are considering this is what it means to be good. (Notice that at work here is a particular view on value in general which, when spelled out in connection with morality, is known as 'Natural Law Ethics'. I will discuss this ethical system in connection with the goodness of God in Chapter 9.) Even on the human level, goodness, power (of the positive sort) and wisdom are very closely interrelated. Subtract from these properties any creaturely limitations and they become one perfectly good, thinking act: God.

I have tried to meet some of the current criticisms of the doctrine of divine simplicity by pointing out that God, in the traditional view, is not considered a property at all, but an act. And sense can be made of the view that the things we want to say about God, such as that He is wise and powerful and good, can all refer to this act. Some very difficult problems remain. First, the doctrine of simplicity entails a position which many contemporary philosophers of religion find incoherent, and that is that God is eternal. He is literally outside of time. We must say this if we are to identify God with His act of being, for if He were temporal He would do first one thing then another. But if His essence is identical with what He does, then He would become a different being as He did different things. If we were to posit some unity underlying but separate from these changing acts we would thereby abandon the doctrine of simplicity. We can solve the problem by saying that God does not change. Rather, He does all He does in one, eternal act. I shall defend the ascription of eternity to a perfect being in Chapter 5. Here there are even more difficult problems to attend to.

It seems that there are all sorts of contingent truths about God. If He created freely, then He might not have done so, and that God is a creator is a contingent truth. If I am writing freely, then I might not have written, and so 'God knows that Rogers is writing' is a contingent truth. But if God's power and His knowledge are identical to the eternal act of being which is His nature, how could He do and know other than He does and knows without being other than God? (The way the question is usually phrased in the contemporary debate has to do with whether or not God's contingent properties could somehow be identical to His necessary properties.)

In the medieval tradition we are considering, Augustine, Anselm and Aquinas each offer different answers to the question about God's contingent attributes. (I do not claim that these exhaust the medieval approaches to the problem.) The different answers become clearer if we look first at the question of divine choice, and then move to the related issue of the effect and status of human choices. Stump and Kretzmann spell out Aquinas' solution to the problem, focusing on the question of whether or not God could have failed to create. In the final analysis the answer is yes, 'there are possible worlds in which God wills not to create . . .'[32] Aquinas distinguishes between absolute necessity and conditional necessity. There are some attributes which are 'absolutely necessary' of God. He is good, He is simple, He does not do evil, and He does not make round squares. That is, He possesses His perfections necessarily and essentially, and He, necessarily, does not 'violate' His nature or the laws of logic. But there are all sorts of ways in which a perfectly good being could 'express' His perfection, and so God can choose among the different ways. No matter what, He wills the good, but He could will it differently . . . for example, through creating a different good world, or even through choosing to simply remain within the dynamic self-expression which is the Trinity. He does not 'have to' create to fulfill His nature.

But given that God is a single, simple, eternal act, what sense does it make to say that He could choose other than He does choose? In answer to this question, Aquinas is willing to admit another sort of necessity in God, conditional necessity. That is, if x, then x follows necessarily. If I am writing, then necessarily I am writing. If God eternally wills to create this world, then necessarily He eternally wills to create this world. But this does not entail any sort of 'constraint' upon God. 'Considered in the abstract, God's not creating is logically possible . . .'[33]

There are problems with this conclusion. First, while the concept of conditional necessity seems clear when applied to the activities of creatures, God's situation is so different that it seems that the same concept cannot apply, except perhaps in a *very* analogical way. When we say that it is necessary that I am writing because I am writing, but that this 'necessity' is only conditional, we have in mind a variety of qualifications with respect to 'necessity'. For example, we know that there was a time when I was not writing and so there was a time when I had the option to choose not to write. Though it is necessary that I write if I am writing I 'could have not written' and I can locate the point at which the choice to write rather than not write was made. God does what He does in His eternal moment. There was never a point at which He chose to create rather than not. From eternity He chooses to create. If the sort of necessity we ought to ascribe to

God's act of creating is less than absolute necessity, still it seems to be more than conditional necessity. Perhaps we could use the term 'actual' necessity for God's eternal and immutable act which is not an absolutely necessary consequence of His perfections and the laws of logic.

But even if we attempt to qualify the notion of conditional necessity to take account of the peculiarities of the divine situation, a problem remains. If Stump and Kretzmann have Aquinas right, there is some sense in which 'there are possible worlds in which God wills not to create . . .' But it is very difficult to see how God in the actual world could be the same being as God in some other possible world, if (1) God in the actual world is identical to His eternal and immutable act in this world, (2) God in a different possible world is identical to His act in that world, and (3) God's act in the actual world is *not* identical to His act in the other possible world. One could suppose that the principle of the transitivity of identity (if A is identical to B and B is identical to C, then A is identical to C) does not hold at the divine level across possible worlds, but I take it this entails the view that we probably can't say anything about what might be possible for God, in which case we have not solved the difficulty of distinguishing the necessary from the contingent in the divine nature.

A second possibility is to deny contingency to God. I take it that this is the move Augustine makes. Certainly God acts freely, but Augustine is a thorough-going compatibilist. Freedom means the ability to do what you want to do, what you are most drawn towards. There is nothing above and beyond God's will to constrain Him, so He is free. Could He choose other than to create? Augustine responds in the negative. In *On the Literal Meaning of Genesis* he explains that,

> if He is not able to make good things then He has no power, and if He is able and does not make them, great is His envy. So because He is omnipotent and good He made all things very good.[34]

Given God's nature He could not do other than He does. There is no contingency in God, so there are no other possible worlds, whatever we may be able to imagine.

Augustine is also a compatibilist with respect to human choices. In *The City of God* (XII, 9) and the *Unfinished Work against Julian* (V, 57) Augustine makes it very clear that if we do good it is because God has given us the grace to do so, and if we do evil it is because we are drawn back towards the nothingness from which we were made . . . because God chooses not to give us the grace necessary to avoid the downward slide. And this is the case both after and before the fall.[35] God is in absolute control of all that happens, there is no contingency anywhere, and so there is no problem of reconciling contingency and necessity in a perfectly simple being.

But on Augustine's compatibilist view the problem of evil becomes acute, and it is very difficult to absolve God of the responsibility for the sin and suffering in this world. Can the simplicity of God be squared with a libertarian analysis of creaturely freedom in which rational creatures function as causal loci of their own such that they can be truly and ultimately responsible for their choices? An example will help clarify the problem. Suppose John and Mary freely commit adultery and Jane is the result of the illicit union. Since Jane exists, God knows her and sustains her in being. God's eternal, immutable act includes knowing and sustaining Jane. On the libertarian account, while God's causal activity is necessary for Jane to exist, it is not sufficient. John and Mary played an independent role without which (barring miracles) Jane would not have existed. Thus John and Mary have determined some of what will be included in God's eternal act which, on the doctrine of simplicity, is identical with His essence. What are we to make of this?

Augustine will simply deny libertarian freedom, and Aquinas may agree with this denial. At least one standard interpretation of Aquinas reads him as a compatibilist when it comes to creaturely choices.[36] If this is correct, and if we take Aquinas' assertion that 'God's knowledge is the cause of things' to cover even voluntary choices we will conclude that Aquinas, though allowing contingency in the divine will, does not see human choices as affecting God.[37] It is Anselm who insists upon libertarian freedom in creatures. He does not *define* freedom as a genuine ability to choose between open options. In fact he explicitly rejects such a definition because it cannot cover the good angels and God. He holds that God inevitably does the best and is in agreement with Augustine on the 'necessity' of God's creating the world.[38] God does not have literal options, but since He exists *a se* this is no limitation on Him. Creatures, though, exist through God. If we did not have literally open options we would not be responsible. We could not do evil or good. And so God has given us the great gift of allowing us to choose on our own to cling to the good that God has given us, or to throw it away. In this way we can contribute to our own creation and reflect His aseity in some small measure.[39] So among the philosophers in the classic tradition the task of systematizing creaturely freedom with a perfectly simple God falls to Anselm.

A first question to ask is: Since the doctrine of simplicity entails that God knows and causes in the same act, and since God is omniscient, does it follow that God somehow causes evil? Anselm answers (and here Augustine and Aquinas agree) that, oddly enough, God does not know evil. This is because evil is not a 'thing' to be known. In the tradition in question evil is consistently analyzed as a lack or corruption of absence of good. This is the only possible answer to the question of the ontological status of evil which will jibe with the classic understanding of a Perfect Being. If God is perfect being, everything that has being is good as reflective of Him, and the 'opposite' of God is just nothing. Moreover if God's omnipotence entails that all that is is made and sustained by Him, then either He causes evil (*absurdissimus*!), or evil is nothing. Certainly there are evil choices. And whatever actually *exists* in the choice . . . the desires, the will that chooses and so on are kept in being by God. It is just in the failure to hold to the good that the will does evil, and God 'knows' that only as one would notice an empty spot where something ought to have been.[40]

But this does not resolve the problems raised by contingent creaturely choices. Do such choices actually have an effect on God? If so, would this entail contingent as well as necessary attributes of God, thus denying simplicity? If not, are we left with the conclusion – rather shocking given where we started – that God's eternal and immutable nature is somehow partially 'caused' by the choices of creatures? I argued above that if God is identical to His act in this actual world, then, in some different possible world, if God* did other things, God* could not really be God. And now the problem seems much worse. On the assumption of libertarian freedom it really is up to free creatures to decide which possible world will be the actual one. But then it seems to be up to John, Mary and every free creature which version of God (If such a thing can be said!) will exist.

Before I suggest a solution it is important to get clear on 'possible worlds' talk in this context. God immutably and eternally knows and causes everything that He Himself does, and He knows everything that anyone ever has or ever will do. From the divine perspective all choices are made. (How we can reconcile this with free choice will be a major topic in Chapter 6.) Thus the actual world is at least conditionally (or in my terminology 'actually') necessary and any other world is conditionally impossible. To use the popular medieval analogy of the eternal God as the center point producing and equally present to all of the circumference of a circle which represents the temporal world, we can say that there is only one possible 'circle' since it has 'already' been drawn. Often possible worlds talk suggests that there are any number of actualizable worlds, of roughly the same ontological status, and all that distinguishes the actual world is that it just happens to be the one that got realized. Given perfect being theology this is a radically misleading way to look at things. There are other imaginable worlds, but the actual world, from God's perspective in eternity, and allowing for the input of free creaturely choices, is the only really possible world. So it is not that free creatures pick and choose among various equally possible worlds and hence 'decide' upon which God will exist.[41]

And now to attempt a solution to the problem of creaturely freedom and divine simplicity. I advance this solution only tentatively and, lest it sound too radical, note that it is indeed based on premises drawn from Anselm's work. First, if creatures are free in a libertarian sense then there seems no way around holding that we do indeed have some sort of effect on God. It really is (partially) up to John and Mary that God keeps Jane in being. If God is simple, then it seems we should deny a real distinction between His obviously necessary attributes like 'being good' and His apparently contingent attributes like 'being the creator of Jane'. I say a 'real' distinction because it seems to me that we can allow an apparent one, a distinction *quoad nos*. From the human perspective, lacking the view that eternity would provide, the distinction between God's absolutely necessary attributes, 'being omniscient' and so on, and God's only conditionally or actually necessary attributes, 'being the creator of Jane' and so on, is a viable one. From God's perspective, if His essence is His eternal and immutable act in this the actual and only really possible world then He could not fail to have any of His attributes and still be Himself. They are equally necessary.[42]

That means that we are forced to conclude that creatures do have some effect on God's very essence. This seems shocking since a major motivation for insisting on simplicity is the absolute aseity of God. And now we have apparently arrived at the conclusion that He is dependent on creatures! Anselm himself does not say this explicitly, but he does provide the key for reconciling God's aseity with His being affected by us. The operant principle comes through most clearly in *Why God Became Man*. Here Anselm claims to argue for the Incarnation through 'necessary reasons'. 'For just as in God impossibility follows upon the smallest unsuitable thing, so necessity attends the smallest reason, if it is not outweighed by a greater.'[43] His underlying assumption is that God, as a perfect being, must do the best. God 'must' respond to human sin by saving His creation, and He must save it in the only way God can do anything, that is, the best way. But this necessity is in no way a limitation on God. It is not a limitation because it arises from His own nature as best. The first cause in this chain of relationships is God Himself. It is not that human sin *causes* God to become incarnate. God 'must' become incarnate because He does the best because He is perfect. A similar point can be made with respect to all of God's 'reactions' to the free choices of creatures. God gives us freedom because He Himself is good. The originating cause of the whole system in which God would respond to free choices is God, and so His aseity is preserved.[44]

Any systematic philosophy of God which incorporated free choice on the part of creatures would have to hold that God is somehow affected by and responsive to something outside Himself. True, the doctrine of simplicity may require us to say that creatures affect God's very nature. But it allows us the move that this is because God chooses to set things up in this way. A denial of the doctrine leaves God dependent on various properties for His existence, and this *not* through His own choice. One can, of course, make the Augustinian move of simply denying any causal efficacy to anything outside God, but the cost is very great in that all responsibility for suffering and (apparent) evil has to be assigned to God.

I must admit that I am not at all sure that this analysis works. Even if we preserve divine independence by insisting that God is the ultimate source of the entire system which includes free choices, we may not be able to eradicate a real distinction in the nature of God between the absolute necessity of the key great-making properties and the conditional necessity of the divine attributes which involve God's response to contingent choices. Could we hold that, in the same way that God thinks many things in one thought and does many things in one act, the single divine act can encompass two kinds of necessity? Perhaps. Clearly there is more work to be done in the effort to portray a simple God who responds to human free choice. But with all its problems, the doctrine of simplicity is worth the effort. And now that we have explained and wrestled with it the rest of perfect being theology should be comparatively . . . simple.

NOTES

1. I defend the doctrine in 'The traditional doctrine of divine simplicity', reprinted as Chapter 2 of *The Anselmian Approach to God and Creation*.
2. Critics include Richard LaCroix, 'Augustine on the simplicity of God'; Alvin Plantinga, *Does God Have a Nature?*; Thomas V. Morris, 'On God and Mann: A view of divine simplicity'; Christopher Hughes, *On a Complex Theory of a Simple God*.
3. Defenders include William Mann, 'Divine simplicity', 'Simplicity and immutability in God', and 'Simplicity and properties: A reply to Morris's "On God and Mann: A view of divine simplicity"'; Eleonore Stump and Norman Kretzmann, 'Absolute simplicity'; Brian Leftow, 'Is God an abstract object?; William Vallicella, 'Divine simplicity: A new defense'. Among the defenders, Stump and Kretzmann do offer the correct analysis of the traditional view of divine simplicity, but their article is devoted to reconciling this doctrine with the idea that God has free choice rather than to making the doctrine itself plausible.
4. Aquinas offers a number of reasons for denying corporeality to God in ST I, Q.3, arts. 1 and 2.
5. He sums up the case in Chapter 17.
6. Leftow, 'Is God an abstract object?'
7. Plantinga, *Does God Have a Nature?*, p. 34.
8. Plantinga, *Does God Have a Nature?*, pp. 52–3, for rejection of simplicity, pp. 140–6, for (tentative) conclusions.
9. For a contemporary discussion see Richard Creel, *Divine Impassibility*, Chapter 4.
10. *Commentary on the Sentences*, Book I (*Ordinatio*), Distinction II, q.4.
11. Peter Burns, SJ, 'The status and function of divine simpleness in *Summa Theologiae* Ia, qq.2–13'.
12. Burns, 'Status and function of divine simpleness in *Summa Theologiae* Ia, qq.2–13', pp. 20–6.
13. See respectively, Stump and Kretzmann, 'Absolute simplicity', pp. 376–8, and Leftow, 'Is God an abstract object?', pp. 595–6.

14. Plantinga, *Does God Have a Nature?*, p. 47.

15. The contemporary debate is rendered complicated by the fact that there is no consensus on the nature and ontological status of properties. See, for example, Mann's attack on what he terms Morris's 'lush and giddy platonism' in 'Simplicity and properties', pp. 347–51. A further difficulty is that contemporary philosophers assume uncritically that an analysis of properties as attributed to creatures can be used unmodified in speaking about God. See Hughes, *On a Complex Theory of a Simple God*, pp. 22–3.

16. Mann, 'Divine simplicity'.

17. Nicholas Wolterstorff explains that the medieval position was based on the idea that a thing's nature was a concrete thing ('Divine simplicity', see especially pp. 541–4). I argue (Rogers, 'Traditional doctrine', pp. 165–6) that this was certainly not the position of either Aquinas, to whom Wolterstorff attributes it, or in fact any but the most extreme realists.

18. ST I, Q.3, art.4. The earlier philosophers, not directly influenced by Aristotle as was Aquinas, would have tended to emphasize God's goodness rather than His being. It seems to me, though, that on the question of whether or not God just is His act of existing, the more Platonic thinkers would be in fundamental agreement with Aquinas. For Anselm see *Monologion* 16. He ends the chapter by describing God's unified nature adverbially. For God to be the highest existence, the highest life and so on is to be 'nothing other than supremely being, supremely living, and the rest'.

19. ST I, Q.4, art.1.

20. Hughes, *On a Complex Theory of a Simple God*, p. 21.

21. Hughes, *On a Complex Theory of a Simple God*, p. 27.

22. *On the Power of God*, Q.7, art.2, Objs. 6 and 9.

23. DP Q.9, art.3.

24. I have found the work of Fr W. Norris Clarke very helpful in coming to an appreciation of Aquinas' concept of being. See Clarke, *Explorations in Metaphysics*, especially Chapter 3, 'Action as the self-revelation of being: A central theme in the thought of St. Thomas'. For a defense of the Thomist position in a more analytic vein see Barry Miller, *A Most Unlikely God*, Chapters 4 and 5.

25. *The Treatise of Human Nature*, Book I, Part IV, Section 6, Personal Identity.

26. Rogers, 'Traditional doctrine of divine simplicity', pp. 172–3.

27. SCG I, 55. Anselm discusses the idea that in knowing Himself God knows all things, in the *Monologion*, especially Chapter 33.

28. SCG I, 31, 3; DP Q.7, art.1.

29. Rogers, 'Traditional doctrine of divine simplicity', pp. 173–4.

30. Rogers, 'Traditional doctrine of divine simplicity', pp. 174–5. See, for example, Anselm's *Monologion* Chapters 33–6.

31. The view that evil is not any sort of 'thing' and is absolutely parasitic on the good is the standard medieval view. Were evil to exist as a positive property, rather than as a lack of what ought to be, then, even if it were never instantiated, it would have to come from and be dependent upon God. The view is often misunderstood in contemporary analytic philosophy of religion. See, for example, Richard Swinburne, *Providence and the Problem of Evil*, p. 32.

32. Stump and Kretzmann, 'Absolute simplicity', p. 368. ST I, Q.19, art.3.

33. Stump and Kretzmann, 'Absolute simplicity', pp. 368–9.

34. Augustine, *On the Literal Meaning of Genesis* IV, 16, 27.

35. See my, 'The irrelevance of original sin in Augustine's doctrine of the will'.

36. See for example, Etienne Gilson, *The Christian Philosophy of St. Thomas Aquinas*, pp. 244–8.

37. ST I, Q.14, art.8. Clarke, *Explorations in Metaphysics*, offers a reading of Aquinas more compatible with human responsibility. God knows our choices, not by literally causing them, nor because we produce any causal power on our own which affects God, but because He knows how His own power is channeled in our choices (pp. 205–6).

38. See my *Neoplatonic Metaphysics and Epistemology of Anselm of Canterbury*, Chapter 2.

39. *On the Fall of Satan* 18. See my 'Anselm's indeterminism'.

40. *On the Harmony of the Foreknowledge, and Predestination, and Grace of God with Free Will* I, 7.

41. Rogers, 'Traditional doctrine of divine simplicity', pp. 184–5.

42. Rogers, 'Traditional doctrine of divine simplicity', p. 186.

43. Anselm, *Cur Deus*, Book I, Chapter 10.

44. Rogers, 'Traditional doctrine of divine simplicity', pp. 185–6.

4

Necessity, Immutability and Impassivity

NECESSITY

The property of Necessary Existence is unique among those we shall discuss, in that attributing it to God seems to imply that we need only cogitate upon the divine nature to see that there is in fact a God. How could a being who *must* exist, fail to exist? Other divine attributes are presented as hypothetical; *If* there is a God, then He is omniscient, and so on. But there seems more at stake in a discussion of divine necessity in that it will turn out that if it is only *possible* that God exist as a necessary being, then (so it is argued) He actually does exist. This is, of course, the thesis of some versions of the famous and infamous ontological argument. This is not the place, *Deo gratia*, to embark upon a study of the checkered history of the ontological argument. Graham Oppy has recently produced a very useful book, *Ontological Arguments and Belief in God*, which attempts the Herculean task of assessing the various versions of the argument and producing a thorough and organized bibliography.[1] Here I want to examine divine necessity as it contributes to the concept of 'that than which a greater cannot be conceived'. But though it will not be the primary focus of this investigation, the fact remains that if a necessary being *can* exist, (arguably) one does exist.

There have been those who held that the very concept of a 'necessary being' is incoherent. Hume argued that 'Whatever we conceive as existent, we can also conceive as non-existent . . . The words, therefore, *necessary existence*, have no meaning; or which is the same thing, none that is consistent.'[2] The apologist for the traditional concept of God can respond that God is a special case, and Hume has not proved the universal application of his (dogmatic) principle. The more Platonically minded among us will add that there are arguably 'things' of a sort, laws of mathematics and logic, which are necessary and which we cannot conceive as non-existent. Kant's most famous contribution to the debate was to note that 'existence is not a predicate'. To which the apologist responds, 'It is so!' Or perhaps, if she is feeling less truculent, 'Well, whatever we say of existence in general, when we ascribe necessary existence to God we say something substantive about His nature.'

Earlier in this century it was often argued (or rather simply mandated) that the very concept of a necessary being is nonsense because 'possible' and 'necessary' are terms which apply only to sentences. Only analytic sentences are necessary. And analytic sentences are about how we have chosen to use language. 'All bachelors are unmarried' is true. It is necessarily true. And it is about how we have chosen to use the term 'bachelor'. By the same token, $2 + 2 = 4$ and *modus ponens* are necessarily true precisely because mathematics and logic are human conventions. On this view, it makes no sense to describe an object as 'necessary' or 'necessarily existent'.[3] One's acceptance of this view will depend upon whether or not one subscribes to the idea, very implausible to my mind, that human beings *invented* the laws of mathematics and logic rather than discovering them. If these laws were there to be discovered, and are necessarily true, then there are necessary existents of a sort. But in any case, the charge of nonsense seems answered by the fact that we can offer a substantive description of what the classical theist means by a necessary being. Some of the groundwork was laid in the last chapter. The classical view may be mistaken, but it is not gibberish.[4]

What, then, does the perfect being theologian mean by necessary existence as an attribute of God? It will be helpful here to distinguish between three senses of 'necessity'. (This is a much debated issue, and the following is just to explain how I shall be using the terms, and to get the question on the table.) Logical necessity derives from the (not necessarily conventional) meanings of terms and propositions. Given the meaning of 'seven', 'plus', 'three', 'equals', and 'ten', it is logically necessary that 'seven plus three equals ten'. Hume in the quotation above seems to view our ability to conceptualize as the test of possibility and necessity, but a proposition may be logically necessary, even if someone imagines it to be false. In thinking of a complicated mathematical formula, I may believe that the right answer is false, but nonetheless the right answer is true, and true by logical necessity. We may 'discover' logical necessity, but we will do so through a careful unpacking of the terms and concepts in question.

Some philosophers allow a much weaker form of necessity, scientific or empirical necessity. Given the actual laws of nature at work in our actual universe some states of affairs must hold and some are impossible. We can discover through a scientific process that the earth must orbit the sun in accord with the laws of gravity, and human beings cannot possibly sprout wings and fly. It is easy to imagine violations of this sort of necessity, and the traditional theist holds that God can work a miracle and bring about cases where the empirically impossible occurs. A third type, metaphysical necessity, derives from the natures of things. Given an everyday meaning of the term 'water' which does not include its atomic structure, the proposition 'Water is not H_2O' is false, but it is not self-contradictory, and so it is not *logically* impossible. Nonetheless, given what it actually *is* to be water, something not H_2O could not be water in any possible world. You might have something *like* what we call water with a different atomic structure, but it is absolutely impossible for something to be water and not to be H_2O. Like scientific necessity, metaphysical necessity can be discovered through an empirical process, as in the case of water being H_2O, but, like logical necessity, a metaphysically necessary truth cannot possibly be otherwise. Even God cannot make it be the case that water is not H_2O . . . this at least will be the standard line in classic perfect being theology, as we will see in Chapter 7. It is this third sort of necessity that will concern us here. That God possesses necessary existence is not a scientific truth, nor is it logically necessary in the sense that 'God does not exist' is a contradiction from the usual meanings of the terms. However, the perfect being theologian holds that it is the very nature of God to exist, and to exist in such a way that it is absolutely impossible that He fail to exist.

'God is a necessary being' entails that ' "God exists" is necessarily true', but the latter is not an adequate translation of the former in that there is more to the concept of God's necessity than that He must 'be there' or even that He must 'be there in all possible worlds'. To say that God is a necessary being describes the *way* in which God exists. (That there are different 'ways of existing' was defended in the last chapter. Both God and the creature exist, but the creature possesses a limited existence and God an infinite existence, just as the Pure Oak and the bonsai oak are both oaks, but the bonsai has stunted oakness whereas the 'Pure Oak' has fully-actualized oakness.) There are a number of ways of defending and analyzing divine necessity. In the last chapter we saw that in the classic tradition, especially as elaborated by Aquinas, God's absolute aseity entails that He is perfectly simple, that is, His nature is identical with His existence. He is simply His perfect act of being. Thus God (if He exists) must be the sort of thing whose very nature it is to exist, who could not possibly fail to exist. He is a necessary being. This radically distinguishes God from all other concrete objects. All things besides God (and the abstract objects like the laws of mathematics which reflect His nature) are contingent. Their essences are separate from their existence. They require an explanation outside of themselves for how they came to be. They might or might not have existed. God is not like this. He must exist, and it is His existence which explains the being of everything else. (Aquinas, though, explicitly criticizes 'ontological' arguments, holding that natural reason must begin with observation of the world.)[5]

There is another way in which God's aseity entails His necessity. In the preceding chapter I argued that divine aseity means that, in addition to the fact that every concrete object not God is dependent upon God, there are no abstract objects, properties or propositions, existing in independence of God. This means that there cannot be a possible world in which God does not exist. He must exist in all possible worlds, and this is another way of expressing His necessity.

What does it say about the nature of God to hold that He 'exists in all possible worlds'? Plantinga's justification for ascribing maximal greatness (the possession of maximal excellence, that is, omniscience, omnipotence and moral perfection, in every possible world) to God is that,

> the greatness of a being in a world W does not depend merely upon its qualities and attributes in W; what it is like in other worlds is also to the point. Those who worship God do not think of him as a being that happens to be of surpassing excellence in *this* world but who in some other worlds is powerless or uninformed or of dubious moral character.

Plantinga notes that, on his analysis, 'existence and necessary existence are not themselves perfections, but necessary conditions of perfection'.[6] It seems to me that the perfect being theologian can wholeheartedly endorse Plantinga's intuition about the maximal greatness and just disallow a real distinction in God between a perfection and a 'necessary condition of perfection'.

But isn't there a possible world containing only a large green marble? If so it is incorrect to say that God exists in all possible worlds.[7] As I noted above, a God who exists in some but not all possible worlds is a very far cry from 'that than which a greater cannot be conceived'. If God exists *a se* in the strongest possible way, then He cannot be dependent on properties which are not identical to Himself. All properties are ultimately 'reflections' of the nature of God, they are ways in which being can be limited. On this view neither contingent concrete objects (green marbles), nor qualities (greenness or roundness), nor the laws of mathematics and logic ('It can't both be a marble and not a marble in the same way at the same time.') are possible without God. The hypothesis of any godless possible world entails that the laws of logic transcend God. They are 'there' independently of Him, and if He is limited to being and doing the logically possible then He is not truly *a se*. Aquinas' God, if He exists, exists in all possible worlds. And conversely, the reason for saying God exists in all possible worlds is that God's *actual way of existing* is so perfectly unlimited that He is not dependent upon anything at all. Richard Gale puts it very well.

> God, as creator, has a standpoint that is 'outside' of or independent of possible worlds – the infinitely many different ways that things could be. God's existence or actuality is absolute, not being in any way relative to one of these worlds: He exists or is actual simpliciter.[8]

There is another way of expressing God's necessary being. In Chapter 3 of the *Proslogion* Anselm writes that God exists so truly that He cannot even be thought not to be. 'Truly, anything which is other than You alone, can be thought not to exist. You alone have existence most actually and therefore most greatly (*maxime*) of all: because whatever is other is not so actual, and therefore has less existence.' With anything (at least any concrete object) but God there is a sort of symmetry with how we think of its existence or non-existence. Either can be conceived. Either could be explained. God exists so perfectly that He cannot fail to exist. If we are operating with a fully-developed concept of *God,* we cannot conceive of or explain His non-existence. James Ross has offered a variant on the ontological argument which underscores the unique incomprehensibility of God's not existing.[9]

The argument depends upon what Ross describes as a weak version of the principle of sufficient reason. For every individual that exists there is a *possible* explanation for its existence, and for every individual that does not exist there is a *possible* explanation for its non-existence. The strong version requires that there actually be an explanation. (Note that, as Ross explains it, neither the weak nor the strong version of the principle of sufficient reason precludes libertarian freedom. I can give an explanation for my choice without that entailing that the choice was determined. For example, I can point to the source of the choice ('*I* made this decision') and the reason for it ('because I *like* avocados!'). This does not mean that the same source could not have produced a different choice, for which there would also have been reasons.) The weak version makes no claim as to the actual existence of something which can serve to explain a given thing. As a claim about the mere possibility of an explanation it seems unarguable. But if we allow this principle we can, according to Ross, prove the existence of a necessary being. In the interests of clarity I am reproducing the argument as Richard Gale reconstructs it in a simplified version. (The brackets are Gale's.)

1. It is impossible that anything prevent the existence of God [conceptual truth];
2. For every individual *x*, if it is a fact that *x* exists or a fact that *x* does not exist, it is possible that there is an explanation for the fact that *x* exists or the fact that *x* does not exist [weak version of the principle of sufficient reason];
3. God does not exist [assumption for indirect proof];
4. It is possible that there is an explanation for the fact that God does not exist [from 2 and 3];
5. It is not possible that there is an explanation for the fact that God does not exist [from 1];
6. It is and it is not possible that there is an explanation for the fact that God does not exist [from 4 and 5]; and
7. It is false that God does not exist [from 3 through 6 by indirect proof].[10]

Gale himself is unsympathetic to the argument. Among his criticisms is one which inadvertently highlights the radical difference between God and creatures which motivates Ross's argument, and which Gale fails to appreciate. Gale assumes that when Ross talks about the possibility of explanation he must be talking about the possibility of some sort of literal cause, a concrete thing with the power to bring something into being. If this is what is meant by 'explanation' then,

> Just as it is not logically possible that anything causally prevents God's existence, it is not logically possible that anything causes his existence either; yet according to this argument, there is an explanation for his existence consisting in this very ontological argument.[11]

Gale seems to have missed the point of Ross's argument. Ross entitles his version the argument from 'self-explanation'. Obviously Ross is not assuming that there can be no explanation for the existence of God. True, there is absolutely nothing, no being concrete or abstract, no state of affairs actual or possible, *outside of God*, that could explain His existence if He exists, or His non-existence if He does not exist. But, unlike with creatures, there is a radical asymmetry between explaining God's existence and His non-existence. If He exists, He exists necessarily, so His existence is eminently explicable. It is His very nature to exist. The point of the argument is that, if He does exist, He is essentially His own explanation for being. He is self-caused and self-explanatory. If He does not exist there is absolutely nothing of any sort which could even *possibly* account for this fact. But this contradicts the weak version of the principle of sufficient reason. So God exists. He exists 'so actually' in Anselm's words, that His non-existence is just incoherent.

It follows from the limitless perfection of God that His existence is His essence. He is the source of all possibilities and so He must 'exist in' or perhaps it is better to say 'transcend' all possible worlds. As self-explanatory, His existence is the most completely explained fact in the universe. If we understand Him properly, His non-existence is incomprehensible. Whether or not we can derive a successful ontological proof from all of this has been passionately debated for the past nine centuries. The perfect being theologian can come down on either or neither side in this debate. But that necessary existence is entailed by the perfect being theologian's concept of God is not negotiable.

IMMUTABILITY

In the classic tradition of Augustine, Anselm and Aquinas God is immutable. *Really* immutable! His essential nature does not change. His will does not change. His knowledge does not change.[12] Since God is simple, so that His will and intellect are identical with His essence, if He were to change in any way at all this would involve a change in His essence. A number of contemporary philosophers argue that, while it must be the case that an adequate object of worship would be steadfast and trustworthy, if God is immutable in the traditional sense He cannot be the God of biblical revelation, a God who is a person and an agent, who loves His people, who responds to prayer. Let us look first at why the medievals were so wedded to the idea that God cannot change, and then see if the contemporary criticisms are damaging to the traditional doctrine.

It is Aquinas who spells out the argument most clearly. In the *Summa Theologiae* Book I, Q.9, art.1 he gives three arguments, the first two of which are drawn from the notion of simplicity. If God is full and unlimited being, perfect act, there is in Him no potentiality. Change involves the actualization of some potentiality. So there is no change in God. Second, everything which changes changes in some respect and stays the same in some respect. There must be some continuity underlying the change, otherwise the thing ceases to exist. But then there would be multiple aspects to God, the part which changes and the part which does not. So there is no change in God.[13] The third argument comes from God's infinity. To change involves to gain some new thing. 'But since God is infinite, comprehending in Himself all the plenitude of the perfection of all being, He cannot acquire anything new, nor extend Himself to anything whereto He was not extended previously.' That which is absolutely the best in every possible way cannot possibly become more. Aquinas does not here consider the suggestion that God might change by becoming less, presumably because to hypothesize the possibility of any diminishing of God's essence would be to hold that God's nature is corruptible. This might even entail that God could cease to be. Absurd! God, if He exists, exists necessarily.

This third argument has been challenged by contemporary philosophers of religion. One might suggest that God could go from one sort of excellence to another without any diminution in His supreme status.[14] On the traditional view, though, God is the best of all possible kinds. If He could leave off having one sort of perfection and adopt another, He would not be the best conceivable either before or after the change, since there would be a perfection He would lack. Nor would He exist *a se*, for He would be the receiver of some new perfection, not the source of all perfection.

Could it be that there are potentialities that are value-neutral such that God could undergo becoming of a sort which makes no difference to His intrinsic value?[15] Within classical perfect being theology, as I have been developing the view, there is no potentiality which is value-neutral. In our universe all existence is actively good, and all action either (ultimately) sustains and enhances the good, or, in the special case of sin, undermines it. But isn't it value-neutral whether or not I have a chocolate ice cream cone right now? Maybe not. (Again, there will be echoes here of natural law ethics, the theory which fits most comfortably with perfect being theology and which will be discussed briefly in Chapter 9.) If eating that ice cream nourishes the body, cheers the individual, and so on, then it contributes to the good. If one is in a situation in which fat and cholesterol are a danger, then it does harm. Even if both hypotheticals are true, then eating the ice cream is not value-neutral: it is good in some ways and bad in others.

Allow that it is good for me to eat this ice cream. While eating chocolate I have the potential for eating pistachio, and the latter is no better or worse than the former, so are there not value-neutral potentialites? On the creaturely level there are. It is not clear that we can carry this over to the divine level, though. If one accepts that God is simple and eternal, as does the classic tradition, then the sort of infinity which God has involves doing all He does and being all He is 'at once' in eternity. On this understanding, to say that God does and is some of what He is capable of now, and then later does and is other things, is to limit God at each instant. To push the ice cream analogy (perhaps just a bit too far), unlike us, God is capable of having all the flavors at once. And that is what perfection entails.

According to traditional perfect being theology, God, in Himself, is immutable. This does not mean that different, even contradictory, propositions cannot be correctly expressed with regard to Him. For example, 'God is believed in by Rogers' and 'God is not believed in by Rogers', when uttered at different times, may both be true. 'God is believed in by Rogers in 1997' is true, and so is 'God is not believed in by Rogers in 1969'. But change in these relational properties, as Anselm makes clear in *Monologion* 25, does not indicate a change in God, any more than the coming into being of someone bigger or smaller than I *ipso facto* renders me smaller or bigger.[16]

But if God is truly immutable . . . and He must be if He is the best . . . how then can He possibly do all the various things that we believe Him to do? In Augustine's day the question was put this way, 'What was God doing before He created the world?' The point was to show that the Christian idea of God as Perfect Being and Creator is just nonsense. Augustine (explicitly eschewing the response, 'He was making Hell for people who ask that kind of question') answers with his famous meditation on the nature of time in *Confessions* XI. Time itself is a function of the created universe, he concludes. It is only temporal things that change. What they were they are not now. What they are now they will not be in the future. God is outside of time. We will use 'eternal' to describe this position and 'everlasting' to describe the view that God is temporal and has always existed in the past, exists now and will always exist in the future. According to Augustine, all of time is present to God, as if His eternity were the center point of a circle which is time. God knows everything that is going on. He keeps everything immediately in being. He acts and reacts. He hears and responds to prayers. And all in His one, eternal and changeless act of being.

That God is eternal is the standard (though not universal) view in the Middle Ages. Many contemporary philosophers have objections to the view, finding it paradoxical or just plain incoherent. The next chapter of this work is devoted to explaining and defending the view that a perfect being must be eternal. Here we are focusing on the issue of immutability, and Augustine is quite right. If God is to be both perfect, and an active person who knows and wills things with respect to His creation, He must be eternal. Aristotle's Unmoved Mover was able to maintain a pristine motionlessness by always doing exactly the same perfect thing, thinking

Itself. But, as the heated debates among Islamic and Jewish philosophers of the eleventh, twelfth and thirteenth centuries proved, an immutable but temporal God could not be squared with the God of revelation.[17]

It is sometimes argued that an eternal and immutable God can't really *do* anything, because conscious action must be temporal. Charles Hartshorne writes, 'A changeless being can have no purposes, for purposes refer to the future and the future is related to the present by change.'[18] Nelson Pike argues that an immutable being,

> could not be affected or prompted by another. To be affected or prompted by another is to be changed by the other. The actions of [an immutable being] could not be interpreted as a *response* to something else. Responses are located in time *after* that to which they are responses.[19]

Richard Swinburne concludes, 'Only a God who acts and chooses and loves and forgives is the God whom we wish to worship, and the pursuit of these activities, since they involve change of state, means being in time.'[20]

The apologist for divine immutability is likely to argue that these assertions are supported only by a dogmatic insistance that God must experience things the way we do. Moreover, even with respect to the human condition, these claims are questionable. Are purposes *necessarily* about the future? Suppose I am right now enjoying reading a book which I choose to read for the very purpose of enjoyment. It seems to me that right now I am reading 'on purpose'. I have an object in mind and I achieve it simultaneously. And surely it is conceivable that a response should not come after the request to which it is an answer. We do not even need to appeal to time-travel scenarios. If I know that my son will ask for his breakfast when he gets up, I may fix it for him before he asks. If he were a very slow talker, and I were an extremely speedy breakfast-maker, I might even be able to make it *as* he asked for it. And why must acting, choosing, loving and forgiving involve changes of state? Certainly if one were not doing something and then one started, that would be a change. If one did not choose or love or forgive and then later one did, that would involve change. But *while* one is engaged in these activities why must one undergo a change of state? We cannot argue that God could not do all of these things simultaneously, since even human beings are capable of performing many actions at once.

There are numerous paradoxes that are raised against the notion of an immutable God. How, for example, could He be truly omniscient, since, unless His knowledge changed He could not always know what time it is 'right now'? We can bypass this issue here, and address it later in the chapter on omniscience, after we have spelled out the traditional doctrine of divine eternity. Suffice it to say that there *is* a solution, although it does involve a slight adjustment in our thinking about time to bring it more into line with contemporary physics.

Among modern philosophers it has been common to jettison the strong notion of immutability, along with simplicity, aseity and eternity. Many hold the much weaker position that so long as a temporal God remains unchangeably powerful and knowledgeable and good in His essence, He is an adequate object of worship, even though what He actually chooses and knows changes over time. One of the few philosophers who has tried to defend a 'medium strength' view of immutability is Richard Creel. God is in time, yet His nature and will are immutable. Human beings are free in a libertarian sense, so God does not know what they will actually choose in the future, but He eternally knows all possibilities and He eternally wills how He will respond to any given choice.[21] But this hardly seems like genuine immutability. If an everlasting God had always willed as a certainty that the world would end at the stroke of midnight GMT, 31December 1999, when the time comes His will must change to this extent, that He wills that the world should end not at some point in the future but *now*. If you add that the divine choice is hypothetical being dependent on what free beings actually choose, then the actual willing to destroy the world seems even more different from the choice to do so in the future *if* certain conditions hold. True, this does not involve God 'changing His mind'. Nonetheless it does involve Him willing something He had not willed before. And since God is the absolute and immediate sustainer of all, should He will to destroy creation He will go from keeping all creation in existence (also known as being a Creator) to not doing so (*not* being a Creator). Though this may not entail a change in the everlasting knowledge or will of this temporal God, it seems to entail a definite change in His nature, the sort of change which an absolutely perfect being could not suffer. (Whether or not the eternal God of the tradition could have failed to create is a very difficult question for Chapter 7.) The attempt to see God as temporal, but nonetheless immutable, does not succeed. It is only the stronger doctrine of absolute immutability which can be squared with perfect being theology.

IMPASSIVITY

Can God feel passions? The Bible speaks of God feeling joy and love and compassion, anger and hate, jealousy and sorrow. But the Bible-believing theist may legitimately approach such language cautiously. The Bible also says that God forgets things and regrets things He has done, but perhaps these terms do not mean just what they do when we use them of our fellow human beings. Perfect being theology will deny that God has the sorts of feelings which are tied to creaturely limitations. When Aquinas writes, in *Summa Theologiae* I, Q.20, that God is 'impassive' he is speaking of emotions which are associated with bodily feelings. God is incorporeal and so does not suffer any of the physical symptoms which can accompany emotions.[22] What can it mean, then, to say, for example, that God shows 'mercy', *misericordia*, literally 'sadness of heart'? Aquinas answers (ST I, Q.22, art.3), as did Anselm in Chapter 8 of the *Proslogion*, that God's mercy consists in the effect of dispelling the sorrow of another, though He does not feel sorrow Himself. He does not feel the physical discomfort associated with sorrow, nor the psychological pain associated with loss and regret.

Is God, then, entirely free of emotions? Not at all. He experiences the 'positive' emotions, love and joy, to an infinite degree. Norman Kretzmann, in his *The Metaphysics of Theism: Aquinas's Natural Theology in Summa Contra Gentiles I*, explains that divine joy and love are the simple act of God's willing Himself and willing other things as the manifold reflections of His perfect goodness.[23] Kretzmann explores the question of whether, on Aquinas' analysis, divine love for the creature, though perfect in itself, may be unrequited and hence fail to achieve the union which is the proper consequence of love. He concludes that the free creature may reject God, and so 'Divine love, too, can be unfulfilled.'[24] Again, the ascription to human beings of freedom poses puzzles for perfect being theology which are worthy of further investigation. But there is no question that in the classical tradition God enjoys complete love and happiness, while 'negative' emotions, like hate and sorrow, which are the falling away from love and joy, are impossible for a perfect being to experience (ST I, Q.20).

Hartshorne argues against this classical conception of God. He writes, 'Love involves sensitivity to the joys and sorrows of others, participation in them – but [on the traditional view] we cannot infect God with our sufferings (since he is cause of everything and effect of nothing), and our joys can add nothing to the immutable perfection of God's happiness.'[25] I argued in the last chapter that the God of Anselm (if not of Augustine and Aquinas) is affected by human choices. But Hartshorne is quite right to hold that no classical theist will allow that we can 'infect' God with our sufferings or add to God's happiness. God is infinitely happy and we can do nothing to lessen it, nor can we (even logically) add to infinity. The medieval position is simply that it is better to be happy than sad, so God must be infinitely happy.

How can we decide between these two views? The medieval view is, obviously, part and parcel of the image of a simple and immutable being. Such a God can't be part sad and part happy or sad then but happy now. He certainly cannot become more happy. If we set aside the background metaphysics and simply focus on the question of the value of divine passibility, it may be that preference for a God who can or cannot suffer or be made happier is ultimately subjective and rooted in the life experiences of the individual theist. I do think there are at least two questions to be raised against Hartshorne's conception, though.

First, suppose it were conceptually possible, as it seems to be, that God does not undergo any suffering and is completely, or infinitely, happy. He would still love His creatures in that He would want only good for them, and extend mercy towards them in that He would help free them from all evil. And suppose it is also possible, as Hartshorne conjectures, that God suffers and experiences only limited happiness. Would Hartshorne *prefer* that God suffer? There seems to be something suspect in prefering that another person not only love and help you but suffer as well. Certainly human preferences in this respect are not going to cause God to be one way or the other. The point is that, if the issue of divine passibility (setting aside related metaphysical questions) boils down to subjective preferences, it seems fair to question the side that would prefer that there should be a God who suffers and is less than perfectly happy.

Secondly (and I grant that this is a *very* subjective point), I have a hard time seeing why one would prefer a God incapable of unconditional love. Hartshorne's view of love seems to be that the lover *needs* the beloved in order to become more joyful. I find in myself (and I can only ask the reader to introspect to see if this is a shared phenomenon) a longing to be loved, wholly and completely, by someone who does not want anything from me. I do not think such love has a place in the created universe, since we are all by nature contingent and hence needy beings. As far as I can tell, the most likely candidate for a being who can perfectly will good for us without demanding anything in return is the God of Augustine and Anselm and Aquinas. Someone unfamiliar with the tradition might respond that the God of the medievals is very demanding indeed. Isn't He quite unyielding in His insistence that we behave well . . . towards other human beings, towards the physical world in general, and towards Him? But in the tradition under consideration here the divine commands directed towards us, also known as natural law ethics, are instructions for the promotion of the well-being of the human animal on its journey to heaven. What God wants *from* us is just that we should act towards our own happiness. Myself, I find the idea of a God who is made to suffer by us, and who needs us to be fulfilled, a depressing conception of divinity. In any case, it does not square with the other attributes of a perfect being, like simplicity and immutability. So if we are committed to perfect being theology we can safely trust that God experiences only infinite love and joy . . . immutably, necessarily and, as we shall see in the next chapter, eternally.

NOTES

1. Graham Oppy, *Ontological Arguments and Belief in God.*
2. Hume, *Dialogues Concerning Natural Religion* IX.
3. J. N. Findlay argued along these lines that the existence of a logically necessary being is logically impossible. ('Can God's existence be disproved?')
4. Kai Neilsen adds the positivist notion that for a proposition to be meaningful we have to be able to say what would count for and against it (*God, Scepticism and Modernity*, pp. 28–9). On the view that God is the ultimate source of all, absolutely everything counts for the claim that God exists, and nothing could possibly count against it. Neilsen is free to conclude that the concept of God is incoherent, but, for those of us who seem to be making sense of it, it is probably better to give up the positivist principle.
5. ST I, Q.2, art.1.
6. Alvin Plantinga, *The Nature of Necessity*, p. 214.
7. David Schrader, 'The antinomy of divine necessity'.
8. Richard Gale, *On the Nature and Existence of God*, p. 179.
9. James Ross, *Philosophical Theology*, pp. 173–82.
10. Gale, *On the Nature and Existence of God*, pp. 203–4.
11. Gale, *On the Nature and Existence of God*, p. 205.
12. For an early and very clear proof text on this, see Augustine's *Confessions* 12, 15.
13. My colleague Michael Rea argues that things can change without having parts. The mereological atom, for example, by definition an object with no parts, may change position. I take it that it is an open question whether or not a spatial, but partless, object could actually exist. In any case, I do not see that there is any change which one might hypothesize of *God* which would not be subject to Aquinas' argument.
14. J. R. Lucas, *The Future: An Essay on God, Temporality and Truth*, p. 216.
15. Thomas V. Morris, *Our Idea of God*, p. 128.
16. This is a standard point. What Anselm calls *relationes* are often called 'Cambridge properties' in the current literature. There is no citation to a previous source in the notes to Anselm's *Opera Omnia* (ed. F. S. Schmitt), and it would not be surprising to discover that Anselm, as the first really analytic philosopher of religion, was the first to make this important distinction.
17. In the medieval debate the question of whether or not the past is infinite really had to do with whether or not God can 'change', that is, can interact with creation. Avicenna and Averroes, for example, held that the world has always existed. Algazali and Maimonides were among those who defended the idea of a finite past. Maimonides seems to have employed the doctrine of divine eternity to solve the problem in the same way that Augustine did, but I do not know that there was any direct influence.
18. Charles Hartshorne, *Reality as Social Process*, p. 159.
19. Nelson Pike, *God and Timelessness*, p. 128.
20. Richard Swinburne, *The Coherence of Theism*, p. 218.
21. Creel, *Divine Impassibility*, pp. 22–4.
22. Daniel Westberg, 'Emotion and God: A reply to Marcel Sarot'.
23. Norman Kretzmann, *The Metaphysics of Theism: Aquinas's Natural Theology in Summa Contra Gentiles I*, pp. 236–7.
24. Kretzmann, *Metaphysics of Theism*, p. 247.
25. Charles Hartshorne, *Man's Vision of God*, p. 114.

5

Eternity

'Now that God is eternal is the common judgement of all who live by reason', says Boethius.[1] And his remark was apt for almost every philosopher or theologian in the Latin West from Augustine at least through Aquinas, that is to say from the fourth century for the next thousand years. Scotus and Ockham questioned the view, but it continued to be the dominant position among Catholic philosophers of religion. A number of contemporary analytic philosophers reject the doctrine, and it seemed to have fallen out of fashion for a time, but today it has a number of staunch defenders. Among them must be anyone who accepts perfect being theology in the classic tradition.

As we saw in the last chapter, it was Augustine's doctrine of divine eternity which shaped the theology of Western Christendom. Confronted with the problem of how an immutable being could nonetheless be the creating agent of the Judeo-Christian tradition, Augustine argued that God is not temporal. All of time is immediately present to Him, and He does all He does in one, perfect, eternal and immutable act.[2] A temporal God could be immutable only if He did not act and interact in creation. Hence the bitter and centuries-long debate in medieval Islam over the everlastingness of the world sparked by many philosophers accepting Aristotle's Unmoved Mover as the temporal but unchanging source of all. Avicenna and Averroes argued that if the source of the world does not suffer any change, then the world must have existed infinitely in the past, and things must have been going on forever pretty much as they go on now. This view is impossible to square with religions founded upon key historical events, as are Judaism, Islam and Christianity. Alternatively, a God who is temporal and mutable cannot be 'that than which a greater can be conceived'. Only through the Augustinian move to eternity can God's perfection be reconciled with His living agency in our world.

Thus it is peculiarly distressing to find that some contemporary philosophers mistakenly trace the doctrine of eternity to a pernicious 'Greek' desire to place God outside of our world. J. R. Lucas presents a vivid example of this misunderstanding. He defends the position that God is temporal and writes,

> A long tradition of Christian theology maintains the opposite, that God is timeless and changeless . . . Boethius . . . resorted to the timelessness of God as the only way of preventing an insoluble problem being posed. Only if God is distanced from the world of space and time can He be acquitted of responsibility for the terrible things that happen within it – an omnipotent Deity who operated in time could have intervened to prevent the holocaust, and if He did not, showed Himself thereby to be insensitive to the sufferings of others, and less than perfectly benevolent.[3]

He goes on to describe the God of the medievals as 'non-interventionist'.

The citation Lucas offers is to Book V, prose 6 of *The Consolation of Philosophy*. Here Boethius says that God is external to time, and he offers his elegant and oft-quoted definition of eternity as 'the whole, simultaneous and perfect possession of boundless life . . .' But he nowhere suggests that because God is timeless He is 'non-interventionist'. *Au contraire*, the very reason that Boethius finds consolation in philosophy is that he comes to see that God's providence governs all things for the ultimate good, and this includes the future. He was writing in prison awaiting execution and the conclusion which Lucas attributes to him would hardly have been consoling. To my knowledge no one in the medieval tradition makes the argument which Lucas sees as the impetus for belief in divine eternity. The philosophers I have taken as my exemplars, Augustine, Anselm and Aquinas, all lived lives of prayerful devotion to a God with whom they believed themselves to be in personal contact.

In the classic tradition the motive for insisting upon a timeless divinity has nothing to do with removing God from interaction with our world. Why were the medievals so adamant that the interaction must be eternal on the part of God? First, as we have seen, it is only by postulating divine eternity that God's immutability can be preserved, and with it His simplicity. If God does first one thing and then another He cannot be simple because His essence must stay the same over time, and thus be something other than the part that does the changing. In addition to preserving the divine attributes of immutability and simplicity, there are a number of other reasons to insist upon God's eternity.

Augustine holds that time is the product of motion and change, and hence it is a category of the physical universe.[4] The author of the space–time continuum could not be bound by it. Recently a number of contemporary philosophers of religion have seen support for this view in Einstein's Theory of Relativity and have used the theory in various ways to explain how an atemporal God could relate to a temporal world. The underlying thesis is that if time is relative to particular observational frameworks, then there is no absolute, universal time which would encompass God and the physical world.[5] Stump and Kretzmann, for example, make use of the theory of Special Relativity to illustrate their doctrine of ET (Eternity/Time) Simultaneity, in which different times could be 'simultaneous' with Eternity, but not with one another.[6] In contrast, some critics argue that this exhibits a misunderstanding of the Theory of Relativity and there can be an absolute time such that God exists in time the way we do (or in a similar way).[7] I am not competent to enter the lists on this particular issue. Nor do I think it is necessary. If the theory of Special Relativity reinforces the view that God is atemporal, splendid. But even if the consensus among scientists should some day come to be that there is an absolute and universal time for the entire physical universe, Augustine's point that being temporal is a limitation would still hold.

As Augustine explains in *Confessions* XI, we temporal beings seem to exist only at the present unextended instant, the point where the not-yet-existent future turns into the no-longer-existent past. A very tenuous sort of existence! We cannot 'possess' all of our lives at once. Our knowledge and our abilities are radically circumscribed by our temporal presentness. We cannot have direct knowledge of the past, but only memory. We cannot act on the past at all, and our effect on the future is not immediate but derived from what we do in the present. God is not like this. God possesses being perfectly because all of His own life is present to Him, and He knows and causes all things at all times because all of time is immediately present to Him.

The one qualification to the last point is that God does not cause sin. Sin is where we become original, and God permits it because of the enormous value of freedom. And herein lies a final motive for adopting the doctrine of eternity. There are a number of reasons for holding that divine omniscience should encompass the future, as I shall argue in the next chapter. On the compatibilist reading of freedom, a temporal God could know the future by extrapolating with certainty from present events. But on the libertarian view of freedom present events do not produce future free choices. A temporal God cannot know the future if it contains choices which are free in the libertarian sense. In the next chapter I shall argue that *only* the doctrine of divine eternity allows an adequate reconciliation between divine foreknowledge and human freedom.

But can sense be made of the idea that God is eternal? What could eternity possibly be like? We are temporal beings and cannot envision a timeless existence. Still, we can achieve some understanding, though the attempt will have to rest on analogies and hence our grasp of the eternal is likely to be tenuous at best. Stump and Kretzmann, in their landmark article in 1981, focusing on Boethius' definition, hold that in the medieval tradition the eternal present 'is not instantaneous but extended . . .'[8] They attempt to explain this durational eternity in a later article through the use of a geometric analogy. Imagine two infinite, parallel horizontal lines, one representing time, the other eternity. On the temporal line the present is an ever-moving point of light, but the eternal line is all light, all present.[9] Brian Leftow also defends the idea of a durational eternity. Paraphrasing Stump and Kretzmann's analogy he writes, 'an eternal God is copresent with the whole of time by His life's being stretched out alongside it'.[10]

It seems to me this is not the right way to express the mode of God's being. In Chapter 3 I argued, agreeing with the medieval philosophers, that unity and simplicity are perfections while multiplicity and extension entail limitation and weakness. A number of the popular analogies which they offer suggest that, as the classic tradition understood it, God's eternity is in no way 'stretched out'. Augustine in the *Confessions* uses the term 'present' to describe the eternal mode of being.[11] And he says repeatedly that what chiefly characterizes the present instant of time is that it has no duration. 'Who would deny that the present time lacks extension since it passes in an instant?'[12] If Augustine chooses to use the word 'present' to characterize eternity, then it seems reasonable to suppose that he does not see eternity as somehow extended. He says that God wills all that He wills, 'in a single act and all at once and eternally' (*semel et simul et semper*).[13]

Boethius writes that God sees 'all things as though from the highest peak of the world'.[14] And Aquinas offers the analogy of a road on which those who travel it can see only what is near them, while someone looking down from a height could see all the travelers at once.[15] Both of these analogies suggest that eternity is an unextended vantage point, from which the expanse of time can be observed. Another analogy which reinforces this view is the oft-cited example of a circle where the center point represents eternity and the circumference represents time. Plotinus and Boethius both use this example. Aquinas, too, adopts it to show how God, in eternity, can be present to all of time. He writes,

> We may see an example of sorts in the case of a circle. Let us consider a determined point on the circumference of a circle. Although it is indivisible, it does not co-exist simultaneously with any other point as to position, since it is the order of position that produces the continuity of the circumference. On the other hand, the centre of the circle, which is no part of the circumference, is directly opposed to any given determinate point on the circumference. Hence, whatever is found in any part of time co-exists with what is eternal as being present to it, although with respect to some other time it be past or future. Something can be present to what is eternal only by being present to the whole of it, since the eternal does not have the duration of succession. The divine intellect, therefore, sees in the whole of its eternity, as being present to it, whatever takes place through the whole course of time.[16]

These analogies clearly imply that whatever the classic tradition thought *could* be said of eternity, they did not hold that it is in any way extended. This is just as well, since, as I have argued at length elsewhere, it is not possible to make sense of a timeless duration.[17] At the same time it would be wrong to dismiss the motive behind the suggestion that eternity ought to be seen as durational. Stump and Kretzmann rightly reject the idea that eternity is 'a static instance' or 'frozen instant'.[18] The reason for insisting upon divine timelessness is that being temporal is being limited. It may be that Augustine is right, and 'present' is the best term we have for God's mode of existence, if we must use a word which has positive, empirical content for us. But whatever God's 'present' is like, it is not, like ours, the unextended point between an inaccessible past and future. I am sympathetic to Paul Helm's suggestion, that since God's eternity is neither instantaneous nor durational, we eschew all positive time-words and simply say that divine eternity is 'time-free'.[19]

Though eternal, God is nonetheless related to the temporal world. He knows what happens. He hears and answers prayers. He sustains all existents in being from moment to moment. How can the temporal and the atemporal interact? Anselm discusses the dilemma in *Monologion* 20–4, and in Chapter 13 of the *Proslogion* which is entitled, 'Therefore because nothing is greater than you, no space or time contains you, but you are everywhere and always'. He offers a final, provocative analogy in a later work, *On the Harmony of the Foreknowledge and the Predestination and the Grace of God with Free Will*. 'Just as the present time contains all place and whatever exists in any place: in the same way all time and what exists in any time is enclosed in the eternal present.'[20] This implies that eternity is a sort of *fifth* dimension, encompassing the other four.

God is neither spatial nor temporal, but He sustains all spatial and temporal things immediately. Space and time are not categories which apply to God, but all spatial and temporal things are immediately known and caused by God. Let us call this relationship one of 'presentness'. 'Present' here is not meant to imply any sort of temporality, and applies equally to the spatial/non-spatial relationship as to the temporal/eternal relationship. God is not 'contained in' any space or time, but He is wholly 'present' to, that is knowing and causing, all of it, and all of it is 'present' to, that is known and caused by Him. (A more developed analysis of divine 'presentness' to all space–time depends upon an understanding of the unique way in which God knows and causes things, which is the subject of Chapters 6 and 7.)

Almost all Judeo-Christian philosophers of religion, past and present, have agreed that God is not spatial, and that nonetheless He is 'present' to all of space and it to Him. In order to try to make some sense of the relationship of time to eternity I shall lean heavily upon the analogy of space to divine aspatiality. We have to stretch our intellectual powers to conceive of God's non-spatial ubiquity. In order to get at eternity we must stretch farther, but in the same direction. So, in order to get at the relationship of time to eternity, first think of (I do not say 'imagine' or 'envision') all of space. Now think of it all 'present' to God and He to it. Now, in the same way, think of all of time, whatever there has been, is, or will be . . . think of it as a temporal continuum, whether finite or infinite is not important here. Now think of it all 'present' to God and He to it. That is the relationship between time and eternity. In what follows I shall elaborate on this relationship by discussing its implications for the nature of time, and by responding to criticisms of the view that God is atemporal.

This statement of the nature of divine eternity in which all of time is 'present' to God entails a particular theory of time. Some find it a bizarre theory, but I do not consider this a problem for the doctrine of eternity, since every theory of time has its eccentricities. Augustine's lament that time is a common and familiar thing until we try to think about it seems as apt today as it did a millennium and a half ago.[21] The 'bizarre' view entailed by the classic doctrine of eternity is eternalism, the view that the past and future are as real as the present, as opposed to presentism, the view that only the present actually exists.[22] On eternalism 'past', 'present' and 'future' are all existent, but can be distinguished relative to a given observer at a given time. What I term 'present' is not what Augustine terms 'present' or what some (from our perspective) future philosopher terms 'present'. The temporal term 'present' is analogous to the spatial term 'here'. 'Past' and 'future' are analogous to 'there' in that, though existent, they are not 'here'. Perhaps they are also analogous to 'right' or 'left' in that the past is 'not here in this direction' while the future is 'not here in that direction'. Absolutely considered, or from the God's eye point of view, time is tenseless in the sense that no given moment is *really* past or future or present. What this means is that the present has no privileged ontological status. What, from our perspective is past and gone, or future and not yet, really exists. As Christopher Kirwan puts it in discussing Augustine, 'the past and the future are in hiding only in the attenuated sense of being absent; but absence, not non-existence, is the true contradictory of being present'.[23]

This may seem a strange view of the nature of things. Usually we think of (what is from our perspective) the past and the future as non-existent. Though not always. Most people do not find time-travel stories incoherent, or so alien from their 'normal' views that they could not be compelling. On the contrary. Most people seem to have no trouble at all in accepting the premise that, if only we had the right sort of vehicle, we could travel from our present to the past or the future . . . and that once we'd arrived there *that* would be our present. At least in the context of time-travel fiction, the assumption is that, while it may be impossible empirically, there is nothing incoherent in the idea that with respect to past and future we can get there from here. Presentism may be our more usual way of viewing time, but we seem to be able to make sense of eternalism.

For understanding eternalism, an analogy with our thinking about space will be helpful. Suppose someone is afflicted with HOPS, 'the-Here-is-Ontologically-Privileged' Syndrome. He is convinced that only the space which is immediately perceptible to him actually exists. He believes that whatever is 'here' is real and whatever is 'there', that is, 'not here', is non-existent. We cannot offer our HOPS victim direct empirical evidence that there really are things out there in the spaces he does not perceive. By definition, he can never have experiential access to such things. While he is in Cincinnati I call him from Philadelphia to try to persuade him that Philadelphia exists even when he does not directly perceive it, but he concludes, consistent with his condition, that all that there is to me at that point is the voice he hears.

Should the HOPS victim be a theologian he will conclude that God must be 'here' because it is only 'here' that exists. And he will go on to point out that this is not a limitation on God. If Philadelphia does not exist when he is in Cincinnati, then that God is not in Philadelphia but only in (a very limited part of) Cincinnati is the inevitable conclusion. God will only know what's going on in Cincinnati, and only be able to affect what happens in Cincinnati. But, our HOPS victim will argue, this does not conflict with God's omniscience or omnipotence. God knows all there is to know and can do all that can be done. But since 'here', Cincinnati, is all there is, then of course God has no access to Philadelphia or anywhere else, except perhaps through memory.

The eternalist holds that those who believe that all that exists in any sense at all must exist in what is to them the temporal present are making a mistake analogous to the one made by our HOPS victim. They are suffering from NOPS, 'the-Now-is-Ontologically-Privileged' Syndrome. They hold that only what is temporally accessible to them is really existent, and even God must exist only 'now' because it is their temporal perspective which sets the standard for what there can be. And, as with our HOPS victim, in favor of their view they have the fact that it is impossible for any of us 'now' to have empirical access to any other time. But it is clearly the eternalist view which jibes better with perfect being theology. A being who can know and act in all of time must be greater than a being who can know and act only in our present. The burden of proof is on those who would hold that such a being is impossible.

There are those who defend divine eternity, but reject the thesis that this entails the view that because all of time is 'present' to God it must be *really* there in some absolute sense. Brian Leftow, for example, in explaining how God and time are related, appeals to the 'framework-relativity of simultaneity'. There may be different frames of reference such that two events which are simultaneous in one are not simultaneous in another. 'If we take eternity as one more frame of reference, then . . . Events are present and actual all at once in eternity, but present and actual in sequence in other reference frames.'[24] The problem with this is that we cannot treat eternity as merely 'one more frame of reference'. Eternity is *God's* point of view, after all. God's 'framework' is not just different from ours; it is the unlimited source of everything. If we see things one way and God sees them another, then what we see is how things appear to the limited perceiver, and what God sees is how things *are*.

Some philosophers introduce William James's concept of a 'specious present' to help explain the relationship of divine eternity to time.[25] James held that we actually experience time as durational. Our present experience is not of an unextended instant, but rather includes perception of the immediate past and anticipation of the future. So even human experience can allow for an actually instantaneous experience of a temporally extended time. The suggestion is then to attribute to God an infinite specious present, so that He can experience all of time in an eternal moment. I think there are difficulties with this approach. If all of our past, present and future are really 'present' to God, then I am not sure what is 'specious' in His experience. If He experiences past and present (and a not-yet-existent future?) *as if they were* present, which I take to be what James is saying about human experience, then God's view of things is inaccurate. So I am not sure that the attribution of a *specious* present to God is helpful. Better just to allow that all of time is actually 'present' to God.

There are a number of remaining questions about this theory of time implied by divine eternity. One might point out that the very reason which the medievals gave for introducing the distinction between eternity and time was to insist upon the radical transitoriness of creaturely existence in comparison to the perfection of God's immutable mode of being, and yet if eternalism is correct and we are four-dimensional beings ever-present to God, then we are not as transitory as we seem to ourselves.[26] The point is well taken, but surely it is good news that ontologically there is more to us than meets the temporal eye. And really, this does not go very far to close the gap between God's being and ours. We are still utterly dependent on God. We are still radically limited. By comparison with God who 'possesses' His unlimited life 'at once', we lead a dreadfully 'disconnected' life in that at each present instant we have little access to or power over all the other instants of our lives.

Another problem involves personal responsibility. If we exist four-dimensionally so that at each moment there is but a temporal 'part' of us present, how can one temporal part be held responsible for the actions of another temporal part?[27] I do not know that the eternalist need commit herself to the doctrine of temporal parts, but in any case she can respond that just as we may hold *you* responsible for what one of your physical parts did, and may inflict harm on one part in punishment for what another did, we can hold *you* responsible when we praise or blame the temporal part to which we have present access.[28]

A number of contemporary philosophers of religion raise a more far-reaching difficulty with the eternalist analysis of the relationship of God to creation. They hold that if God's eternal presence to all of time renders (our) past and future existent, then time is somehow illusory. If all temporal events are just 'there' eternally then change, sequence, causation do not really exist. William Hasker, for example, holds that if God were eternal He could not know temporal events immediately, for anything really present to God in eternity would have to be itself eternal, not temporal.[29] Richard Creel writes that, if the future is known as actual by God, then because God cannot be mistaken our belief that the future lies before us must be false, and the occurrence of change must be an illusion. Time becomes the Platonic peephole through which we observe things that God knows to have been always in existence. We thereby come to the mistaken impression that things occur sequentially when in fact, as God knows, they exist simultaneously. In brief, either a thing is changing or it is not. If God does not know it as changing but we know it as changing, then one of us is mistaken, and it surely is not God. Therefore if eternalism is true, then experience of change is an illusion.[30]

But this charge rests on a misunderstanding. To say that all of time exists and is 'present' to God's eternity does not render temporal events eternal any more than to say that all of space exists and is 'present' to God's ubiquity renders spatial objects ubiquitous. Space continues to be its usual extended self, and spatial objects continue to be 'here' and 'there', 'right' and 'left', with distance between them, even though the entire spatial universe is immediately 'present' to God and He to it. The whole point is that God is not subject to the category of space. His presence to spatial events does not involve being a spatial object in contact with other spatial objects. And so He can be 'present' to all space without being some huge, all encompassing, body. And space and spatial objects can be 'present' to Him without ceasing to be the spatial objects that they are. And time is analogous. God does not have to be temporally extended to encompass all of time. And temporal events do not cease to be temporal because they are 'present' to God. It is true that 'now', 'past' and 'future' are relative to the given temporal observer, just as 'here' and 'there' are relative to the spatial observer, but that does not do away with temporal extension and relationships.

There is no reason to conclude that God's eternal 'presence' to time should somehow render time frozen or static. Augustine offers a helpful analogy when he says that God's knowledge of (what we call) the future, and presumably of all of time, is like our knowledge of the past.[31] Suppose there were a very good (*very* good) historian who could think about the American Civil War with perfect accuracy and in a single instant. (That this is impossible is just a result of human frailty. When we think about history we do something like this, only with a lesser degree of speed and accuracy. We get some things right and we are capable of capturing a durational event like a war in a single concept.) The event, being past, is 'fixed' in that it cannot turn out otherwise than it actually has turned out. Our historian's knowledge of it is *ex hypothesi* instantaneous. Now does it follow that the remembered events do not include sequence and change and causal connections? If our historian's knowledge is accurate then he remembers the Battle of Gettysburg occurring after the firing on Fort Sumter and before the surrender at Appomadox. And he appreciates events which led up to the battle, and the importance of the battle for the future conduct of the war. His fixed and instantaneous memory does not rob the event of any of its activity and motion. Nor does God's 'fixed and instantaneous' immediate knowledge of all events somehow render them non-temporal or non-sequential. (I will argue in the next chapter that God's knowledge of the 'future' does not render human choices unfree any more than does the historian's knowledge of the past.) Time is no more illusory than space. Nor is our experience of time somehow 'defective'. We experience things as we were made to experience them. The only mistake is when we insist that what we now call 'the present' is all there is.

The traditional doctrine of divine eternity does entail eternalism. This view is not incoherent, nor does it render time illusory nor destroy sequence and causal connection. Thus I do not include this entailment among the problems for the doctrine of eternity. However, there are a host of problems which need to be addressed. To begin with, some contemporary philosophers of religion accuse the doctrine of being 'non-biblical' and, even worse, 'Greek' or 'Platonic'.[32] And there certainly are scriptural passages which *prima facie* imply that God is temporal. There are passages which imply that He is corporeal. There are scriptural passages which imply that He is radically imperfect . . . forgetful, for example. The question of how and by whom such passages are to be interpreted has deeply divided Western Christendom, and here is not the place to address the issue. Suffice it to say that all sides agree that the Bible is not a treatise in metaphysics. There are passages which suggest that God is not a being bound by time, so the philosophical question is open. Paul Helm goes farther than this and argues that, 'only a God who is immutable in a particularly strong sense can (logically) perform all that Scripture claims that God performs, and a God can only be immutable in this strong sense if he exists timelessly'.[33] Moreover, many of those who level the charge of being 'non-biblical' against the doctrine of eternity recognize that, if human beings are free in a libertarian sense, then a temporal God cannot know the future, and so they jettison the idea of divine foreknowledge. The Bible expresses, clearly and often, the view that God knows the future, whereas it never addresses the question of the metaphysical nature of time. Thus it seems a suspect biblical exegesis which will deny foreknowledge and reinterpret prophecy because it conflicts with the eternalist theory of time.

There is more to be said here, though. The reason many contemporary philosophers of religion see the doctrine of eternity as 'non-biblical' is that they think it is incoherent to suppose that a timeless being could be a *person*, an agent who chooses and acts. After all, the persons we know best, human beings, are one and all subject to time. Swinburne writes,

> so many other things which the theist wishes to say about God – that he brings about this or that, forgives, punishes, or warns – are things which are true of a man at this or that time or at all times. If we say that P brings about x, we can always sensibly ask *when* does he bring it about?[34]

The classic tradition is adamant that God is indeed a person. But the insistence that God be so similar to human beings seems a mistake. The very same argument could be used to show that God must be a spatial being. Human persons are spatial and, 'If we say that P brings about x, we can always sensibly ask *where* does he bring it about?' Presumably Swinburne does not want to hold that God must be embodied as we are.

Is the argument just that mental processes which do not 'take time' are inconceivable? Certainly there are some mental activities in which God cannot engage. He cannot *remember* or *anticipate*. He can understand these terms in the sense that He knows what a temporal being is doing when it remembers or anticipates. Is this a limitation on the divine intellect? Of course not. To remember and anticipate require that there be times, one's past and future, to which one does not have immediate experiential access. But this is a limitation. A being 'present' to all of time has no past or future to remember or anticipate.

Alternatively, there are certain activities which the Judeo-Christian God does engage in. He knows, He wills, He loves. Do these require time? Well, it should be noted first of all, that we human beings engaged in these activities only actually do them in the present. When I am thinking or willing or loving, I am doing it *now*. We do not experience or act in the past or the future, but in the present. It is just that what I am thinking one instant is immediately superseded by some new thought and another and another. We live in the now, but each succeeding now is different from the one before. So when the eternalist says that God thinks or wills or loves in a single, eternal act, he need not be postulating mental activities which are different in kind from our own. The radical difference lies in the fact that God's thoughts do not change, flickering in and out of being as ours seem to do.

St. Augustine implies an analogy between the human and divine mind when he writes,

> But if only their minds could be seized and held steady, they would be
> still for a while and, for that short moment, they would glimpse the
> splendour of eternity which is for ever still. They would see that time
> derives its length only from a great number of movements constantly
> following one another into the past, because they cannot all continue
> at once. But in eternity nothing moves into the past: all is present . . .
> If only men's minds could be seized and held still! They would see
> how eternity, in which there is neither past nor future, determines
> both past and future time.[35]

We do not think in the past, present and future, but only in the present. If
our present thoughts were not constantly changing we could have an idea
of what the eternal present is like.

But how could an eternal God interact with His temporal creation?
'Such two-way interaction', writes Richard Gale, 'makes no sense on the
theory of a timelessly eternal God, for all of his states and actions occur
within a single timeless present and cannot be the effect of anything that
happens in time'.[36] Now it is quite true that on the traditional doctrine of
divine eternity all of God's 'states and actions occur within a single timeless
present' but it simply does not follow that they 'cannot be the effect of
anything that happens in time'. The classic tradition equally insists that
God is incorporeal, which could be expressed as saying that all of His
'states and actions occur within a single spaceless here'. Presumably Gale
would not take it to follow that in that case God's states and actions
'cannot be the effect of anything that happens in space'. Just as God is non-
spatial but 'present' to all of space, He is eternal, but 'present' to all of
time. I occupy space and time when I pray. God occupies neither when He
hears and responds.

But doesn't the very term 'responds' suggest a temporal relationship?
How can God respond unless it is *after* I have prayed? Certainly the
concept of a response requires that there be a certain sort of causal
connection such that the prayer 'prompts' the response, and the response
'answers' the prayer. At the end of Book IX of the *Confessions* St.
Augustine asks that we who read the book should pray for his deceased
mother Monica. Suppose I (following the logic of my eternalism) include in
my prayer, formed towards the end of the twentieth century, a request that
God give Monica the strength to persevere through all those years when
her son rejected Christianity. And suppose God, to whom the fourth and
the twentieth centuries are equally present, eternally and in His single,
immutable act of being, gives Monica strength in part (very small part)
because of my prayer. Then He has responded to my prayer. There is no

reason to insist that a divine response must be made in time unless one is already committed to the view that time is absolute and God cannot transcend it.

A different sort of problem arises from a too literal reading of the doctrine of divine eternity. Or perhaps it is better to say that the doctrine has sometimes been incautiously expressed. Augustine, for example, says that all of God's years, 'stand simultaneously' (*simul stant*) and they are all but a 'single day . . . today' (*dies unus . . . hodie*).[37] But 'simultaneous' means 'at the same time'. One might then argue, as some contemporary philosophers have done, that if the year 499 and the year 1109 and the year 2001 are all 'at the same time as' God's present then they must be 'at the same time as' one another. But that is absurd.

It is this problem which Aquinas addresses with his analogy, cited above, of the center point being equally present to all the points on the circumference of a circle. Stump and Kretzmann speak to this problem when they propose that the relationship of ET Simultaneity is not transitive. A temporal event simultaneous with eternity need not be simultaneous with another temporal event, though the second event is also simultaneous with eternity.[38] This solution is basically correct, though it might be better to eschew the term 'simultaneous' entirely. I prefer to say that two different times can be equally 'present' to God (immediately known and sustained by Him) without being present to one another temporally or otherwise.

And again, the analogy with space is helpful. One might express divine ubiquity (badly) by saying that Cincinnati, for example, and Philadelphia are both 'in the same place as God'. But then one might draw the conclusion that the two cities are in the same place as each other. Better to say that both cities are 'present' to God. This terminology would not mislead people into arguing that if God is 'here' in Cincinnati and 'here' in Philadelphia then Cincinnati is here in Philadelphia.

Some have argued that if God is eternal He cannot be omniscient. If past, present and future are equally present to God then there is at least one sort of thing he cannot know and that is what time it is *now*. The way A. N. Prior explains it is that a tensed statement, such as 'Clinton is president now', spoken in 1997, does not mean exactly the same thing as the tenseless, 'Clinton is president in 1997'. A timeless God could, timelessly, know the latter, but He could not timelessly know the former. And so there are an almost limitless number of facts which an eternal being could not know.[39]

But this criticism presupposes that there is an absolute *now*. If what I call 'now' is all that really exists, and if God, seeing all times as equally actual, fails to appreciate this fact, then God is mistaken. But that is not possible.

If God sees all times as equally actual, then, if I suppose that there is some ultimate reality to 'now', I am the one that is making the mistake. The criticism simply begs the question against the traditional doctrine of eternity. The eternalist will hold that God can certainly know what I mean when I say, in 1997, 'Clinton is president now', and He also knows what I mean when I say, in 1990, 'Bush is president now', and He knows both eternally. If I go on to add, in 1997, that this year (or this instant) is the only one with ontological status and past and future are absolutely non-existent then I am making a mistake.

Our hypothetical HOPS victim might address an analogous criticism to the view that God is non-spatial and ubiquitous. If all of space is equally present to God then He cannot know what place it is *here*. 'Clinton is here' uttered in Washington D.C. does not mean exactly the same thing as 'Clinton is in Washington D.C.' And so, although God can know the latter, and He can know what I (the HOPS victim) mean when I utter the former in Washington D.C., He cannot know that Washington D.C. is *here* (in the sense that it alone of all places is currently existent). But of course it is the HOPS victim who has made the mistake. All those places which are not perceptible to him and which he therefore considers non-existent are 'present' to God and do in fact exist. Just as there is no absolute *here*, the doctrine of eternity entails that there is no absolute *now*.

It is quite true that God cannot know things from the perspective of a limited perceiver. He can know what I mean when I use the terms 'here' or 'now'. He knows that I am a spatio-temporal being and that when I use these terms I am referring to the only time and place to which I have experiential access. However, God cannot know any 'here' or 'now' as the only place or time to which He has access since He is 'present' to all time and place. It would be logically impossible for Him to both be and not be eternal and ubiquitous, and even God cannot do the logically impossible. He cannot know what it would be logically impossible that He should know. And so it is not a limitation on God's knowledge that He does not experience 'here' and 'now' the way we do. (There will be more to say on this issue in the next chapter on divine omniscience.)

A final difficulty remains for the doctrine of eternity. If my explanation is correct, and all of time is equally present to God, doesn't this do away with the possibility of human freedom in the libertarian sense? It is not just that God *knows* the future, which would be damaging enough. The future is 'already' *there*. It exists as much as what we call past and present. But past and present are 'fixed'. So the future must be equally unalterable. Whatever I 'will' choose is 'already' chosen. My 'future' choice is eternally 'present' to God, and so I cannot do otherwise. Paul Helm, who mounts a ringing defense of the view that God is eternal, writes, 'the existence of an omniscient, timelessly eternal God is logically inconsistent with the libertarian freedom in any of his creatures . . .'[40] I think this conclusion is a mistake. It is in fact *only* the doctrine of divine eternity which allows for an adequate reconciliation between freedom and foreknowledge. But since this issue falls more squarely under the topic of divine omniscience I shall save it for (what is to us) the future, that is, the next chapter.

NOTES

1. Boethius, *The Consolation of Philosophy* V, 6 (I am following the translation in the Loeb Classic Library edition).
2. The phrase 'all of time' might seem to imply that there is such a *thing* as time above and beyond temporal objects. Augustine himself would, I think, deny this. For the purposes of this chapter it is not important to decide whether or not time has any substantive being. I shall talk about time as well as temporal objects, but this is not intended to suggest that 'time' *per se* exists, or that there could be an 'empty time'.
3. J. R. Lucas, *The Future: An Essay on God, Temporality and Truth*, pp. 209–10.
4. Augustine holds that time comes into being through the angelic consciousness. I try to analyze his position in 'St. Augustine on time and eternity'.
5. See Michael D. Robinson, *Eternity and Freedom*, pp. 67–76.
6. Eleonore Stump and Norman Kretzmann, 'Eternity'. Pages cited refer to the reprint in Thomas V. Morris (ed.), *The Concept of God*, pp. 219–52.
7. William Lane Craig, 'God and real time', and 'The special theory of relativity and theories of divine eternity'; Alan Padgett, 'Eternity and the special theory of relativity'.
8. Stump and Kretzmann, 'Eternity', p. 225.
9. Eleonore Stump and Norman Kretzmann, 'Atemporal duration: A reply to Fitzgerald'.
10. Brian Leftow, *Time and Eternity*, p. 117.
11. Augustine, *Confessions* XI, 11.
12. Augustine, *Confessions* XI, 28.
13. Augustine, *Confessions* XII, 15.
14. Boethius, *Consolation of Philosophy* V, 6.
15. ST I, Q.14, art.13, reply to Obj.3.
16. SCG I, 66, 7.
17. Katherin Rogers, 'Eternity has no duration'.
18. Stump and Kretzmann, 'Eternity', p. 220.
19. Paul Helm, *Eternal God*, p. 36.
20. Anslem, *On the Harmony of the Foreknowledge and the Predestination and the Grace of God with Free Will*, I, 5. This analogy might not be applicable to an Einsteinian universe if the theory of Special Relativity implies that it cannot be 'the same time' everywhere. But a minor modification might salvage it. One could say that just as, within a given observational framework, an instant of time is present to all of space, so God's eternity is present to all of space–time absolutely.
21. Augustine, *Confessions* XI, 14.
22. These views have also been dubbed the B-theory and the A-theory of time from J. M. E. McTaggert, 'The unreality of time'.
23. Christopher Kirwan, *Augustine*, p. 183. Kirwan argues that this is what Augustine should have said and didn't, while I hold that in fact this is Augustine's view (Rogers, 'St. Augustine on time and eternity').
24. Leftow, *Time and Eternity*, pp. 234–5.
25. Alston, *Divine Nature and Human Language*, pp. 136–8, and James F. Harris, 'An empirical understanding of eternality'.
26. Delmas Lewis, 'Eternity, time and tenselessness', especially p. 83.
27. Delmas Lewis, 'Persons, morality and tenselessness', especially pp. 306–7.
28. I argue this at more length in 'Omniscience, eternity, and freedom', see especially p. 408.
29. William Hasker, *God, Time and Knowledge*, pp. 165–70, 184–5.
30. Creel, *Divine Impassibility*, p. 96. See also, Richard Gale, 'Reply to Helm', especially p. 258.

31. *On Free Will* III, 4, 11.
32. See, for example, Gale, *On the Nature and Existence of God*, pp. 53–5; Lucas, *The Future*, pp. 210–11; Richard Swinburne, *The Coherence of Theism*, pp. 224–5; Edward Wierenga, *The Nature of God*, pp. 173–4; Nicholas Wolterstorff, 'God everlasting', in Steven Cahn and David Shatz (eds), *Contemporary Philosophy of Religion*, p. 93.
33. Helm, *Eternal God*, pp. 21–2.
34. Swinburne, *Coherence of Theism*, p. 228.
35. Augustine, *Confessions* XI, 11. Here I am following the Pine-Coffin translation in the Penguin edition.
36. Gale, *On the Nature and Existence of God*, p. 54.
37. Augustine, *Confessions* XI, 13.
38. Stump and Kretzmann, 'Eternity'.
39. A. N. Prior, 'The formalities of omniscience'.
40. Helm, *Eternal God*, p. 144.

6

Omniscience

Knowledge is good. So a Perfect Being must have the most possible knowledge in the best possible way. Traditionally this has been expressed by saying that God is omniscient, 'all-knowing'. In the contemporary literature 'omniscience' is often defined as something like this; 'S is omniscient if for any proposition p, if p is true, S knows that p is true, and if p is false, S knows that p is false.' And by 'knowledge' the contemporary philosopher of religion is very likely to mean 'justified true belief', or at least 'true belief plus ____'. Fill in the blank with some additional property which bestows upon the true belief the exalted status of knowledge. This definition fails, and fails radically, to capture what the tradition intended by 'omniscience'. On the assumption that mere 'true belief' requires something in addition to enhance it to genuine knowledge, it is probably right to say that, on the classical understanding, God does not possess beliefs at all. According to Augustine, Anselm and Aquinas God's knowledge is immediate; it is (in general) non-propositional; and it is identical with God's power. God's omniscience entails direct knowledge of all objects, states of affairs, propositions and possibilities. This traditional approach is entailed by perfect being theology, and, once it is grasped, it becomes easier to solve the puzzles associated with omniscience.

GOD'S DIRECT AND CAUSAL KNOWLEDGE

The best possible way of knowing something would be to have it immediately present to cognition rather than to have to deduce it or learn about it through other things. As Thomas V. Morris says,

> God cannot be conceived of as having to depend for his knowledge on any independent sources, intermediaries or carriers of information . . . His knowledge rather consists in his being in the most intimate contact possible with the objects of that knowledge. In brief, God's knowledge is as direct as it is possible for a state of knowledge to be.

He goes on to explain that this position is motivated not only by a consideration of what would be the best manner of knowing but also by the premise that God is the absolute creator.

> And how could such a creator God be thought to depend on any intermediary for his knowledge? For he would have to be conceived of equally as the creator of both the intermediary and the ultimate object of knowledge. But then, given the thoroughgoing intelligence and rationality of creation, he *as creator* would have to be every bit as well acquainted with the properties of the object as of the inter-mediary.[1]

William Alston defends the view that God's knowledge is direct, or 'intuitive' as Alston calls it. On this view 'knowledge of a fact is simply the immediate awareness of that fact'. Unlike belief,

> Knowledge is not a state that could be just what it is intrinsically without the actual existence of the object; it has no intrinsic character over and above the presence of that object to consciousness. Thus knowledge, on this construal, is infallible in a strong sense; its inherent nature guarantees the reality of the object . . . Immediate awareness of facts is the highest form of knowledge just because it is a direct and foolproof way of mirroring the reality to be known.[2]

It will turn out that even Alston's analysis falls short of the traditional thesis in that, on the classic view, God's knowledge does not 'mirror' reality, but causes it. In any case, contemporary philosophers of religion (outside the Thomist tradition) by and large do not seem to have embraced Alston's position, and at least one has argued against it. William Hasker agrees that, 'immediate, intuitive knowledge . . . does indeed represent a cognitive ideal, a maximally favourable mode of cognitive access to reality . . . [however] I shall claim that if made into a *comprehensive* account of the divine knowledge, it becomes simply incoherent'.[3] The problem, as Hasker sees it, is that if we say that God is eternal, and 'sees' all things as present to Him, then things must exist in two ways, in time and in eternity. But then God cannot know things as they exist in time. As he explains in *God, Time and Knowledge*, on the eternalist view, at least in its Thomist version, God 'knows us only by contemplating in eternity his own unchangeable "similitudes," "images," or representations of us'.[4] But then God does not know *us* as we really are at all. So Hasker rejects the view that God is eternal. But if God is temporal, Hasker continues against Alston, then His knowledge of the past and future cannot possibly be direct. It must be like ours, grounded in memory and anticipation.

In the preceding chapter I argued that the eternalist position does not entail that temporal objects cease to be temporal, or bi-locate into temporal and non-temporal 'versions' of themselves. God is simply not subject to any spatial or temporal limitations. All of space is 'here' to God and all of time is 'now' but spatial objects are not a-spatial, nor are temporal objects eternal. All of time is immediately 'present' to God and directly known by Him. This is the traditional view, the one espoused by Augustine, Anselm and Aquinas.

Hasker argues, with apparently powerful textual evidence, that Thomas holds the 'God knows us only in our eternal representations' view.[5] William Lane Craig concurs. He explains that according to Aquinas,

> God has no direct knowledge of anything other than Himself . . . although the divine essence is the only direct object of the divine knowledge, nevertheless God possesses indirect knowledge of all other existents . . . In effect, what Aquinas seems to have done is simply to have substituted a mental realm of particulars for the physical realm of particulars as the objects of God's knowledge.[6]

This interpretation is mistaken, and it will be useful to take a little time here to clear up the misunderstanding. This will serve the dual purpose of setting the historical record straight and of providing a framework for elaborating on the traditional view of omniscience as Aquinas sets it out.

In looking at the text of Aquinas it is easy to see how the misinterpretation could come about. As Hasker quotes *Summa Theologiae* I, Q.14, art.5, adding emphasis, Thomas says, 'He [God] sees himself through His essence; and He sees other things *not in themselves, but in Himself*; inasmuch as *His essence contains the similitude of things other than Himself*'.[7] At first glance this might seem to mean that God knows things outside himself only indirectly, and that His immediate 'perception' is only of His own essence. But it is difficult to reconcile this reading with Aquinas' doctrine of 'knowledge of vision' discussed in the preceding chapter. In explaining God's eternal knowledge of the temporal world Aquinas says, 'The divine intellect, therefore, sees in the whole of its eternity, as being present to it, whatever takes place through the whole course of time'.[8] Craig notes that this 'seems to entail the actual existence of the temporal series of events as the proper object of God's knowledge'. He finds the apparent inconsistency puzzling.[9]

To appreciate what Aquinas is saying will require a note on his epistemology. Aquinas was an empiricist and also a realist about natures. Knowledge begins with sense observation of the world, but goes beyond it. I cannot grasp an object's nature without some sort of contact with the object, but the merely passive reception of sense data will not suffice. According to Aquinas the rational mind is so constituted that, from the sense evidence, it can set aside the inessential features, and pick out the essential ones, thus 'abstracting' the nature of the object. Once I have the nature in my mind – Aquinas refers to this mental object as the 'intelligible species' – I can recognize and understand what this thing is.[10]

Now a question arises which will prove relevant for solving the puzzle about God's knowledge. Aquinas asks whether or not it is the intelligible species which is the primary object of our understanding. That is, is what we are actually understanding a mental object? No, he answers. It cannot be that what we have cognitive access to is just the furniture of our own minds, for then science could not talk about the external world at all, and, since people could only know intra-mental impressions, 'it would lead to the opinion of the ancients who maintained that *whatever seems, is true* . . .' He concludes that the intelligible species is that *by which* the intellect understands. *What* it understands is the extra-mental object itself, for example a cat. The intelligible species can become an object of knowledge when I am doing epistemology. That is, when I ponder how it is that I understand an object's nature I may cogitate directly upon the abstracted object in the intellect. But to recognize the object it is enough that the intelligible species be present so that I can understand the thing 'through' it.[11]

On Aquinas' analysis, God's knowledge is both like and unlike ours. Like us, God understands things through their natures. But whereas our understanding depends upon our coming in contact with an object which exists independently of ourselves and then abstracting its form, it is God's understanding of the thing which brings it into being. We understand things in or through their 'similitudes', the intelligible species which may or may not be an object of our thought, but which is necessary for our understanding. And we understand things directly in the sense that, although we require the sense data and intelligible species to understand the thing, it is the thing itself and not some mental representation that is the object of our knowledge. God, too, knows things directly, in or through their similitudes, which is His understanding of their natures. God knows this cat directly in, or through, the divine idea of catness, which is in turn, one of the myriad ways in which His essence, perfect being, can be imitated. For us, individual corporeal things are the primary objects of our cognition, and from them we can learn about natures and even about God. The order is logically reversed for God. He Himself is the primary object of His cognition, then (this is a logical 'then' not intended to imply any temporal sequence or any step-by-step inference) come natures (catness and so on) which exist in logical dependence upon His nature. And then come individuals which He creates through willing the existence of the form (nature) and matter of the individual. So when Aquinas says that God knows only Himself 'primarily and essentially' he is not denying that God has direct knowledge of individuals. He is explaining the logical order of divine cognition. The point is that human understanding starts with things outside and independent of ourselves, while God's does not. As Aquinas says, 'It is true that God knows nothing outside Himself if the word *outside* refers to that *by which* He knows. However, God does know something outside himself if this refers to *what* He knows'.[12]

Aquinas holds that God knows all things directly. This is a necessary consequence of perfect being theology. A perfect being, existing absolutely *a se*, must be simple. God's power is His knowledge. He creates by thinking. Whatever is is sustained immediately by the knowledge of God. If God did not *know* this particular planet, cat or sub-atomic particle, and know it directly, right now, it would blink out of being. And that is why Augustine, Anselm and Aquinas would dispute Alston's description of divine knowledge as a perfect 'mirroring' of reality. The mirror passively *reflects* the objects present. God's knowledge *produces* them.

Notice that we have been speaking thus far about concrete objects, and that the term 'proposition' has not been used yet in the discussion of omniscience. Many contemporary philosophers see propositions as the primary, or only, objects of God's knowledge. And this produces confusion when these philosophers approach the traditional doctrine of God's causal omniscience. William Lane Craig, for example, writes,

> For what does it mean to say God's knowledge is the cause of something? Does this mean God knows certain propositions to be true and His knowing them to be true causes the corresponding states of affairs to obtain in reality? If so, what makes the propositions true to begin with? How can God know them to be true unless they correspond with reality so as to be true? And how can knowing a proposition to be true be the existential cause of the corresponding

state of affairs? Aquinas's answers to such questions are not at all clear.[13]

What it means to say that God's knowledge is the cause of something is that God's thinking has the power to make things exist . . . rather like Shakespeare's thinking has the power to make Hamlet exist. It is the immediate presence of divine cognition which sustains creation. (This sounds very like idealism, and in Chapter 9 I will argue that perfect being theology does entail a moderate, sober and innocuous version of this doctrine.) Aquinas does not address Craig's questions because, on the classic understanding of God's causal knowledge, such questions do not arise. The traditional doctrine of divine omniscience cannot be squared with the popular contemporary assumption that the primary objects of knowledge, including God's knowledge, are propositions. What, then, should the contemporary perfect being theologian make of propositions? The first question, and a nasty one it is, is 'What in fact are propositions?' A discussion of this vexed issue lies beyond the scope of this work, but a few sketchy remarks may help forward the project of appreciating the doctrine of omniscience within perfect being theology. I take it that a number of contemporary philosophers of religion see the contents of the universe in this way: there are concrete objects (God, planets and so on) with their various properties including how they could behave, be related and so on; there are states of affairs which are concrete objects behaving, being related and so on; there are sentences, which are the expressions in actual languages, and which can be about concrete objects and states of affairs; and then there are propositions. Propositions, as portrayed in much contemporary philosophy of religion, transcend sentences in that many different sentences in different languages might express the same proposition. And propositions transcend, or at least exist separately from, concrete objects and states of affairs as well. Note Craig's assumption that there are states of affairs and, apparently in addition, propositions whose truth value comes from correspondence with these states.

Some propositions, such as '2 + 2 = 4', are generally considered true necessarily, eternally and immutably. There is debate, among those who accept this view of propositions, as to whether or not propositions about contingent states of affairs are equally necessary, eternal and immutable (indexed to the actual world). Some hold that if, in the actual world, the cat did in fact sit on the mat at time t then the proposition '(In the actual world) The cat sat on the mat at time t' has always been true and could not have been otherwise. Others hold that there is no truth value to propositions about the future. It is only at time t and thereafter that 'The cat sat on the mat at time t' becomes true. This debate plays an important role in current discussions of divine foreknowledge, as we shall see.

Perhaps the most puzzling thing about propositions in the contemporary discussion is their ontological status. Are they objects of some sort? That they 'exist' beyond the states of affairs to which they refer and the sentences which express them seems to imply this Platonic conclusion. Clearly they are not dependent upon contingent knowers, since they can be eternal while we are not. Jonathan Kvanvig holds that 'propositions are necessary *beings* [emphasis added] composed of properties which are bearers of truth-values'.[14]

Within the system of perfect being theology, if propositions are held to have some sort of ontological status then they must be supposed to depend upon God for their existence. God is the absolute creator, and the classic tradition, having roundly rejected the Platonic image of a demiurge, a divinity who makes the world through an independently existing world of forms, will resist reintroducing the image in the guise of a god whose plans must take account of an independently existing world of propositions. The status of propositions becomes even more opaque when the propositions express facts about the choices of free beings. Shall we say that it is up to the free creature to make the proposition true or false, while it is up to God to sustain its existence? The classic tradition must say at least this; propositions cannot be objects which exist independent of any knower including God.

Further, as will become clear in the discussion of divine foreknowledge, insistence that God knows only or primarily propositions precludes the sort of direct knowledge that constitutes ideal cognition. If propositions are beings which 'correspond to' states of affairs then knowing propositions allows, at best, only indirect knowledge of the reality to which they correspond. This is not to say that '2 + 2 = 4' and 'The cat sat on the mat at time t' are not truths to be known, and known eternally, by God. But God knows that 2 + 2 = 4 because, in knowing His own immutable nature which is perfect being, He knows necessary truths as the ways in which being must exist. He knows that the cat sat on the mat at time t because, in His eternal present by the power of His omniscience, He sustains in existence the cat, the mat and everything else at time t and at all times. And He knows all that He knows in His one, eternal act. He knows everything immediately and in a unified way, in a single thought. There is no multiplicity, no extension, no discursiveness. Clearly this is not propositional knowing.[15]

Human knowers understand in a way that is discursive, temporally spread out. Our appreciation of reality, and how we express our beliefs, must be piecemeal and extended. In Chapter 5 I imagined an impossibly good historian who could grasp all of 'the Civil War' instantaneously and with perfect accuracy. In fact, though, our limitations require us to move from point to point, and, at least with many types of belief, we can only understand propositionally. And so there is a sense in which God may be said to understand 'propositions' of a sort. God knows all the capacities of His creatures. God knows all the possible ways we can and do think about reality and express it in language. In Aquinas' terminology, He knows all *enuntiabilia*. But of course He knows them after the manner of His own power, in His single unified act.[16]

On the traditional understanding God's knowledge must be direct because He is simple and His omniscience is identical with His omnipotence. But the notion that God's thought is causal raises difficulties. Does this mean that if something does not exist, God doesn't know it? But then God's knowledge is limited, for you and I can think of the unicorn as a mere possibility, even though we suppose that there are no actual unicorns. Aquinas responds that God, too, can think of mere possibilities. (We must be careful of the term 'possible' here. If God knows that He will never create any unicorns then God knows that unicorns are 'actually' or conditionally impossible in accord with the analysis of 'actual' necessity presented in the discussion on divine simplicity.) Non-existent but possible beings have a sort of shadow existence as ways God might be imitated and as thoughts in the minds of limited beings. So it is God's omniscience which sustains the being of all things, both actual and possible.[17]

Does God know evil? Here it is crucial to remember that God causes *things*. God's thought sustains every created object in being. Evil is not an object. It does not exist *per se*. As Augustine explained in the *Confessions* (VII, 12), and as the medieval tradition in the Latin West unanimously agreed, evil is when good is harmed or diminished. Whatever is is good, and evil is the loss or corruption of being. It has no ontological status. So God knows evil only as an absence of a good that should have been present.[18]

But what of evil choices? If I have sinned, surely God knows that I have sinned. If His knowledge is causal, must we say that He brought about the evil state of affairs? Again, to say that all that exists is sustained in being by God's knowledge is to speak of *objects*. It is not to say that it is God who actualizes all states of affairs. That the earth revolves around the sun is a state of affairs brought about by God, since He created the earth and the sun with natural properties which would determine how they behave. Human beings He made with free will. On Anselm's libertarian analysis, we have the option to throw away the good He has given us by choosing in opposition to His will. Now the will itself, and whatever there is in the choice that can be said to have any sort of ontological status, must be kept in being by God and is known by Him. But the turning from the good originates in the will of the sinner, and the evil which is a loss or diminution of the good is the responsibility of the free creature, and is known by God only as a failure to adhere to the good.[19]

THE FUTURE

Almost everyone agrees that knowledge which encompasses the future would be better than knowledge which is limited to the past and present. But is knowledge of the future possible? The problem is pressing because, apparently, there is a conflict between libertarian freedom and infallible foreknowledge. The compatibilist on free will need not find anything paradoxical about foreknowledge of free choices. If our choices result from pre-existent causes then they can be known with certainty beforehand even by a time-bound being. But the libertarian focuses on an 'ability to choose otherwise' as the key criterion of the sort of freedom which permits of praise and blame. If God knows today what I will do tomorrow then, since I cannot change the past, it is not possible that tomorrow I should do other than what God foreknows today. God's foreknowledge seems to render my choice necessary, and hence unfree.[20]

Some philosophers solve the paradox by giving up on divine foreknowledge. J. R. Lucas, insisting upon libertarian freedom and a temporal divinity, concludes that

> He will have a fair idea of my future course of action, far from complete, of course, since I have not made up my mind about many things, and do not know myself what I am going to do, but enough none the less to predict some things with a fair degree of certainty.[21]

Lucas goes on to explain that God changes His mind and makes mistakes. Sometimes His prophecies are false.[22] Most contemporary philosophers of religion are not willing to go as far as Lucas in limiting God. Creel and Morris, for example, while agreeing that God cannot know a future containing free choices, hold that God's will is nonetheless immutable. God's omniscience entails knowing all possibilities, and God also knows just how He will respond to whatever possibility is actualized by the free choice of creatures.[23] But He does not know what creatures will actually choose, so while He has complete knowledge of what *might* happen, He is ignorant of what *will* happen.

This is a hard pill for the believer to swallow. Not only does it not jibe with perfect being theology but also it raises serious problems for ordinary religious belief. Most notably, in the face of all the suffering which sentient creatures undergo, it is a comfort to trust that God permits it because He knows that in the final analysis things will turn out for the best. But if He has only an educated opinion on how things will turn out, if He permits all the suffering *hoping* that ultimately all will be well . . . then the believer's trust seems misplaced.

And certainly the God of scriptural revelation makes prophecies without qualification. Jesus does not say to Peter that He *strongly believes* that before the cock crows it is *quite likely* that he will betray Him three times. It is ironic that some philosophers who quote chapter and verse to show that God is changeable and fallible apparently feel comfortable downplaying the texts that imply that God knows the future with certainty.[24] Moreover, if God is in time and does not know the future then presumably His predictions with respect to the future become less accurate the more temporally distant from Him the time to which they refer. But if that is the case then the biblical message will speak less and less directly to succeeding generations as the times in which it was revealed recede further and further into the past. At the end of the second millennium since Christ it is the philosophers who hold that God knows the future infallibly who have the best reason for taking the Bible seriously as the living word of God.

There are excellent reasons not to abandon the traditional insistence that God knows the actual future completely and infallibly. Can this be reconciled with the view that human beings have libertarian freedom? I will argue that the best solution to the apparent paradox starts with accepting the eternalist position that God 'sees' all of time as present to Him. But first it will be useful to look at two other popular approaches to the problem which do not situate God outside time. I will argue that both suffer from a number of weaknesses.[25]

One popular contemporary strategy for reconciling God's omniscience with human freedom draws on the work of the fourteenth-century philosopher, William of Ockham. Ockham viewed God as temporal. God does not 'see' the future, for the future does not exist. Nonetheless, and *pace* Aristotle, propositions about future contingents, including future free choices, have a truth value in the present. And, since God knows everything, He must know the truth value of those propositions. Notice that this position, though it does allow God knowledge of the future, has abandoned at the outset the belief that all of God's knowledge fits the cognitive ideal of direct access to the thing known. That is, God knows the proposition *about* the future, but He does not have direct cognitive access to the objects and states of affairs which make the proposition true.

On the Ockhamist understanding God today knows infallibly what I will do tomorrow. But while it is true that 'If God knows today that I will do x tomorrow, I will do x tomorrow', it does not follow that I am unfree with respect to x. That is, it does not follow that 'I *must* do x tomorrow'. Being free, I could instead do not-x. And if I do not-x tomorrow than *that* is what God knows today.[26] The point has been elaborated by appealing to a distinction between 'hard' and 'soft' facts, a distinction which has been debated and analyzed at length in the recent literature with a subtlety that is almost appalling.[27] For our purposes here a quick definition will suffice. A proposition states a 'hard' fact about time t if it is about only time t. 'Sophie went to the store yesterday' expresses a 'hard' fact. But 'Sophie went to the store before I wrote' expresses a 'soft' fact because its truth depends not only on what Sophie did at time t but also on what I did at a later time. The Ockhamist holds that propositions concerning divine foreknowledge such as 'God knows today that I will write tomorrow' express 'soft' facts. Their truth depends not only on God's knowledge at time t but also upon the occurrence of the foreknown event at t + n. 'God knows today that I will write tomorrow' may express an immutable truth, but since that truth depends in part on what I will actually do the fixity of God's knowledge does not impose any necessity which could interfere with my freedom.

There is a great deal of debate among contemporary Ockhamists on just how to analyze the distinction between 'hard' and 'soft' facts, and some critics of the Ockhamist position make the plausible case that propositions about God's knowledge at a given time are 'hard' facts plain and simple.[28] But allow, for the sake of argument, that the Ockhamist move does permit a bare reconciliation between freedom and foreknowledge. A question remains which Ockham's theory does not answer. *How* could God possibly know the present truth value of propositions about future free choices? Presumably it is the fact that I will freely make a certain choice in the future which brings about the present truth value of the proposition about my choice. But I have not made the choice yet. It does not exist. So what grounds God's knowledge? Ockham holds that God's knowledge comes from His cognition of His own nature, but, in answer to the question at hand he responds with characteristic candor and elegance that 'I do not know how to describe the way [in which He has it]'.[29] Apparently God 'just knows' which propositions are true, and there is no more to be said.[30]

A second popular strategy for reconciling freedom and divine fore-knowledge is based on the doctrine of 'middle knowledge' originated by the sixteenth-century philosopher Luis de Molina. God has 'natural' knowledge of all necessary truths and all the possibilities he might actualize. He has 'free' knowledge of what world he will actually create and of all that will actually happen. And He also has 'middle' knowledge, 'middle' because logically it falls in between God's knowledge of all possibilities and of all actualities. 'Middle' knowledge encompasses knowledge of all that *would* happen given any possible creative choice by God. God's knowledge is so perfect that for any creature, actual or merely possible, in any set of circumstances, actual or merely possible, God knows infallibly what that creature would do, including whatever free choices it would make. Thus, since God knows what any creature *would* do in any given situation, He knows what any creature *will* do in the situations which He chooses to actualize. Yet creaturely choices can be entirely free. God's middle knowledge is 'prevolitional', that is, unlike His free knowledge, it is not the result of His will. God does not choose the truths of His middle knowledge. They simply exist as the framework within which He can create.[31]

Molina's theory is subject to a number of criticisms. Like Ockhamism it entails that God's foreknowledge cannot be direct. God, in time, knows *about* the future through a series of premises and a discursive process. And, as with Ockhamism, the question arises: How can God possibly know the truth of the propositions which give Him foreknowledge? In fact, the case with Molinism is even more puzzling in that middle knowledge supposes, not just that events which do not exist *yet* can furnish the conditions for the truth value of present propositions, but that events which will *never* exist can do so.[32] Since free choices do not follow from any preexistent facts about the universe or the actor, it seems that only the fact of the agent actually choosing could possibly ground the truth of a proposition about the choice. Molina's middle knowledge allows that there can be a truth value for propositions about what *non-actual* (that is, never to exist) agents freely choose in *non-actual* situations. But it is extremely puzzling to see how it could be true of a non-actual agent in a non-actual situation that 'X *would* freely choose Y rather than Z in situation S' when Z is an equally open option, and there is absolutely nothing about X or S which precludes Z. Even more puzzling is how God could possibly *know* such a truth. Molina himself postulates a divine 'supercomprehension', an omniscience so powerful that, in knowing Himself, God knows creatures so well that He knows even what they would freely choose in non-actual situations.[33] This does not seem to solve the problem, though. Libertarian freedom means that there is literally nothing about the creature that would preclude its choosing one or another out of a set of options. Thus, no matter how well God knows the creature, He cannot know what is not there to be known. He cannot know how it *would* freely choose. If it is argued that

God knows the truth of the counterfactual of freedom, not from His knowledge of Himself and the creature, but simply because it *is* true, then we are back to saying that God 'just knows'. And if the Molinist reconciliation of divine omniscience with freedom ultimately rests on holding that God 'just knows' counterfactuals of freedom then we might as well apply Ockham's razor, return to the simpler theory of its namesake, and jettison middle knowledge altogether. Propositions about future free choices have a present truth value and God 'just knows' it.

A further problem for the Molinist arises when we consider the doctrine of middle knowledge in the light of the problem of evil.[34] If God knows what any possible free creature would freely choose in any situation then it seems that He could actualize those creatures and situations such that the creatures would freely choose only the good. Obviously God allows an enormous amount of evil. If He could have prevented it, then is He not responsible to some extent? One of Molina's favorite scriptural proof texts for God's knowledge of counterfactuals of freedom makes the point vividly. Jesus tells the people of Chorazin and Bethsaida that 'if the miracles done in you had been done in Tyre and Sidon, they would have repented long ago in sackcloth and ashes'. As for Capernaum, 'if the miracles done in you had been done in Sodom, it would have been standing yet' (Matt. 11: 22–4). One wonders, then, why God did not see to it that some such miracles were performed in those infamous towns so their citizens would be led to repentance, as they certainly would have been on Molina's reading.[35] God could have saved them with no infringement on their freedom, yet He did not. Why, indeed, did God not simply create free beings who would always choose the good?

In response Plantinga introduces 'transworld depravity'. 'What is important about the idea of transworld depravity is that if a person suffers from it, then it was not within God's power to actualize any world in which that person is significantly free but does no wrong . . .' It is possible that every creaturely essence suffers from transworld depravity. If so, 'then it was beyond the power of God himself to create a world containing moral good but no moral evil'.[36] The doctrine of transworld depravity, while logically possible, seems extremely implausible, and is unlikely to satisfy the believer concerned to discover why a good God would permit evil. As Hasker remarks, 'the need to maintain that these things are so must constitute a heavy burden for the theodicist – a burden, however, which is easily shed once we relinquish middle knowledge'.[37]

A final difficulty with the Molinist position, and this is the problem which most concerned Molina's opponents in his own day, is that the doctrine of middle knowledge places severe restrictions on God. Molina advanced the view in order to avoid the conclusion that God 'learns' about future free choices from those choices themselves. He was motivated by a desire to safeguard divine aseity. But the counterfactuals of freedom which comprise God's middle knowledge 'obtain prior to and hence independently of God's willing or permitting them to obtain'.[38] God cannot actualize just any possible world because the 'creation situations' which God knows to be actualizable given His natural and middle knowledge 'constitute the antecedently fixed framework within which God operates as a cause'.[39] 'Antecedently fixed' here means prevolitionally. God is bound to create within certain guidelines which are not necessary truths and which do not arise from or depend upon His choice. He is limited by contingent truths existing eternally yet independent of His nature and will. The doctrine of middle knowledge fails to defend the absolute aseity of God.[40] I take it that this criticism of Molinism is a version of the problem mentioned earlier, that if propositions are granted independent ontological status then one risks reducing God to a sort of Platonic demiurge who looks to a separate realm of intelligible objects to make the world.

Ockhamism and Molinism are riddled with problems, and both deny that God's knowledge of the future could be the best sort of knowledge, that is direct cognitive access to the thing known. Only the view that God is eternal and present to all of time permits direct divine foreknowledge (*fore*knowledge only from our perspective). God knows what is to us future in the same way He knows what is to us present and past. It is all immediately there before Him. Aquinas calls this 'knowledge of vision' in that God just 'sees' everything in all time and space, somewhat as (though even more directly than) we see what is present to us in time and space. How does God know today what choice I will make tomorrow? My tomorrow is eternally present to God, and He eternally 'sees' me choosing.

But how does this solve the original paradox concerning divine omniscience and human freedom? If it is true that 'God knows today that I will do x tomorrow', and that I cannot change the past, then when tomorrow comes I cannot fail to do x. How then am I free? One strategy for solving the problem is to deny that 'God knows today that I will do x tomorrow'. If God is not in time at all then He knows things in eternity, not at a given time. But then the issue about the fixity of the past does not arise. True, I cannot change the past, but God's knowledge was not 'in the past'. Brian Leftow writes,

> as we are temporal agents, our options are closed off only if they are closed off (temporally or causally) *before* we have the chance to choose among them . . . If God's knowledge is wholly outside time, it

cannot have the sort of temporal relation to our actions which would let it determine them.[41]

I do not find this an adequate solution for a number of reasons. For one thing, what are we to make of prophecy? If God provides the prophet, who certainly is a temporal being and hence knows *before* the event, with knowledge involving a future choice, must we say that this choice cannot be free? Even if in every other respect it is exactly like a free choice? But it seems radically implausible to suppose that your freedom and hence your moral status should depend upon whether or not God has happened to mention to someone in the past what you are up to today.[42]

Moreover, though God is eternal we are not. Douglas Lackey writes that appealing to God's eternity will not resolve the freedom/omniscience paradox because *we* have to say, ' "it is true now that God knows what I will do tomorrow" . . . for us, it is now true that he knows'.[43] Paul Helm explains, 'If it is proper to speak of God's knowledge in this timeless way, then from the point in time of the temporal agent God knows beforehand'.[44] Most telling perhaps, as Linda Zagzebski points out, if it is the immutability of God's knowledge which generates the problem at hand then saying that 'God knows timelessly' rather than 'God knows beforehand' does not solve the difficulty. God's knowledge will be as fixed if it is eternal as it would be if it were past.[45] How then does appealing to God's atemporal nature solve the paradox of human freedom and divine foreknowledge?

The view that God knows what I will do in the future because, being eternal, He 'sees' me doing it can be called the 'Concomitance Theory', and it is the standard solution to the freewill/foreknowledge paradox in the Latin West from Augustine through Aquinas.[46] The first move for the concomitance theorist is to bite the bullet on the principle that God's eternal knowledge that I will choose x renders my choice for x necessary. But the necessity involved is entirely innocuous and does not in any way conflict with libertarian freedom. The necessity in question is what Boethius and Aquinas called 'conditional necessity' and Anselm 'consequent necessity'. It is a *non-causal* sort of necessity which follows from, rather than determines the event in question. Suppose I know that you are walking because I see you walking. If I know that you are walking it is necessary that you be walking. My knowledge is indeed a necessitating factor, but it is a non-causally necessitating factor. Though it is necessary that you be walking, you may be walking quite freely since my knowledge neither caused you to walk, nor precluded the possibility that you might choose not to walk.[47]

But isn't it a problem that God knows what I will do *before* I do it? No. The reason God knows what I will choose is that I do in fact choose it. It is my choice which causes God's knowledge. On some interpretations of Aquinas he would reject this conclusion, holding that God, since He is not *in potentia* in any way at all, cannot 'learn' from His creatures. It seems to me that on the libertarian view of freedom the causal flow of information with respect to free choices *must* go from creature to Creator. W. Norris Clarke resolves the apparent paradox, explaining that, without qualifiying God's nature as pure act and absolute creator, one can still hold that God 'learns' about our choices.

> God knows my choice by knowing his own active power working within me, as thus determined or channeled determinately here and now by me. Hence God knows by acting, not by being acted on, but I supply the inner determination or limit of this power at work – which I repeat is not a new positive being at all but only a limiting down of an indeterminate plenitude.[48]

Thus God's knowledge is causal in that it sustains the being of all things by its power. Nonetheless our free choice produces God's knowledge of that choice. Logically we might say there are three 'events' involved in my foreknown choice. The logically first 'event' is my freely made choice. The second is God's 'perceiving' my choice. The third is my making the choice as necessitated by God's timeless knowledge. Logically the first 'event' is prior to the third, but the choice in question is one and the same. When I choose x, I set in motion the series of 'events' which results in my 'necessarily' choosing x. But, of course, once I choose x it is necessary, simply by the law of non-contradiction, that I cannot choose not-x in the same way at the same time. This is true even if we set aside divine foreknowledge, and it in no way vitiates my libertarian freedom. So since it is my choosing x initially that necessitates that I choose x, the fact of God's eternal knowledge as a non-causally necessitating factor does not conflict with my freedom. It is only the view that God is eternal, and the future 'there' to be perceived, which permits the conclusion that God's foreknowledge depends upon my actual choice, and so allows us to construct a coherent reconciliation between human freedom and divine omniscience.[49]

KNOWLEDGE *DE SE*

Thus far in the present chapter, by insisting that divine omniscience is direct, causal (in that it keeps all existents in being) and timeless, I have emphasized how different God's knowledge must be from ours. But this in itself raises a problem with respect to omniscience. If God does not know things as we know them then must there be things which He cannot know at all? What are we to make of *de se* knowledge, that is, knowledge which one has *from one's own perspective*? If I know that I am writing now, don't I have a unique sort of knowledge? From within, as it were? Is there not, then, knowledge which is private to each of us, which even an omniscient being cannot share? Certainly God has *de se* knowledge with respect to Himself. But is there information to which others have access which is unknowable to God?

There are several ways of expressing the question about omniscience. If one insists that omniscience is to be defined as 'believing of all true propositions that they are true, and of all false propositions that they are false', the question is, what do we make of *de se* propositions such as 'I am writing now', which is true if presently uttered by me? Does God believe it? But He isn't writing now. He certainly believes, 'Rogers is writing now'. But 'Rogers is writing now' does not seem to express the same proposition as 'I am writing now'. I have argued that God's knowledge is not primarily propositional, so I am not committed to saying that, without qualification, He 'believes of all true propositions that they are true and of all false propositions that they are false'.[50] For my purposes it is quite adequate to say that He knows that I am writing, and He knows what I mean when I say, 'I am writing now'.

But this does not really solve the problem about *de se* knowledge. Does our perspective as limited creatures allow us to know things which God as perfect, unlimited and eternal cannot know? In the previous chapter on eternity the question arose of whether or not God could know what time it is *now*. Once the implications of divine eternity are appreciated, the answer to the question is relatively simple. In fact it is entailed by casting the question as one concerning *de se* knowledge, in that it can be expressed as, 'Does God know what time it is *for us*, or *as we do*?' If we are asking the question at time t then God knows that 'now' is time t, for us. For any temporal creature, God can know what it means by 'now', just as He can know what a spatial creature might mean by 'here'. If the question implies that my 'now' is all there really is then it is misguided because the temporal present is relative to the perceiver. There is no universally absolute 'now' any more than there is a universally absolute 'here'.

What about sense knowledge? Anthony Kenny held that according to 'the philosophers' God, having no senses, is incapable of sense knowledge.[51] He cites the *Summa Theologiae* I, Q.3, arts. 1 and 3, where Aquinas discusses divine simplicity. Aquinas certainly does say that God is not a body. He does not go on to draw the conclusion that God does not have sense knowledge, though. And in *Summa Contra Gentiles* I, Chapter 65, section 6, he explicitly says that God knows whatever we know, including what we know through our senses.[52] This is striking in that it seems to grant sensible qualities a more exalted status than most modern philosophers would allow. The ancient atomists, the early modern empiricists and (I take it) the majority of contemporary philosophers hold that sense phenomena are 'mere appearance' in that, as Locke explained it, they are not qualities in the thing perceived, but effects in the perceiver. It may be that Aquinas does not disagree. Perhaps he holds that what God knows in knowing sensible qualities is that that is how the perceiver experiences things. But even so, there is a sense in which colors, tastes, smells and so on have the status of genuine objects of knowledge eternally known by God. So, though God does not know sensible qualities as we do, through corporeal senses, He does know them.

A more serious problem remains. Are there not some concepts which can be fully comprehended only through having the sorts of experiences which an omnipotent being could not possibly have.[53] An omnipotent being could not fully understand fear or frustration or despair, and hence could not be omniscient. God might believe, in some abstract way, that 'Rogers is terrified at time t' but He cannot have complete comprehension of the meaning of 'terrified', and thus He is lacking in knowledge. One might raise an analogous problem with respect to divine goodness. In the tradition of perfect being theology, God is perfectly and *necessarily* good. It is not possible for Him to behave badly or to want to behave badly. How then can He have complete comprehension of lust, greed, unjust anger and so on?

There are a number of things to be said in response to this problem. First, it does not speak to the central thesis of the traditional doctrine of omniscience which sees God's knowledge as direct and causal. That God is all-knowing means that everything which has any ontological status is kept in being by the power of God's thought. On the traditional view God knows *that* 'Rogers is terrified', through keeping every sub-atomic particle of me in being. Whether or not God knows 'what it is like' to be terrified, He is omniscient in that He knows every *thing*.

More needs to be said, though. It seems vital for religious commitment that God really understand our pain and sorrow. Perhaps we can move towards this conclusion by questioning the claim that comprehension of some concepts requires experience. Even human beings are capable of 'vicarious' experience. As a movie-goer I can appreciate the gangster's joy in the violence which expresses his personal power and freedom without literally doing the things he does and without (I hope) incurring the guilt that, were he a real human being, he would incur. I can understand, and in a sense even share, his feelings, without being him or even being at all like him. Perhaps God is the perfect audience, able to understand and appreciate our feelings fully, without becoming us or becoming like us.

And here it ought to be said that, though the extremely difficult doctrine of the Incarnation falls outside the scope of this work (*gratias tibi domine!*), the view that the author of all has somehow written Himself into the story goes a great way to resolve the issue of *de se* knowledge. If one can accept that God, eternal, immutable, unlimited, could take on humanity's limitations then it follows that He can see things to some extent as we see them.

Even the Incarnation could not give God complete knowledge, though, for even if God became a man, that man saw things from His own perspective, and not from the perspective of anyone else. If He felt pain, it was His pain and only analogous to *my* pain. But here it becomes clear that if 'complete knowledge' means knowledge from all perspectives as if one were every knower such knowledge is not possible. I cannot see things from a perspective which is not *my* perspective. For example, I can know what it is like to be female and I can know this *de se*, in the way a woman knows it. I have some grasp on what maleness is, and perhaps can enter imaginatively into 'what it is like to be male'. But being not-male I cannot understand maleness the way a man does. It is not logically possible. As Paul Helm explains, in this context 'knowing what it is like' is essentially the same as 'knowing for oneself', and it is just not possible to know the experience of someone other than oneself 'for oneself'.[54] Even God cannot do the logically impossible, and so to ask that He know, not only all objects and states of affairs but also *as other beings know them*, is making impossible demands.

There is one last point to be made here. God knows something of fear, frustration and even sinfulness, through knowing us. He certainly does not know them *as we do*. But perhaps there is a sense in which He understands these feelings even better than we do. The experiences that God cannot have for Himself are experiences associated with limitation, weakness, or even, as in sin, willful failure. They all represent a falling away from the best. Just as God knows evil as the absence of some good which ought to be there, perhaps He knows fear, frustration, sinfulness and so on as the absence of the positive feelings which they negate . . . feelings of trust and security, of adequacy to the task, of being in harmony with things as they should be. And since it is God who has the most complete comprehension of the positive feelings, it is He who can most fully appreciate what is lost. For a human analogy, take the case of a sane person and an insane person. Neither can fully comprehend what it is like to be the other. Nonetheless the sane person has a better understanding of what insanity entails than does the insane person, not just because the sane person understands things better in general, but because he knows what's lacking in the experience of the insane person. In the same way a sighted person cannot know what it is like to be blind from birth, but the sighted person has a better grasp of what blindness *means* in the sense that she grasps what is missing. God does not understand us *as we understand ourselves*. That would be impossible. But perhaps He understands us *better* than we understand ourselves. Surely that, along with direct knowledge of all other objects, states of affairs, possibilities and propositions, is sufficient for perfect knowledge.

NOTES

1. Morris, *Our Idea of God*, p. 84. Morris does not follow this position out to its traditional conclusions.
2. William Alston, 'Does God have beliefs?'. Page numbers refer to reprinting in *Divine Nature and Human Language*, p. 187.
3. William Hasker, 'Yes, God has beliefs!', see p. 389.
4. Hasker, *God, Time and Knowledge*, p. 184.
5. Hasker, *God, Time and Knowledge*, pp. 168–9.
6. William Lane Craig, 'Aquinas on God's knowledge of future contingents', see pp. 67, 68 and 69.
7. Hasker, *God, Time and Knowledge*, p. 168.
8. SCG I, 66, 7.
9. Craig, 'Aquinas on God's knowledge of future contingents', p. 68.
10. ST I, Q.85, art.1.
11. ST I, Q.85, art.2.
12. *On Truth* Q.2, art.12, reply to obj.11. Theodore Kondoleon cites this text in a response to Craig's article; Kondoleon, 'God's knowledge of future contingent singulars: A reply', see p. 131.
13. Craig, 'Aquinas on God's knowledge of future contingents', p. 73.
14. Jonathan Kvanvig, *The Possibility of an All-Knowing God*, p. 66.
15. Alston, 'Does God have beliefs?', defends the immediacy and (at least relative) simplicity of God's manner of knowing. Hasker, 'Yes, God has beliefs!', pp. 392–3, agrees that for God to know things propositionally implies a less than ideal manner of cognition. He proposes that, in knowing the solar system, for example, it is not the case that God knows all the propositions about where this body will be when and so on but rather knows through a sort of cognitive 'working model'. Aquinas, in contrast, will hold that God has no need of a model, since He has the solar system itself right there immediately present to His intellectual 'vision'.
16. ST I, Q.14, art.14.
17. ST I, Q.14, art.9.
18. ST I, Q.14, art.10. I discuss some of the early medieval history of this position in 'Eriugena and Anselm on God's causal omniscience'.
19. See Anselm's *On the Harmony of the Foreknowledge, the Predestination, and the Grace of God with Free Choice*, Question I, section VII.
20. Perhaps the most famous modern expression of the problem is Nelson Pike's 'Divine omniscience and voluntary action'.
21. Lucas, *The Future*, p. 221.
22. Lucas, *The Future*, p. 224.
23. Creel, *Divine Impassibility*, Chapter 2; Thomas V. Morris, 'Properties, modalities, and God'.
24. Lucas, *The Future*, is an especially vivid example: see Chapter 11.
25. This discussion of Ockhamism and Molinism draws heavily, sometimes verbatim, on the first part of my 'Omniscience, eternity and freedom' and on my 'Middle knowledge versus knowledge of vision'.
26. *Treatise on Predestination and on the Foreknowledge of God and on Future Contingents*.

27. See, for example, the collected essays in John Martin Fischer (ed.), *God, Foreknowledge, and Freedom*.
28. See William Hasker, 'Hard facts and theological fatalism'.
29. *Ordinatio* d. 38, q.u., M (Appendix 1, p. 90 in Adams and Kretzmann, *Predestination, God's Foreknowledge, and Future Contingents*).
30. William Lane Craig suggests that God's belief in propositions about future choices may be justified by His also possessing the belief in the necessary truth that 'God holds only and all true beliefs' (*Divine Foreknowledge and Human Freedom*, p. 230). He goes on to propose that 'it is indeed the future events themselves that furnish the truth conditions for such propositions [about future choices]'. But this temporally backward 'furnishing' from a non-existent event to a present proposition is incoherent. And if what God knows is just propositions then, again, God's knowledge is not direct. Kvanvig, too, holds that God does not directly know future events, for they do not exist, but rather knows the truth value of propositions about the future (*Possibility of an All-Knowing God*, p. 3).
31. Molina, *Liberi Arbitrii cum Gratiae Donis, Divina Praescientia, Providentia, Praedestinatione et Reprobatione Concordia*, Part IV.
32. Hasker, *God, Time and Knowledge*, pp. 39–52.
33. Molina, *Concordia* IV, Disputation 50, 15. Freddoso, in the Introduction to *On Divine Foreknowledge*, pp. 79–80.
34. See Robert Adams, 'Middle knowledge and the problem of evil'.
35. One who denies that there are true counterfactuals of freedom will offer some alternative understanding of the scriptural text. Given the context it seems likely that Jesus is saying, 'You people are even worse than the Sodomites, and so on . . .'
36. Plantinga, *Nature of Necessity*, pp. 186, 189.
37. William Hasker, 'How good/bad is middle knowledge? A reply to Basinger', see p. 117.
38. Freddoso, Introduction to *On Divine Foreknowledge*, p. 36.
39. Freddoso, Introduction to *On Divine Foreknowledge*, p. 48.
40. This last problem has hardly been touched in the current literature and is the focus of my 'Middle knowledge versus knowledge of vision'.
41. Leftow, *Time and Eternity*, p. 246. See also Eleonore Stump and Norman Kretzmann, 'Prophecy, past truth, and eternity'.
42. I argue this in Section 2 of 'Omniscience, eternity and freedom'.
43. Douglas Lackey, 'A new disproof of the compatibility of foreknowledge and free choice', see p. 317.
44. Paul Helm, 'Timelessness and foreknowledge', see p. 527.
45. Linda Zagzebski, *The Dilemma of Freedom and Foreknowledge*, pp. 60–3.
46. Classical texts include Augustine's *On Free Will* (Though Augustine is a compatibilist, his work introduces the elements which will be required for a successful solution to the paradox.), Boethius' *The Consolation of Philosophy*, Anselm's *On the Harmony of the Foreknowledge, the Predestination and the Grace of God with Free Will*, and Aquinas' *Summa Theologiae* I, Q. 14, art. 13 and *Summa Contra Gentiles* I, Chapter 66, sections 7 and 8, and Chapter 67.
47. Linda Zagzebski, *Dilemma of Freedom and Foreknowledge*, argues this point in the contemporary idiom (though she does not go on to emphasize the conclusions entailed by God's eternity). Her definition of freedom can be found on p. 161.
48. W. Norris Clarke, 'A new look at the immutability of God'. The quotation is from p. 205 in the reprint.
49. I have argued this at length in 'Omniscience, eternity and freedom'.
50. Jonathan Kvanvig, *Possibility of an All-Knowing God*, defends the view that God is omniscient in that He 'justifiably believes that p if and only if *p* [a proposition] is true'. He leaves open the question of whether or not *de se* propositions can be reduced to *de dicto* propositions (propositions which objectively express a state of affairs), but introduces a distinction between 'directly or indirectly grasping' a proposition. There are some true propositions which it is logically impossible for God to 'directly grasp' but which He can nonetheless justifiably believe.
51. Anthony Kenney, *The God of the Philosophers*, p. 29.
52. Anselm, too, insists that God knows sensible qualities. I discuss this point in *Neoplatonic Metaphysics and Epistemology of Anselm of Canterbury*, pp. 32–6 and 171–3.
53. David Blumenfeld, 'On the compossibility of the divine attributes'; p. 204 in reprint.
54. Paul Helm, 'Omniscience and eternity', see pp. 81–5.

7

Omnipotence

In the contemporary literature a great deal of time is spent on the question of the proper definition of the term 'omnipotence' for 'some being x'. It is notoriously difficult to arrive at a coherent definition because, as Aquinas noted in his discussion of the issue in the *Summa Theologiae* Q.25, art.3, different sorts of activities are appropriate to different sorts of beings. Certainly, 'some being x' can scratch his nose, forget his phone number, and deceive his mother. God can do none of these things. But we need not conclude that God is not omnipotent, or, what amounts to the same thing, that the God of perfect being theology does not exist. Our mission here is not to arrive at a definition of 'omnipotence' for 'some being x', but rather to try to assess the scope of the power of 'that than which a greater cannot be conceived'.

According to the classic tradition, God is indeed 'all powerful'. As the absolute creator of the world *ex nihilo* He is the source of all being and hence of all powers and abilities possessed by His creations. Whatever anything is able to do, it is able to do it because it is immediately sustained in being, with all of its properties, right now by God. 'What do you have that you have not received?' asks St. Paul rhetorically (1 Cor. 4: 7). Augustine and the classic tradition answer for the whole created universe, 'Absolutely nothing!' This might suggest that it is a mistake to ascribe natural causal power to created things so that we ought to explain the rock's falling in terms of God's will rather than gravitational attraction, and some important philosophers of religion have argued just that. There are ways around this counterintuitive position, but how we reconcile creaturely power, termed 'secondary causality', with divine power depends upon the more fundamental issue of the ontological status of creation relative to the Creator, so we will save the discussion of secondary causes until the next chapter.

Whatever else can be said about divine omnipotence, it is crucial to keep in mind that the fundamental divine act is the immediate sustenance of all creation, and that all ability or power which is not God's is received from and is a dim reflection of the divine power.[1] There are a couple of important corollaries which follow from this initial premise. The ability to create *ex nihilo* is absolutely unique to God. At the best, human makers can rearrange things. In order to understand divine omnipotence we cannot start with the sorts of actions we do and the sorts of powers we exercise and then stipulate that God does 'all' this sort of thing. The human knower can conceptualize, if not imagine, what it means to bring something into existence from nothing, but there is only a very distant analogy between the processes by which human makers go about their business and God's immutable, eternal act of creation.

A second corollary is that any 'ability' for which a creaturely limitation such as being corporeal or weak or caused is a prerequisite will be an 'ability' not possessed by God. And so there will turn out to be, as the tradition spelled out very clearly, all sorts of tasks that God 'cannot' perform. For example, if, with Tomis Kapitan, we hold that intentional action requires that one 'form' an intention, which in turn requires a change of mental state, then God does not act intentionally.[2] But rather than conclude, as Kapitan does, that God is impotent, the tradition will argue that our ability to act is radically restricted by the limitations of our spatio-temporal nature and *of course* God's action is not like that. But God does act (eternally and immutably) through reason and will and choice. It's just that He never dithers over what to do. If Kapitan prefers not to call this 'intentional action', fine. We can call it 'intentional action*'. The point is that we cannot suppose that our power is much like God's, and we must suppose that God's power is not circumscribed by any creaturely limitations.

Not only is God 'all-powerful' but also He is the *most* powerful being possible. This, at least, is what the tradition held. Some contemporary philosophers of religion are apparently comfortable with the view that there could be a more powerful being than God, a being who possesses *real* omnipotence, unhampered by such divine attributes as perfect goodness.[3] Richard Gale finds it conceivable that there could be a being, whom he names 'Pinrod', who possesses only one of the divine attributes, omnipotence, without God's other perfections. He suggests that Pinrod could do everything God can do, and then some. He could have a body, and so play football. He could commit suicide, and behave in a generally immoral fashion.[4]

Clearly these philosophers do not have the traditional conception of omnipotence in mind. On that conception Pinrod is impossible. Given the doctrine of simplicity God's omnipotence is not separable from His 'other' attributes. God does what He does through His omniscience, and this act of thought is the standard for value. Gale notes this, but dismisses simplicity too easily. And even if we set aside the traditional doctrine of simplicity, it is difficult to make sense of a being who has omnipotence, without the other divine attributes. Gale's suggestion is that Pinrod is omnipotent, but not omniscient. Suppose we grant Pinrod some knowledge, short of omniscience. He knows all there is to be known except that there is a can of soda on my desk. But then the soda exists independently of Pinrod since, presumably, he cannot sustain in being by the power of his thought something which he does not know to exist. He cannot even act deliberately upon the soda. He cannot possess the sort of omnipotence attributed to the God of perfect being theology. For an unlimited being who brings things about simply by willing, perfect power requires perfect knowledge.

What of immoral actions? We will address the question more fully below, but here suffice it to say that, on the traditional understanding at least, good behavior is that which reflects the nature of God as pure act, and *God's* perfect power and knowledge are identical to His goodness. Gale's Pinrod, if he is supposed to have the same sort of power that the traditional God has, is not a conceivable being after all, and presumably the same would hold true of any hypothesized 'being who was more powerful' than God . . . more powerful precisely in virtue of lacking some of God's perfections. There is no possible being more powerful than the traditional God who brings creation into being from nothing, and on whom all positive properties depend.

Shall we then say that God, according to the classic tradition, can do absolutely anything? In fact there are all sorts of 'things' God cannot do. First and foremost, God cannot do the logically impossible. He cannot, for example, make a round square. To my knowledge this was the unanimous opinion of the medievals, Christian, Moslem and Jewish. Even Ockham, whose insistence on the supremacy of God's will leads him to a radical voluntarism, takes it for granted that God's will could not violate logic. Descartes, apparently, was of a different opinion, and a very quick look at his view and the problems with it should establish the importance of the traditional approach in our project of perfect being theology.

There has been a lot of debate recently about just exactly what

Descartes' position on God and necessary truth really was. In a series of letters Descartes makes statements such as this one:

> To one who pays attention to God's immensity, it is clear that nothing at all can exist which does not depend on Him. This is true not only of everything that subsists, but of all order, of every law, and of every reason of truth and goodness . . .[5]

In Descartes' view the laws of logic and mathematics seem to depend upon God's will in such a way that they could have failed to be or could have been other than they are. Harry Frankfurt has taken this to mean that God is 'a being for whom the logically impossible is possible', while 'necessary truths' are only necessary in the sense that our human minds *must* structure perceived reality in accord with them. Reality itself need not comply. Frankfurt finds the view that it is possible that the impossible be possible just incoherent.[6]

Certainly, from the standpoint of perfect being theology, if we accept this position we cannot accept anything else. If, for example, the law of non-contradiction does not hold for reality, then when we say that 'God exists' we must allow that it is possible that 'God does not exist'. He may be omniscient and yet ignorant, good and bad, ubiquitous and situated in and only in Los Angeles. On this analysis of the Cartesian doctrine, there is unreason at the heart of things, and thinking will not help us to understand what is the case, since what is the case, in reality, is equally possibly not the case. Perfect being theology must give up any pretensions to having anything ultimately correct to say about the nature of God, and religion must admit that what it worships is beyond comprehension in the sense that God might be anything or nothing.[7] If this is where commitment to the absolute sovereignty of God has led us, we had better backtrack a few steps.[8]

Richard LaCroix offers a more sympathetic reading of Descartes.[9] He holds that the Cartesian position entails neither that God can make the impossible possible, nor that necessity and possibility are merely functions of human cognition. He writes,

> According to Descartes' general doctrine of divine creation God's creative will cannot be determined by any antecedent knowledge of possibilities or goods or truths which he has not already created because there are no possibilities or goods or truths prior to God's creation of them.[10]

Nonetheless, 'the eternal truths are *eternal* and *unchangeable* because they were established by the will of God which is eternal and unchangeable'.[11]

Having established these eternal truths, even God Himself cannot violate them. The crucial distinction to be made is between God's absolute power, that is, His power 'before' He has made any creative choices, and His self-determined power which is limited by the truths He has chosen to create.[12] Reality is as God has chosen it to be, and human cognition recognizes what are genuinely eternal and necessary truths which (now) even God cannot alter or evade.

Problems remain. If LaCroix is correct, Descartes grounds the objective immutability and necessity of the eternal truths in God's 'eternal and unchangeable' will. But God's will, being eternal and immutable, could nonetheless be time-bound and changing, unless the law of non-contradiction holds with objective necessity. This seems to involve a vicious circularity. In any case, on this Cartesian view, perfect being theology will still have to go. We have operated on the assumption that, if there is a God, certain propositions with respect to His nature, while they may require a great deal of discussion, are nonetheless non-negotiably true. Such propositions include 'God is wise', 'God is powerful', 'God is good', 'God is eternal (or at least everlasting)'. The Cartesian account, at least as LaCroix spells it out, entails that God *creates* all 'possibilities or goods or truths', so He *chooses* that these should be true. He might have chosen differently. But that God 'might have been' ignorant, powerless, wicked and deceased (or both omniscient and ignorant, omnipotent and powerless and so on) is incoherent. The Cartesian view entails that God has no pre-volitional nature, that is, no nature 'in Himself'. The doctrine of simplicity is abandoned in that we now have to acknowledge an absolute God beyond comprehension and a self-determined version with the various attributes God has chosen for Himself. And moreover, since Descartes' God could have failed to possess the great-making properties, He does not have them necessarily and hence is not as great as 'that than which a greater cannot be conceived'.

If Descartes responds that whatever properties God chooses to give Himself are *ipso facto* great-making, the tradition replies that in that case 'great' is a term without meaning. If the ignorant, powerless, wicked and dead divinity that God could have been is 'great' then there is no virtue in greatness. And if Descartes responds that God has *made* it necessarily true that 'God is good' and so on, although He could have made such propositions necessarily false, the tradition replies that this is incoherent *simpliciter*. What it means for something to be necessary is that it could not have been otherwise. If we are going to think about God, we must deny that He transcends the laws of logic.

Is God then *limited* by the eternal and immutable necessary truths?

Aren't there things He cannot do, such as make square circles? No. 'Square circles' are not possible things to be made. All there is to these 'things' is the words we have strung together, and it is no lack of power to be 'unable' to make something fitting the contradictory or incoherent description. This is not to say that the laws of logic and mathematics exist independently of God, outside of and somehow circumscribing Him. They are not independent of Him nor are they *chosen* by Him. Rather they follow from His nature as perfect being. The creation which participates in Him reflects this being. The laws of logic and mathematics describe the way being must exist as an image of the necessary being which is the source of all.[13]

God, as creator, sustains all creation in being *ex nihilo*. This power entails the ability to bring about any possible state of affairs, with perhaps one class of exceptions. As we will see, there is some debate among the classical philosophers of religion over the relationship between divine power and the freedom of rational creatures. But, with the possible exception of free creaturely choices, if it is possible, God can bring it about. (Remember that we are temporarily setting aside the question of secondary causation. It may be appropriate to say that both God and natural causes 'brought it about' that Comet Hale-Bopp passed close to the sun in the spring of 1997. A further warning to the reader: it may turn out that what states of affairs are genuinely possible are surprisingly limited.)

Saying that God can actualize (almost) all possible states of affairs is not at all the same as saying that 'If it can be done, God can do it.' There is a crucial difference between performing a task and bringing about a state of affairs.[14] There are many possible tasks which God cannot perform because it would be logically impossible for Him to do so. Socrates can sit. God can bring it about that Socrates sits. God cannot sit Himself because to sit is to assume a certain position with your body. No body, no sitting. The inability to sit is not a limitation on God. It is a consequence of God's freedom from corporeal constraints. God cannot perform any task for which limitation and weakness is required on the part of the performer. He can bring it about that someone forget, or trip, or die. He cannot do these things Himself, because it would be logically impossible for an omniscient, incorporeal and necessary being to do these things. As we have seen, God cannot do the impossible.

If we were beginning from scratch and attempting to construct a working definition of 'omnipotence' as it applies to 'some being x' the above move might be questionable. Isn't there something circular about saying that God is omnipotent because He can do everything possible *for Him*? Might we not find ourselves in the foolish position of having to attribute omnipotence to Mr. McEar, the gent who is, by definition, able to scratch his ear and *only* able to scratch his ear?[15] But we are not trying to define 'omnipotence for some being x'. We have saved the present question of what states of affairs God can actualize and what tasks He can perform until well into our discussion of perfect being theology. We have already established a great deal about the nature of 'that than which a greater cannot be conceived', and it does not beg any questions to take as given the divine attributes which we have previously established. It is no limitation on *divine* omnipotence that God cannot do what it is logically impossible that a simple, necessary, eternal and so on being should do. So, though He can actualize all possible states of affairs (save only the aforementioned possible exception), He cannot perform all possible tasks . . . and more power to Him!

Does this mean that God can change the past? That Comet Hale-Bopp did not pass close to the sun in the spring of 1997 seems a possible state of affairs. Can God 'go back' and bring it about? Some contemporary philosophers, Richard Swinburne, for example, have felt compelled to add to the qualification with respect to the logically impossible a further condition that omnipotence does not entail the ability to change the past.[16] The tradition will certainly agree that even God cannot change the past, but it will not see this as an *additional* qualification on divine omnipotence. First, it must be remembered that the God of classic perfect being theology is not time-bound at all. Being eternal, there can be no issue of His 'going back' or 'going forward' for that matter. Whatever God does, all the beings He sustains and all the states of affairs He actualizes, He does immediately in His eternity to which all of time is present. According to the tradition, to ask whether or not God can change the past is essentially to ask whether or not God can make it so that what is the case is not the case. And the same holds for the present and the future. If I am writing, even God cannot make it be the case that at the time I am writing I am not writing. And if it is the case that the sun will eventually expand into a red giant, God cannot make it not be the case. But we have already allowed that God 'cannot' do the logically impossible.[17]

The tradition responds to the old chestnut about 'the stone too heavy for God to lift' by noting that that, too, is just a logical impossibility. *I* can make something too heavy for me to lift, but this is because I am not the creator of all *ex nihilo* for whom the ascription of physical limitations is a category mistake. This paradox has received a serious hearing in the contemporary literature, and it is worth devoting some time to it, in order to underscore again how completely some contemporary philosophers have abandoned the God of Augustine and Anselm and Aquinas. Richard

Swinburne's 1973 article, 'Omnipotence', is a prime example. Swinburne writes that the stone paradox is perhaps not a happy one.

> One may wonder whether it makes sense to talk of a disembodied agent, such as God, lifting things. However, a paradox in all essentials the same can be constructed with different examples in which there is no question but that the action is of a kind appropriate to a disembodied being. We can, for example, ask whether God can make a planet too massive for him to split apart, or a universe too independent for him to annihilate.[18]

Swinburne concludes that an omnipotent being 'is able to make a stone too heavy for him to cause subsequently to rise, that is to lift. So he will be able to abandon his omnipotence.'[19]

Assuming that what Swinburne has to say about his omnipotent being is supposed to be applicable to God, it is clear that Swinburne's divinity has little in common with the God of the classic tradition. It is not just that Swinburne has abandoned divine simplicity, necessity, eternity and immutability. Many contemporary philosophers of religion do the same. But Swinburne, in this article at least, apparently does not accept the traditional interpretation of the credal principle that God is 'the maker of heaven and earth, of all that is seen and unseen'. On the traditional understanding the most fundamental aspect of divine omnipotence is that it is God who keeps all things in being. Creatures are contingent. They would just blink out if God's power were not immediately present to them. For any stone that God feels moved to 'cause to rise', there is no possible impediment which could affect the God who keeps the stone and the rest of the universe in being by an act of will. God, if He took a mind to, could cause the stone to leave the surface of the earth by relocating the planet to the Andromeda Galaxy and leaving the stone marking a lonely path around the sun between Venus and Mars. Size and weight have no relevance with respect to the scope of God's power. 'A stone too heavy for God to lift' and 'A planet too massive for God to split' are logical impossibilities, as is 'a universe too independent for Him to annihilate'. In the classic tradition the universe just is God and what He sustains in being.

There is one qualifier to the above discussion of the stone paradox. Suppose God erects a stone somewhere (perhaps as a reminder of His omnipotence) and promises that, 'This stone shall stand here undisturbed until the sun turns into a red giant and the earth itself is destroyed!' In that case, God would have indeed endowed the stone with a property which renders it immovable, even to Him . . . the property of having been promised by God to be kept in place. God cannot break His promises, because that would be wicked. (Should we add a *ceteris paribus* in case the ingenious philosopher is able to come up with some situation in which even God *ought* to make a promise and later break it?) But now, don't we have a genuine paradox since there is, indeed, a stone which God 'cannot' lift. If God 'cannot' do evil, as we certainly can, isn't He limited? Again, the tradition responds that for God to do evil would entail a logical impossibility. This can be analyzed starting with the nature of God, or starting with the nature of moral activity.

'That than which nothing greater can be conceived' is good necessarily. In the classic tradition this does not mean that God always complies with the laws of morality, always 'does His duty' or some such thing. It means that God's nature itself is the source and standard for all value of any kind. The morally good act, the good painting, the good dog, all are good insofar as they imitate God in their various ways. (We will say more on this in Chapter 9.) Evil is a falling away from this standard. God, the necessarily existent standard for what goodness is, cannot 'fall away from' Himself.

If we approach the question from the perspective of moral activity, it is again clear that God cannot sin. What is it to sin? Anselm puts it well when he explains that to sin is to choose to act contrary to the will of God. Note that this need not, and in Anselm's case, does not, imply voluntarism, the view that whatever God wills is *ipso facto* good, and God can will just anything. Anselm's position (though not thoroughly spelled out) accords nicely with Aquinas' version of natural law ethics which takes it that what God wills is that we should do those things which promote our well-being here and in the hereafter. So sin is both choosing contrary to the will of God and choosing contrary to what will promote one's well-being. (Again, more of this in Chapter 9.) But if sin entails a choice contrary to the will of God, God cannot both will and not will the same thing at the same time. He cannot sin. Some have argued that this makes God *less* virtuous than the being capable of evil who freely chooses good. The tradition responds that it is incoherent to propose that the source and standard of all good should be 'less good' than a lesser being. (This is yet another issue for Chapter 9.)

Anselm goes one step further. It is logically contradictory that God cause *anyone* to sin. God cannot make anyone abandon goodness, since that would mean that He 'does not wish him to will what He wishes him to will'.[20] In Anselm's view not only can God not perform the task of sinning Himself, but in addition there is one class of possible states of affairs which we can bring about and God cannot, and that is the state of our own sinning. And thus we do have to qualify divine omnipotence by saying that it can bring about any possible state of affairs, *except* that of an individual's choosing to sin.

Augustine's compatibilist position is rather different. He holds that God does not actively will people to sin, but rather He withholds from them the irresistible grace required for not sinning. If they had received the grace they would not have sinned.[21] So, though perhaps we can stop short of saying that God 'causes' the sin, in the final analysis it is 'up to' God whether or not the sin occurs. Since this position seems to lay the ultimate responsibility for the existence of evil on God, I prefer to opt for the Anselmian solution and simply bite the bullet on the conclusion that *we* can bring about a possible state of affairs which it would be logically impossible for God to bring about.

This is related to a question which is phrased in the contemporary literature as a paradox: can God create a creature whose will is so free that He cannot control it? If not, He is not omnipotent, since there is a logically possible being which He cannot create. If so, He is not (necessarily) omnipotent because there exists (at least possibly) a being He cannot control. This is an important issue because it figures in free will theodicy, the attempt to absolve God of the responsibility for moral evil by holding that such evil is the result of the choices of free beings, that the existence of free beings is so great a good that it is *worth* the cost in evil, and that having made free creatures God 'cannot' step in and control them.

One solution, derivable from Anselm's work, goes like this.[22] In one sense no creature is beyond God's control. God can produce in a rational being beliefs, feelings, actions and so on. He can shut down your free will. He can make you blink out of being. But there is another sense in which He cannot control a free being. On Anselm's analysis, for a human agent in this life, a morally significant choice requires options and, for *any* agent, the free choice is the one that originates solely with the chooser. If it is caused by anything outside the will of the one choosing then it isn't really free. If God produces your choice it isn't free. On this understanding of freedom, a choice (hence a being) who is both free and controlled is a contradiction. God can no more make a controlled free being than He can make a round square. And, as we have often repeated, it is not a limitation on divine omnipotence that God cannot do the logically impossible.

I find this an adequate solution, indeed the only possible solution if one depends on free will theodicy to argue that God is not responsible for moral evil. Augustine would disagree, and would, I take it, resolve the paradox differently. He would argue that it is misleading to say that 'God can no more make a controlled free being than He can make a round square', and leave it at that. The difficulty is that when we say that God can't make a round square what we mean is that there is nothing there to be made. God's power can encompass the whole universe, but the said universe will not include round squares. But when we say that God can't make a controlled free being what we are saying is that God can indeed make a free being whose morally significant choices, so long as the being is genuinely free, will be beyond divine control. Anselm's solution entails that there will be in the universe, in addition to God, other 'sources of power'. Anselm does not fall into Pelagianism, the view that we can achieve virtue and salvation on our own, because he insists that our freedom extends only to the ability to keep or reject the good that God has given. We do not cause anything from scratch, even our good choices. God gives us the ability to cling to the good, and this same ability enables us to reject it if we choose. But still, it is up to us whether or not God's will will be realized in our regard. We are only really *original* when we choose evil, but when we do we choose from ourselves.[23] Our free choice, unless God steps in to cancel our freedom, is outside God's control.

Augustine apparently found this view insupportable.[24] If God is *omnipotent* then all power everywhere belongs to Him. Period. Augustine can solve the paradox of the being so free that God cannot control it by insisting that such a being is logically impossible. Given the nature and scope of God's power, no choice and no being could possibly fall outside of it. Both Anselm's and Augustine's solutions are adequate to solve the paradox. If Augustine is right, the hypothetical free being really is not possible, and if Anselm is right and such a being *is* possible, then it cannot be both controlled and not controlled in the same way at the same time. Which way to go depends on one's analyses of freedom and evil.

A final question remains on the issue of divine omnipotence, and that is, 'Could God have done other than He does?' The most interesting and most widely discussed variant on this question is, 'Must God have created a world, and must He have created *this* world?' Within the classic tradition no one doubts that God's actions, including creation, are free. But what does divine freedom consist in? Augustine is clear that God, while absolutely free in the sense of acting purely from His own will, inevitably does the best. The Supreme Good is necessarily self-diffusive, and so God could not fail to create.[25] Anselm follows Augustine in this view. Given Anselm's insistence on libertarian freedom for rational creatures, this may seem surprising. But Anselm does not *define* freedom as an ability to do otherwise. 'Freedom' is the ability to hold fast to the good ('uprightness of will') for its own sake. He adopts this definition precisely in order to include the freedom of God who is unable to sin.[26] God has (indeed, *is*) goodness *a se*, from Himself, and could not be any better. It is important for rational creatures to have the option to choose evil, so that, if they cling to the good, there is a sense (a very limited sense) in which they have given this good to themselves, they have made themselves better, and so they can be praised and rewarded by God.[27] But God Himself cannot get any better. He is the best. He does the best. He does whatever He does freely, and He could not do otherwise. He could not fail to make a world, and (with one key qualification) ours is the best and only world God could actualize.[28] It is important here to note that this is not quite the same as saying, with Leibniz and Voltaire's Pangloss, that this is the best and only *possible* world. Given that rational creatures have libertarian freedom, we could do other than we do and hence produce any number of alternative possible worlds. If human beings had not consistently behaved so dreadfully we might now live in a better world. God takes our free choices into account and actualizes the best world compossible with these choices. This is in fact the driving assumption behind Anselm's proof for the 'necessity' of the Incarnation in *Why God Became Man*.

Aquinas adopts a rather different position.[29] It is true that the Good is necessarily self-diffusive, but nonetheless God's perfect act need extend no farther than the internal self-begetting which occurs within the Trinity. God *must* will the best as an end, but the means to that end are open, and God is equally good no matter what He chooses. God could have chosen to create a different world, or not to create at all. It is, of course, conditionally necessary that whatever God eternally chooses could not be otherwise, but the eternal choice could have been different. (I noted in the chapter on divine simplicity that this seems a bit difficult since God is identified with His eternal act. Could He really be other than He is?) God's act of being is already perfect. Creation does not add anything to it. Our world is neither the only nor the best world God could make. This is not to say that our actual world could have been somehow better ordered. Given its contents, it is as good as it can be. But God could have made a different world with different beings, and that world could have been better than ours. This might seem to imply that God fails to do the best, but on Aquinas' view there is no best. For any possible world, there is a better, and so we cannot fault God for failing to create the best, since 'the best' is a logical impossibility.[30]

The two sides in the classic debate are reflected in the contemporary discussion.[31] It has been fairly common for contemporary philosophers to hold that God must be free in a libertarian sense and be able to choose evil, or at least do more or less good, so that He can get credit for doing well when He could have failed to do so.[32] We will address this issue more fully in Chapter 9. Here suffice it to say that, within the parameters established by perfect being theology, it is incoherent to suppose that God, who is Goodness Itself, could do evil or even less than the best. While Aquinas holds that God could make a better world, he holds that the divine activity itself could not be any better.[33] For the perfect being theologian the question is not whether or not God has the freedom to choose in ways which would make Him better or worse. He doesn't. He is absolutely and necessarily perfect and incorruptible. The operant questions are, 'Is God's activity of creating somehow related to His nature, such that failure to create or create the best would be symptomatic of some lack or limitation?' and 'Is there a best possible world?' Augustine and Anselm answered both in the affirmative, and Aquinas answered them in the negative.

My own inclination is to follow Anselm. There is no need to posit for God the sort of choice which is necessary for the creature if it is to be morally responsible. Given the doctrine of simplicity it is hard to see how God's act as creator can be dissociated from His nature. Further, I am not convinced that the idea of a best actualizable world is incoherent. From the point of view of divine creation, why not say that being is good, and God could create a universe with an infinite number of creatures and/or kinds of creatures? Such a universe would be the best possible reflection of divine infinity, but could never equal it, since the creature is necessarily on an ontological level radically inferior to the creator. If logic requires that God create only a finite number of creatures, I am not sure that there is something contradictory about a possible world containing the most compossible creatures.[34]

Paul Helm has argued, and I agree, that there is no value in ascribing to God an ability to choose which, in the final analysis, renders His choice arbitrary.[35] Both the Anselmian and the Thomist hold that God *must* will the best. But Aquinas holds that there is no reason why God chooses our universe or *any* universe as a means to this end, rather than choosing otherwise. It is hard to see the advantage in this. Laura Garcia, in an effort to defend the Thomist approach against Helm, insists that we should not say that God chooses for 'no reason', but she proposes an analogy which, in my view, supports Helm. She says if someone were in a room that suddenly caught fire and there were four doors equally accessible, we would not say that whatever door our endangered example should choose as an exit was chosen for 'no reason'. Obviously there was a reason, to escape the fire.[36] But the motive and moral status of the person in the burning room would be exactly the same if there were only one door and that's the one he chooses. True, if there are three other possible exits, he has the ability to choose between them, but what does that ability profit him or anyone else? The willing to save one's life counts for something, as does God's necessarily willing the best, but since it doesn't matter which door is chosen, the choice between them is arbitrary. In insisting that God has His choice of possible worlds one loses the explanatory value of being able to suppose that there is some reason for His creating rather than not, and creating this world rather than some other. One has to drive a wedge between God's act as creator and His nature. And the benefit of ascribing to God the ability to make arbitrary choices between means is puzzling given that, as both sides within the perfect being theology camp agree, He necessarily wills the best as an end.

Does the thesis that God 'must' create the best actualizable world contradict the earlier conclusion that He can bring about any possible state of affairs (with the exception of someone's choosing to sin)? Certainly there are no possible states of affairs which are *beyond* God's power . . . too difficult for even Him to actualize. God's power is unrestricted. Nonetheless it is one with His (equally unrestricted) knowledge and goodness. So what is in one sense possible to His power, in abstraction, may not be 'possible' *simpliciter*. God could do less than the best if He chose, but He could not possibly choose to do so. On the Anselmian understanding, given the choices of free creatures, our world is the only world God could make. All those other imaginable worlds are 'possible' only from the perspective of limited creatures unable to see why a perfect and necessary being would not make them. Thus, as I warned earlier, what states of affairs are really possible turns out to be much more limited than one would at first suppose.

I grant that intuitions may differ here. If you are convinced that an ability to choose, even when the choices are ultimately arbitrary, is a great-making property, then adopt the Thomist line. The debate between Augustine and Aquinas takes place within a framework of non-negotiable postulates of perfect being theology, including that, whatever God does, His action is perfect, and is the source and standard for all value. God has, in fact, chosen to create our world. Our next question will be, 'What is the relationship of creation to the creator?'

NOTES

1. Thus I am reluctant to surrender the term 'omnipotent' to those who would use it to mean something like 'capable of performing all possible actions'. The tradition had it first. If the debate gets confusing, let those who would import new meanings adopt new vocabulary. Peter Geach, in contrast, advocates use of the term 'almighty', when speaking of the Judeo-Christian God, so as to avoid the problems attendant on 'omnipotence'. Geach, 'Omnipotence'.
2. Tomis Kapitan, 'Action, uncertainty and divine impotence'.
3. Schlesinger, *New Perspectives on Old-time Religion*, p. 1.
4. Gale, *On the Nature and Existence of God*, p. 23.
5. René Descartes, *The Philosophical Works of Descartes*, 2, p. 250.
6. Harry Frankfurt, 'Descartes on the creation of the eternal truths'. See also Plantinga, *Does God Have a Nature?*, pp. 95–126.
7. Walter Glannon holds that Descartes' position must be that certain eternal truths are uncreated and *do* apply to God. He does not support this from the text, nor does he try to sort out

systematically which truths are which. He mentions as an uncreated eternal truth 'God exists', but without non-contradiction this simultaneously allows the possible truth of 'God does not exist'. Glannon, 'Omnipotence and the transfer of power', see p. 95.

8. Earl Conee defends what he calls the 'intuitive' conception of omnipotence, which is that for any proposition, including those we call logically necessary and logically contradictory, it is up to God to decide on their truth value. He does not suggest any explanation or qualification to mitigate the radically unpalatable consequences I have mentioned. Conee, 'The possibility of power beyond possibility'.

9. Richard LaCroix, 'Descartes on God's ability to do the logically impossible'; pages cited refer to reprint in LaCroix, *What Is God?*

10. LaCroix, 'Descartes on God's ability to do the logically impossible', p. 155.

11. LaCroix, 'Descartes on God's ability to do the logically impossible', p. 158.

12. LaCroix, 'Descartes on God's ability to do the logically impossible', pp. 160–4.

13. This is the conclusion of Augustine's proof for the existence of God from the possibility of true reasoning in human beings in Book II of *On Free Will*. Some contemporary philosophers of religion ground the necessity of mathematics and logic in God's eternal knowledge of necessary propositions which exist as His ideas. The classic tradition would not deny such knowledge to God, but would hold, in keeping with the doctrine of simplicity, that what God knows are the ways in which His being can be reflected.

14. See Thomas Flint and Alfred J. Freddoso, 'Maximal Power'; reprinted in Thomas V. Morris (ed.), *The Concept of God*, see p. 137.

15. This fellow was first hypothesized by Plantinga in *God and Other Minds*, p. 170, and baptized 'Mr. McEar' by Richard LaCroix in 'Swinburne on omnipotence'.

16. Richard Swinburne, 'Omnipotence', p. 232, and Flint and Freddoso, 'Maximal power', p. 144.

17. ST I, Q.25, art.4. Here Aquinas focuses only on the past, but, if I am correct that his doctrine of divine knowledge of vision commits him to eternalism, then I take it he would agree with what I say here with respect to the future.

18. Swinburne, 'Omnipotence', p. 233.

19. Swinburne, 'Omnipotence', p. 235.

20. *On the Freedom of the Will*, 8.

21. See the discussion of the fall of the angels in *City of God* XII, 9, or my 'Irrelevance of original sin', pp. 85–9.

22. *On the Freedom of the Will* 8 combined with *On the Fall of Satan* 14 and 18 make it very clear that God cannot control a free creature if the creature is to have moral responsibility.

23. See, for example, Anselm's *On the Harmony of the Foreknowledge, the Predestination, and the Grace of God with Free Will*, Q. I, Chapter 7 and Q. III, Chapter 5.

24. See note 21.

25. *On the Literal Meaning of Genesis* IV, 16, 27.

26. *On the Freedom of the Will*, 3.

27. *On the Fall of Satan*, 18.

28. See 'The "necessity" of creation', Chapter 2 in my *Neoplatonic Metaphysics and Epistemology of Anselm of Canterbury*.

29. This is only the quickest sketch of Thomas's position. Kretzmann argues that there is a tension between the libertarian and the necessitarian strains throughout Thomas's work (Norman Kretzmann, 'A general problem of creation').

30. ST I, Q.25, arts. 5 and 6. For a brief overview with further references see Gilson, *Christian Philosophy of St. Thomas Aquinas*, pp. 120–9.

31. Recent discussions include: Laura Garcia, 'Divine freedom and creation'; Helm, *Eternal God*, pp. 171–94; Kretzmann, 'A general problem of creation' and 'A particular problem of creation'; Ross, *Philosophical Theology*, pp. 280–319; William Rowe, 'The problem of divine perfection and freedom'.

32. Thomas V. Morris makes the 'more or less good' move in 'Duty and divine goodness'.

33. ST I, Q.25, art.6, reply to obj.1.

34. I have argued this at length in 'Anselm on praising a necessarily perfect being'.

35. Helm, *Eternal God*, pp. 171–94.

36. Garcia, 'Divine freedom and creation', pp. 198–9.

8

Creation

It is, of course, a rhetorical question when God asks Job who it is that laid the cornerstone of the foundations of the earth when the morning stars sang together. God is the author of everything other than Himself. What this means according to perfect being theology is that all creatures which have any sort of being at all are kept in existence from moment to moment by the immediate will of God. Deism, the view that at the beginning of the world there was a supreme being who made the world and then left it to run on its own, cannot be squared with the concept of a perfect being who possesses all power. Nothing can exist independently of God and in His absence. Divine creation *ex nihilo* is absolutely unique. Whatever sort of 'creation' creatures engage in is but the dimmest reflection of divine creation. When we make a chair or a baby we merely rearrange preexistent things. When we create a literary character we just piece together properties that we find in the world. Even if it were possible for me to produce a corporeal object just by wishing . . . let's say I wish for an ice cream cone, and there it is . . . I have not produced it *ex nihilo*. I had to receive my own being and power to think and wish from another source, and I am not the source of any of the qualities that go into making an ice cream cone what it is.[1]

On this analysis of creation, the question of whether or not the world has always existed is not an especially telling one. The issue was extremely pressing seven centuries ago because those who defended the infinity of the past, thinkers like Avicenna and Averroes, did so based on the Aristotelian premise that an immutable God must produce an essentially unchanging effect. Certainly there is the cycle of birth and death, of production and corruption, but the cycle itself has always been going on as it goes on now and will go on always in the future. Such a view is necessarily at odds with the religions of the Book, Judaism, Christianity and Islam, which insist upon a genuine *history* involving watershed events, miraculous divine interventions which change the world forever. Without the Aristotelian corollary that an immutable cause must produce an unchanging effect, there is no philosophical reason for the perfect being theologian to deny the infinity of the past. The argument that contingent beings require a necessary being as their cause is unaffected by how many contingent beings there are and how long they have been around. It is entertaining that contemporary physics has accepted a story about the beginning of our universe which accords with a more literal reading of Genesis, but should the present theories about the Big Bang be abandoned in the future perfect being theology will not suffer any setback.[2]

Nor does the theory of evolution pose any threat to perfect being theology. Science is not up to the task of dealing with the question of whether or not the processes of nature are and must be designed and guided by a creative intelligence. And perfect being theology has no quibble with a natural history which includes the formation of stars, life from inanimate matter, dinosaurs and the rest. The story the scientist tells is not exactly that of Genesis, but, as Augustine warned in the fifth century, we should probably not stake our faith on a *prima facie* reading of Scripture. Augustine's *On the Literal Meaning of Genesis*, which is motivated by a desire to interpret the first book of the Bible both literally and in a way which is consistent with the rest of Scripture, advances a reading of Genesis which accords nicely with the theory of evolution.[3]

At least two of the key problems which arise in attempting to analyze the nature of God as the creator have already been addressed in this book. One is the question which inspired Augustine's meditation on the nature of time in Book XI of the *Confessions*. What was God doing before He made the world? The question is intended to show that an immutable being cannot be a creator. Augustine's answer, accepted by the majority of traditional philosophers of religion, is that God is eternal and does all He does in one, perfect and eternal act to which all of creation and hence all of time is 'present'. We looked at the question of divine immutability in Chapter 4, and Chapter 5 was devoted to the issue of divine eternity.

Several problems connected with the concept of creation came up in the previous chapter on omnipotence. On the question of whether or not God could make other, perhaps even better, worlds, or no world at all, the tradition is divided, as are contemporary philosophers of religion. I lean towards the view that God inevitably does the best, and this world is it, with the qualification that if creatures possess libertarian freedom then God works with the free choices which creatures make. Many find this too restricting on God and suppose that He must be able to do other than He has done. As we will see in the next chapter, the non-negotiable point for the perfect being theologian is that, whatever God does, He is necessarily good, the source and standard for all value.

To the question of whether or not God can do the logically impossible, the classic tradition answers unanimously in the negative. It is not that God is circumscribed or dependent upon the laws of logic and mathematics. Nor does He, as Descartes suggested, 'create' them, for if God transcends logic then all bets are off with respect to saying anything meaningful about Him, and perfect being theology must be abandoned. The tradition insists that the laws of logic and mathematics are somehow reflections of God's nature. The Augustinian expression of this point holds that the truths of logic (including what is necessary and what is possible) and mathematics are divine ideas eternally thought by God, to which Aquinas adds the clarification that these ideas depend upon God's perfectly unified knowledge of Himself. Since God is pure being, in understanding Himself He understands all the ways in which it is possible for being to exist.[4]

There are at least two remaining issues relevant to the concept of God as creator which we have not seriously touched on thus far in this study. Both deal with the question of how to analyze the relationship of creatures to their maker. The first is the ontological question of how the existence of creatures relates to the being of God. A subsidiary of this first question is that of whether or not creation 'adds' to God. The second has to do with the issue of 'secondary' causation. Do created beings really have the power to produce effects, or is all that is done in this universe (with the possible exception of human free choices) done by the power of God alone? How we answer the first question will help in addressing the second.

We have seen that perfect being theology rejects Deism. It is not that God makes things and then leaves them to themselves. Contingent things cannot exist independently. Whatever has creaturely existence in any way at all is kept in being in all its aspects from moment to moment by the power of God. God is simple and His power is His thought. For a creature to be, then, is to be thought by God. There is nothing more to a creature than what God is thinking. For want of a better name, call this view 'theistic idealism'. I hesitate to use the term 'idealism' as it carries a great deal of negative historical baggage, but a better has not occurred to me, and I will try to show that the idealism I will suggest, with the necessary addition of 'theistic', is a sane and sober doctrine, in keeping with the basic system of traditional perfect being theology.

The core of theistic idealism is the view that in describing the relationship of God to creation the best analogy is that of a mind to its ideas. God
is to the created world as Shakespeare, let's say, is to Hamlet. I take it that
one can adopt a strong or a weak version of this position. The weak
version will focus on the fact that we are drawing an analogy. It will say
that the relationship between God and creation is *sui generis* and ultimately perhaps inexpressible. The created mind and its ideas is the best
analogy we have, but it does not begin to capture the actual creature/
Creator relationship. A follower of Aquinas, if he could get over the term
'idealism', might find this version congenial. He could go so far as to hold
that we can *say* that things are God's ideas but, as with all theological
language, our understanding captures only a semblance of the reality, and
an ineradicable element of mystery remains.

The strong version will allow that not only is the created mind with
its ideas the best analogy for God and creation but also it is just right to
say that things *are* God's ideas. Those who hold that we can speak
univocally of God can argue that whatever created things exist do so
because they are produced by God's thought which is roughly the same
kind of thing, though radically different in degree, from our thought.
And since what are produced by thought are ideas, things are God's
ideas. Anselm's metaphysics of participation says basically this.[5] This
does not conflict with the doctrine of simplicity which I have defended
since, as I argued in Chapter 3, we can say that God thinks all He thinks
in one thought.

It is important not to confuse this brand of theistic idealism with
Berkeley's sort. Berkeley, with his empiricist motivations, was apparently
ambivalent about the status of 'objects' in the world. Sometimes he
describes them as simply the coming together of the characteristics which
the creaturely perceiver perceives, so that the tree outside my window just
is the collection of my perceptions. Sometimes he says that they exist
independent of limited perceivers because they are always perceived by
God, thus the tree is 'out there' whether I or any created perceiver perceives
it.[6] Theistic idealism owes nothing to empiricism, and does not admit of
ambivalence on the status of objects. There are indeed things out there in
the world independent of any created mind, and created minds themselves
exist because they are thought by God. Nor need the theistic idealist have
any objection to atoms and their constituents. She will agree with Berkeley
that it is a mistake to suppose that our world of 'middle-sized' objects is a
sort of illusory shadow-world cast by the 'real' world of the particle
physicist, but she can be quite sanguine that objects are composed of
imperceptible particles . . . just so those particles, too, are kept in being,

structured and arranged by the mind of God. The theistic idealism is quite congenial to the most robust scientific realism, the view that the explanatory laws, principles and objects which are posited by the scientist to explain the observed behavior of 'middle sized' objects have objective existence. Optimism about the ability of science to describe reality seems a reasonable attitude on the part of the theistic idealist, since the view that things are thoughts entails that on some level at least the universe is intelligible. If the question is what sorts of things are most 'real' or most important, the answer lies with what God finds most interesting and valuable. All that the theistic idealist denies is that there is some underlying matter like Aristotle's prime matter or Locke's substance which is in principle imperceptible and unthinkable. If all contingent being exists because it is thought by God then if something is by definition inconceivable (*simpliciter*, that is, inconceivable by anyone including God) then it cannot exist.

There is nothing in theistic idealism to worry the scientist, but some have suggested that it poses a serious threat to orthodox religious philosophy. Phillip Quinn argues that if we see the created universe as 'merely' an idea of God's then we have fallen into pantheism. Theistic idealism entails that 'the universe is an affection or modification of God, and all truths which ostensibly make reference to the universe can be analyzed into truths which make reference to God and not to the universe'.[7] The underlying justification for this conclusion seems to be an acceptance of Chisholm's doctrine of 'ontological parasitism', in which propositions about thoughts can be correctly translated into propositions about thinkers.[8]

Whatever one says about Chisholm's paradigm cases of appearances or sense data, the thesis seems wrong with respect to the paradigm case of the theistic idealist which is the idea of a fictive character while it is being thought by its 'creator'. (The analogy works best if we think of the fictive creation not as it is printed on a page or acted on stage or recorded on film, but as it exists in the mind of its creator, immediately sustained by his thought.) Hamlet, the character, is entirely dependent upon Shakespeare, it is true, and so every proposition about Hamlet *entails* a proposition about Shakespeare. But propositions about Hamlet cannot be *reduced to* propositions about Shakespeare. If Shakespeare had not conceived it thus, the proposition 'Hamlet kills Polonius with a sword' would not be true. But 'Hamlet kills Polonius with a sword' is a different proposition from 'Shakespeare thinks "Hamlet kills Polonius with a sword"'. There is no way to translate the former correctly into a proposition about Shakespeare. Hamlet, the fictive character, is entirely dependent upon Shakespeare, and there is absolutely no more to him than what Shakespeare is thinking, and yet he has enough independent existence that he can function as the irreducible subject of a proposition.[9]

We can say the same of the created universe with respect to God. To be an idea of God's is not to be God or 'part of' God. As long as we maintain a distinction between the act of thinking and the object thought, we can hold that created things just are what God thinks and wills to exist in His one, perfect act which is identical to His nature, and yet that the objects of divine thought are not identical to that thought itself and hence are not God.

One might ask how, according to theistic idealism, rational creatures could possibly have libertarian freedom. Hamlet, after all, is not going to make any choices which Shakespeare has not decided he will make. There are at least two things to be said. First, the problem is not unique to theistic idealism. Any orthodox view of the relationship of God to the world is subject to the same difficult question. If it is God's power which sustains everything from moment to moment, how can one of His creatures possibly choose on its own, even against His will? Secondly, the theistic idealist can happily admit that God's ideas are not just like ours. God is a more powerful thinker than we, and the supreme instance of this power is that He can endow some of His ideas, those made most closely to His image, with a trace of aseity such that they can choose on their own, if only to the very limited extent of being able to hold onto or reject the good they have been given. It may be that human libertarian freedom does not fit snugly into the system of perfect being theology, but that moral evil is illusory or ultimately traceable to God fits worse. In any case libertarian freedom is not a difficulty with theistic idealism *per se*, but with any doctrine entailing a strong view of divine omnipotence.

Moreover, there is a distinct advantage to adopting theistic idealism in that it helps one to keep in mind the radical ontological difference between God and creation. I argued above that there is a sense in which the fictive character Hamlet exists. He has certain properties, he performs certain actions. But his existence is very 'thin'. He is utterly dependent. There is not much to him, only the very limited collection of properties which Shakespeare thinks him to have. He exists, but on an ontological level very different from that on which Shakespeare exists. There is much more to Shakespeare. He is not dependent on any created mind. He has a much richer set of properties. And, so the analogy goes, God surpasses Shakespeare in ontological richness by more than Shakespeare surpasses Hamlet. He does not depend on anything at all to exist, and goes beyond having an infinitely rich set of properties by encompassing them all as perfect being. Thinking this way protects us from the temptation to treat God as just another object in the universe, bigger and better than the others, perhaps, but still an instance of the same kind of thing. (Shakespeare, of course, could write himself into one of his plays, and this may be an apt analogy for the Incarnation.)

Once we are firmly committed to the position that God exists on an ontological level as superior to ours as ours is to Hamlet's we can address further difficulties with the concept of creation. A good question for perfect being theology is that of whether or not creation adds to the Creator, making somehow *more* than if there had been just God alone. And if there is more once God creates, then God is not absolutely infinite and ubiquitous since there was 'room' for Him to make things, and He is not what has been made. As Robert Oakes puts the question, 'how can it rationally be denied that an Existent whose unique essential nature ensured freedom from all limitation or finitude would – simply *by virtue* of being absolutely unlimited or infinite – exhaust reality i.e., constitute a Being who is *all-inclusive?*'[10] The question does not arise within theistic idealism because God and creation occupy different ontological levels. Hamlet may express something about Shakespeare, and it may be a valuable activity for Shakespeare to think about Hamlet, but you cannot really add Hamlet's being to Shakespeare's and come up with more existence. The existence of Hamlet does not make Shakespeare's world more crowded, nor does the existence of Shakespeare make Hamlet's world more crowded. This is not because Hamlet and the fictive world of the play are simply aspects of Shakespeare, but because fictive existence and extra-mental existence (that is, existence outside of the created mind) are two different 'levels' of existence. You can compare them as in Anselm's famous dictum that existence in reality is greater than existence in the mind alone, but they are sufficiently different that adding them doesn't produce more of either. And the same goes for God and creation. There cannot possibly be more of God, and no matter how much created universe there is it does not add to or impinge upon the being of God at all.

Keeping in mind this point about the distinction in ontological levels will prove very useful in addressing the problem of secondary causation. The question is this: If all that exists is absolutely and immediately dependent upon the will of God, how can we ascribe to objects the power to cause effects on their own? The discussion, past and present, has produced three main answers. One possible approach can be called 'mere conservationism'.[11] On this view God merely keeps things in existence, and the things act and hence produce effects on their own. Jonathan Kvanvig and Hugh McCann, in defending the view (though they later repudiate it), explain it this way,

> As Creator, God is directly and primarily responsible for the fact that there is something rather than nothing: that is, it is His creative activity that is causally responsible for the *existence* of the physical universe. To say this is not to say He is directly responsible for the states of things in the universe, or the changes they undergo.[12]

This position does not jibe with perfect being theology, nor does it allow for a metaphysically adequate account of what it is to be an existent object. Take the time-honored example of fire burning cotton. Mere conservationism holds that God causes the existence of the fire and the cotton, but it is the fire which causes the cotton to be reduced to ashes. This implies that God causes the existence of the cotton, but not its subsequent blackness and powdery texture nor, by the same token, its previous whiteness and cottony texture. It conflicts with perfect being theology to hold that the myriad properties which fall under the heading of 'the states of things' should not be caused and sustained in being by God.

Moreover, mere conservationism presupposes an incoherent analysis of what it is to be an object. While it is possible *in intellectu* to distinguish the essence (nature) from the existence of a thing, a thing cannot exist without an essence. God produces things, essence and all. But a thing's essence cannot be divorced from its role in the system of causes and effects. To be a certain kind of thing is to behave and respond in a certain way. That cotton is fluffy and white, flammable, possessed of a certain genetic code and so on are all the effects of certain causes, and the causes of certain effects. A ball of cotton that behaved and responded like a parrot would not be a ball of cotton. It is incoherent to hold that God could cause the existence of a certain kind of thing without causing it to behave and respond as the kind of thing it is.[13]

A second view, very forcefully defended by the Islamic fideist Algazali in the eleventh century, and prominent today, is known as occasionalism.[14] This position answers the question about the causal power of objects by holding that objects simply do not have the power to produce effects at all. Algazali argues, as would Hume seven centuries later, that there is no conceptually necessary connection between cause and effect, nor does observation reveal any necessary connection. Using the example of fire burning cotton, Algazali notes that his opponent

> has no other proof except the observation that burning occurs when there is contact with fire. However, observation only proves that one occurs together with the other, but it does not prove that one occurs through [the agency of] the other. Indeed, there is no other cause but [God].[15]

The occasionalist holds that the only agent (with the possible exception of free rational creatures) is God. It is not the fire, but God, which causes the cotton to turn to ash. This does not mean that the material world cannot be counted on to behave in a regular fashion. By and large we can trust that God will continue to cause one event following another in the order to which we are accustomed. But, and this was the great advantage which Algazali claimed for occasionalism, there is no necessity in the things themselves which means they must behave and respond in a certain way, and which might preclude the possibility of miracles.

At first glance this view, that there is no causal power at work anywhere in the universe except for the immediate power of God, might seem the ideal position for perfect being theology. But there are deep difficulties with occasionalism. First, it is subject to the same problem as mere conservationism with respect to the status of existent objects. Again, the claim is that God causes the objects to exist, but without causal powers. Algazali does not deny that there are such things as fire and cotton. He just denies that one acts causally on the other. But, again, if things do not behave and respond in certain ways then they do not have the natures we suppose them to have, and what we call 'fire' and 'cotton' are not really anything like we suppose them to be. The result is a radical skepticism about the external world.

A possible move for the occasionalist here is simply to deny the objective reality of objects. (To my knowledge Algazali did not make this move, although it would have followed from his arguments.) Given that sense perceptions are commonly taken to be the effect of some sort of causal connection between perceiver and perceived, if we claim that all effects are produced immediately by God then we must say the same for all perceptions. And if all perceptions are caused by God, only by God, and not by perceptible objects in the external world, then we have no cognitive connection with any extra-mental world at all. Things may be 'out there' but all we have access to is the perceptions 'fed' to us by God. Thus occasionalism entails a brand of idealism (*not* theistic idealism) which has no role for objects existing outside of the created intellect.

This subjective idealism (subjective in that objects 'exist' only as the perceptions of a particular subject without any sort of extra-mental objectivity) is neither conceptually incoherent, nor irreducibly at odds with experience, nonetheless the perfect being theologian would do well to reject it, and the occasionalism which gives rise to it, for a number of reasons. First, subjective idealism conflicts with the almost indubitable deliverance of common sense that objects continue to exist and behave in an orderly manner when unperceived by a created perceiver. This general criticism has led the vast majority of philosophers to reject subjective idealism.

The perfect being theologian of a classical stripe might also object that the view that all there are are minds and their ideas, and that there are no objects outside of the created perceiver, violates the principle of plenitude, the idea that being is good and an excellent universe will have as much as possible. It is a better universe if the sub-atomic particles and galactic clusters are really existent beings 'out there' in the world. This gets back to the question of whether or not one can expect God to have made the best world or even a very, very good world. On the view that God is pure being, if one holds that He does the best, subjective idealism is an unlikely worldview.

There are a number of further arguments against occasionalism. Aquinas' primary complaint is that it 'would imply a lack of power in the Creator; for it is due to the power of the cause, that it bestows active power on its effect'.[16] To say that God cannot produce creatures capable of exercising causal power is to limit God. We have seen that it is no limitation on divine omnipotence that God cannot do the logically impossible, He cannot make a stone too heavy for Him to lift, He cannot sin. But to say that He cannot create fire with the power to burn cotton is a limitation. The occasionalist may respond that it is logically impossible for there to be other powers in a universe sustained by an all-powerful being, but we will try to offer a coherent account of just that situation when we come to the third answer to the problem of secondary causation.

A final difficulty with occasionalism is that it forecloses one possible move in attempting to solve the problem of evil. If all causal power is God's then the responsibility for all evil effects belongs to God. We might separate out the causal power of free beings and hold that the effects of the free created will are not ultimately produced by God. But then we have departed from a pure occasionalism. And on the issue of natural evil, the pain and suffering caused by natural phenomena may be partially justified if they are the result of a system of natural causes and effects which constitute our universe and which, in the final analysis, are a very good thing. This move cannot be made if every instance of pain and suffering is immediately caused by God.[17] More will be said on this question in Chapter 10, on evil.

A third solution to the problem of secondary causation is concurrentism. On this view it is God and the created being together which operate to produce an effect. But if it is God who sustains everything in being from moment to moment, how can the created being contribute causal activity of its own? And if it is really the fire that burns the cotton, isn't God's activity superfluous in the final analysis? Alfred Freddoso attempts to defend concurrentism by offering examples of causation in which two agents achieve a single effect through cooperating in one action. For example, two people might lift a car, or a cooling and a heating agent might together raise the temperature of the room fifteen degrees where either alone would have produced a quite different effect.[18] It seems to me that these examples are not sufficiently analogous to suggest an adequate analysis of the relationship of God to the secondary cause. In both examples each of the agents alone lacks the power to produce the effect, whereas concurrentism holds that both God and the natural cause have the power to produce the effect. Moreover, neither example takes account of the unique relationship of creature to creator. In neither example does the existence of one agent including its causal power totally depend upon the other. If the example included this relationship it would simply raise the problem of secondary causation again, not illuminate it.

Here is where theistic idealism can suggest an analogy which really does help show how two causes can produce one effect. The crucial point, which Freddoso's examples fail to capture, is that in the case of secondary causation, in the words of Aquinas, 'One action does not proceed from two agents of the same order.'[19] If we hold that God is to the created world as the author is to his fictive creatures we will see that the primary and secondary cause operate on different ontological levels such that there is no question of them 'interfering' with each other. For example, in *The Wizard of Oz* a tornado blows Dorothy's house to Oz. Here, L. Frank Baum is the primary cause . . . the author of the created world in which the event occurs . . . and the tornado is the secondary cause. On the ontological level of the story it is the tornado which acts through the powers it has as the kind of thing it is. If Baum had imagined that a tomato blew the house to Oz the story would have been quite different. The analogy entirely resists a mere conservationist or occasionalist reading. It is not the case that Baum caused the existence of the tornado, that is, imagined it in the story, and then the tornado blew the house to Oz on its own. Nor is it the case that it was really Baum who blew the house, as if he had chipped in with his own lung power. It is both Baum and the tornado which cause Dorothy's house to be set down among the Munchkins, but they operate on entirely different levels, and which cause we focus on depends on which level we have in mind. If we are thinking of the level of the creator then it is Baum, not some other author, who made it the case that the tornado would blow the house to Oz. On the level of the story it is the tornado, not some other house-lifting force, which picks up and moves the house. There is not the least parity between these causes. Baum can exist without the tornado, but not vice versa. Still, there is a concurrence of causes. Presumably Baum could have simply written that the house flew to Munchkin Land with no cause at all, that is, no cause within the story. But if Baum chooses that the house in the story shall be lifted by a tornado then the tornado is not superfluous with respect to achieving the effect. And God is to the real Kansas with its real tornadoes as Baum is to the Kansas of his story. If a building in Kansas is destroyed by a tornado and we should wonder whether it was *really* God or the tornado that caused the destruction, the answer will depend on which ontological level we are thinking of. Does God produce and sustain the tornado including all its powers, activities and effects? Certainly. Could God have destroyed the building simply by willing it destroyed? Of course. But given that there was a tornado, is it the tornado that destroyed the building through the force of its winds? Yes, again.

Perfect being theology holds that God sustains everything in being by the power of His thought. This suggests a theistic idealism, more or less literal depending upon one's view of how concepts apply to God (and perhaps upon how negative are one's associations with the term 'idealism'). One issue which theistic idealism clarifies is the ontological gap between creature and Creator. It gives more content to the idea that creation is a 'reflection' of the divine. In so doing it highlights the failure of mere conservationism and occasionalism as solutions to the problem of secondary causality, and proposes the analogy of the author and his creation to show how two causes of radically different orders can 'concur' to produce an effect. This last example of the tornado does raise, in a very stark fashion, the problem of why a good God allows such things . . . not only allows them, but causes them immediately. We will turn to this most difficult question in Chapter 10, on evil, but it seems appropriate before we look at evil to address some remaining issues on the subject of divine goodness.

NOTES

1. Swinburne in *The Coherence of Theism* presents a very different understanding of divine creation and holds that if we could bring matter into existence by thinking then we would be creators in the same way that God is (pp. 130–43).
2. William Lane Craig and Quentin Smith debate the question of the religious implications of the Big Bang in *Theism, Atheism, and Big Bang Cosmology*.
3. In Book I, Chapter 19, Augustine cautions against insisting on a particular biblical interpretation when the issue is a scientific question. The chapter is entitled 'On interpreting the mind of the sacred writer. Christians should not talk nonsense to unbelievers' (Taylor translation in Ancient Christian Writers, Vol. 41). For a contemporary discussion of how the contemporary reader committed to the position that Scripture is the word of God might take Genesis, see Peter van Inwagen, 'Genesis and evolution'.
4. ST I, Q.15, art.2. Richard Creel argues for a 'plenum', a sort of Platonic world of possibilities, existing external to God. He holds, rightly in my view, that this is the logical consequence of

Plantinga's argument in *Does God Have a Nature?* which rejects both the traditional account of divine simplicity and the Cartesian position that modal truths are 'made' by God. Creel accepts the conclusion that God does not create *ex nihilo* (*Divine Impassibility*, Chapter 4).

5. I argue this historical point, as well as offering an extended defense of theistic idealism, in 'How a perfect being creates: Anselm's theistic idealism'. Eriugena offers an even more explicit defense of idealism, but in making the case that one's views are 'sane and sober' one may not particularly want Eriugena in one's corner.
6. John Foster and Howard Robinson in the introduction to *Essays on Berkeley: A Tercentennial Celebration*, pp. 1–17(10).
7. Phillip Quinn, 'Divine conservation and Spinozistic pantheism', see pp. 298–9.
8. Roderick Chisholm, *Person and Object*, pp. 48–51.
9. Rogers, 'How a perfect being creates', pp. 235–40.
10. Robert Oakes, 'God and cosmos: Can the "mystery of mysteries" be solved?', see p. 315.
11. This is the term used by Alfred Freddoso in his article 'God's general concurrence with secondary causes: Pitfalls and prospects'.
12. Jonathan Kvanvig and Hugh McCann, 'Divine conservation and the persistence of the world', see p. 16.
13. Averroes makes this point in arguing against Algazali's occasionalism (*Tahafut al-Tahafut*, 1, p. 325. I take it that Aquinas is saying something similar in his second criticism of occasionalism in ST I, Q.105, art.5.
14. Algazali, *The Incoherence of the Philosophers*, the section 'Concerning the natural sciences', pp. 283–91. (For contemporary defenders of occasionalism, see Jonathan L. Kvanvig and Hugh J. McCann, 'The occasionalist proselytizer', and William Vallicella, 'Concurrentism or occasionalism?')
15. Algazali, *Incoherence of the Philosophers*, p. 284.
16. ST I, Q.105, art.5.
17. Alfred Freddoso makes this point in 'Medieval Aristotelianism and the case against secondary causation in Nature', p. 116.
18. Freddoso, 'God's general concurrence with secondary causes', pp. 149, 153.
19. ST I, Q.105, art.5, reply obj.2.

9

Divine Goodness

God is good. Perfect being theology would have it that God is perfectly good necessarily. In this chapter we will examine what this means and why we should say it, and then look at two perennial questions that arise in connection with the goodness of God: 'Is a being who is good necessarily really praiseworthy?' and 'What is the relationship of God to the principles of morality?' In the tradition which I have been defending God Himself is considered the absolute source and standard of all value. Whatever sorts of goodness creatures have, they have it as caused by and reflective of this perfect goodness. Thus descriptions of divine goodness which isolate divine 'actions' fall short of the mark. It will be incomplete to sum up God's goodness as Swinburne does when he writes that 'God is so constituted that he always does the morally best action (when there is one), and no morally bad action'.[1] And Morris's premise that 'Divine moral goodness is understood basically on the model of human moral goodness' is certain to generate puzzles when we attempt to square it with classical perfect being theology.[2] Human moral goodness is certainly reflective of divine goodness, but it makes a difference that God is the absolute source of all value and 'that than which a greater cannot be conceived'.

In earlier chapters in this book I defended the traditional position that a perfect being must be simple and exist necessarily and *a se*. It follows from the doctrine of simplicity that God does not *have* goodness as a property in addition to His nature. He *is* goodness, *per se*. He is unlimited being, that is, He is a person who is entirely act, with no unrealized potential. He does all He does in one, eternal act of thinking, and this act, as perfect being, is identical with perfect goodness, the source and standard for all value. In the contemporary literature it is not uncommon to distinguish between metaphysical goodness, that is possessing the 'fullness of being', and moral goodness, that is a propensity to do the right thing, and to ascribe both to God.[3] The contemporary philosophers who make this distinction seem to view these two sorts of good as irreducibly different and do not address the question of what their relationship might be such that both are appropriately called 'good'. The God of traditional perfect being theology is absolutely simple and does not possess goodness under two radically different species. In discussing the divine attributes, metaphysical goodness takes priority. God in Himself just is perfect being, pure act. It is fitting to describe God in terms of moral goodness. He *does* always and necessarily 'do the right thing'. But His relationship to the principles of ethics is not the same as ours. This point requires discussion. First, though, let us take a brief look at the motivations for adopting the view that God is necessarily goodness itself.

It seems intuitively obvious that 'that than which a greater cannot be conceived' could not lack the attribute of goodness, and that it is greater to possess it necessarily than contingently. A being that might cease to be good is corruptible even if not now corrupted, and so is not as good as a being that is intrinsically incorruptible.[4] Of course, one philosopher's 'obvious' is another's 'clearly wrong'. One could argue that a being who was always good contingently would be better than a being who was good necessarily in virtue of the fact that the former could engage in a whole set of good actions impossible for the latter. A contingently good being could refrain from doing evil. A necessarily good being could not because it is not possible to *intend* not to do something which you know to be logically impossible for you to do.[5] The perfect being theologian will respond that the literal number of good acts one performs is not the determining factor of the extent of one's goodness. If it were, the God of the classic tradition would be the least possible good being in that, in the final analysis, He only engages in *one* act of goodness. But that one act encompasses the greatest extent (perhaps an infinite extent) of perfect good possible for an unlimited being, that is for a being who does not possess any 'abilities' which require weakness or imperfection. True, there are all sorts of good actions which God cannot do. (Setting aside the Incarnation) He cannot have faith or hope, He cannot struggle bravely against fear or lust, He cannot honor his parents. Only a being which is not omniscient, omnipotent and *a se* can do these things. It would be logically impossible for God to engage in the good act which is His nature, His simple, eternal act of unlimited wisdom, power and love, and also in acts requiring that

He be limited. But just as it is not a limitation on divine omnipotence that God cannot do all sorts of things which creatures can do (forget His phone number, scratch His nose), it is not a limitation on divine goodness that He cannot engage in many of the virtuous activities open to rational creatures. God's goodness consists in being just as good as a perfect being can be. This raises the problem of whether or not the God of classic perfect being theology can be said to have 'morally significant freedom'. Might one not insist that it is just morally better to be tempted and freely overcome the temptation than never to be tempted at all? We will address this question after we look at two more motivations for insisting that God be good necessarily.

If God is good, then it follows from His other attributes defended in earlier chapters of this work, that He is good necessarily. If He is simple and necessarily existent then His goodness is identical with His essence which is identical with His necessary being. If He exists absolutely *a se* then His goodness cannot consist in conforming to a standard or set of principles which exist independently of Him. He Himself must be the standard, the perfect good which all other goods reflect. (We will discuss this point more below in dealing with the question of why it is theologically inadequate to hold that God 'creates' values.) But then, again, God's goodness is just identical with His nature, and His nature is to exist necessarily.

Finally, only a God who cannot do evil is an adequate object of religious worship. The God of the people of the Book demands obedience. Is it possible that God may defy His own standards, His very nature? Do we owe perfect obedience to a God who may turn hypocrite? I do not think I am setting too high a standard when I hold that the God to whom we pray must be absolutely trustworthy. When it comes to whether or not God will do right by us, whether that means justice or mercy, *almost* certainly is not good enough. If God is not to be absolutely trusted then there is no safe harbor anywhere in this universe, and one might as well turn to the meaningless chaos of atoms and the void for comfort. At least they haven't held out any hopes. Luther's magnificent hymn, based on Psalm 46, does not have the same ring if we insert that our God is a mighty fortress, a bulwark failing *almost* or *probably* never.[6]

Contemporary philosophers have raised a question about the necessity of God's goodness. If God cannot fail to do the good, does He have 'morally significant freedom'? It is argued that in order to be good morally or ethically one must *choose* the good, and one can only really choose the good if one has the option to choose otherwise. A God who must do the right thing is not morally good at all, and hence is not the best possible being and is not worthy of worship. We have seen that the God of perfect being theology described in this work, especially in Chapter 7, does not have the option to choose evil. If such an option is necessary for moral or ethical goodness then there is no doubt about it, the God of Augustine and Anselm and Aquinas is not morally good. This may seem shocking, but at this stage it is just a matter of definitions. The substantive question is whether or not having the option to choose evil would really make for a better divinity.

First it would be well to clarify the concept of 'morally significant freedom'. I take it that in this context contemporary philosophers mean libertarian freedom, the real ability to choose between options. This must be stronger than a bare logical possibility, since it could be logically possible that I can choose between options in a completely determined universe in which I obviously do not have morally significant freedom. In a determined universe it might be true to say that, though my choice of A over B is necessitated by the physical causes operant in the actual world, there is nothing *logically* necessary about those physical phenomena and so it is logically possible that I could, had the universe been differently constituted, have chosen B. I take it that the operant notion of morally significant freedom requires more than this.

Some contemporary philosophers of religion insist that if God is good 'by nature' then He is not good in an ethical sense. But they go on to argue that God is absolutely trustworthy because given His character and disposition doing evil is totally repugnant to Him. It is unthinkable that He do evil.[7] This analysis is puzzling. If God's choices simply flow from his character and disposition, if there is something about him that forecloses evil as a really viable option, how is there choice and hence morally significant freedom involved? If it is possible for God to be tempted by evil and choose against His character, then it is not unthinkable that He would do so. I take it that ascribing morally significant freedom to God entails allowing that He really might (or really has) chosen evil.

What if we allow that God may have in fact, once in a great while, done wicked deeds, of which an example might be His insistence, recorded in 1 Samuel, that the Israelites destroy all the Amalekites along with their livestock?[8] Should we continue to worship Him? If this peccable God is the only game in town then perhaps on some grossly prudential level it does make sense to ally oneself to Him, but just what that means may be problematic. Shall we obey Him when He orders us to commit atrocities? If we do so, will He blame us later, when and if He repents of His evil?[9]

It has even been suggested that God's creation of beings to whom He can have moral responsibilities opens the logical possibility for a significantly free God to choose to fail in His duty. Moreover, if God ceases to be good He ceases to exist, so any instance of divine dereliction would result in self-extinction.[10] Of course, the bare logical possibility of God's doing evil may leave it very, very unlikely that He will do so. But again, its being merely 'very probable' that God will be good ought to cause the believer some concern. This is especially true on the present analysis which holds that if God commits an evil deed He ceases to exist. Since He is the absolute sustainer of all, if He commits suicide He takes the rest of the universe with Him. This God is a sort of divine time bomb.[11] It is unlikely to go off, but given the length of the divine life span, and God's morally significant freedom, we are not safe from the possibility that God may fail in His duty and blink out of being carrying the rest of us with Him into oblivion.

A God who has done or might do evil is not the perfect divinity I have argued for in earlier chapters. It cannot be Goodness *per se*, and the standard for all value. This God must be in time since the claim is that God is good *now* but might not be good always. Nor does the only-usually-good God or the divine time bomb seem adequate objects of worship. Is ascribing to God morally significant freedom worth the price?

It seems fair to ask: 'Why is it important that God have morally significant freedom?' In the face of all that is lost if we attribute this sort of freedom to God it begs the question to say that someone who can choose between good and evil is 'just better'. The question is, why? In the tradition I have been defending it is Anselm who offers the first philosophically developed discussion of the importance of libertarian free choice in connection with morally significant freedom.[12] But Anselm is careful to limit libertarian freedom to rational creatures, that is, to beings that do not exist independently and *per se* but *per aliud* in almost total dependence on God. The reason the creature needs to have the option to choose between good and evil is that if it freely clings to the good God has given it, when it could fall away, it will, though in a very limited sense, give goodness to itself and participate in its own creation. And because a measure of its goodness comes from itself it is a better being than if it received all that it has immediately and irresistibly from God. In a radically limited way, the free creature who chooses good reflects the aseity of God. But God does not exist *per aliud*. He is perfect goodness *per se* and does not need to choose the good over the evil to make Himself better.[13] If the importance of morally significant freedom for rational creatures is that they should be able to make themselves better *on their own*, it is clear that such freedom is irrelevant to an absolutely independent being. Given that it would involve sacrificing the rest of perfect being theology it seems unreasonable to insist that God have morally significant freedom.

This is not to say that we should deny that God can engage in moral activity, if moral activity means roughly doing the right thing. (We will address the question of divine 'obligations' below.) God can keep His promises. He can treat us as is most fitting, whether that means justly or mercifully. He can love us unconditionally and want only our welfare. The point is that we can trust, with absolutely no qualification, that He will not do the wrong thing.

Thomas V. Morris, while allowing that the God of perfect being theology must necessarily be good, attempts to preserve the intuition that God would be better if He chose among open options. Noting that we do not praise people when their actions simply flow from their natures, he argues that God may indeed choose between merely doing His duty, in an analogical sense, and engaging in acts that are supererogatory . . . above and beyond the analogical call of divine duty. By nature God cannot fail to do His 'duty', and hence be good, but He becomes genuinely praiseworthy when He does more than His nature requires.[14] This approach, while not as extreme as that which insists that God can do evil, is subject to analogous problems. God cannot fall below a certain level, but He can certainly do, and hence be, less than the best. On Morris's account we have no reason to believe that God has performed *any* supererogatory actions, let alone all compossible ones. Thus it is possible that there be a being who behaves better and is more praiseworthy than the Lord of our actual creation. So God is not necessarily 'that than which a greater cannot be conceived'.

Moreover, given divine simplicity and aseity, it must be the case that God Himself is the standard for all good. And given that His nature is identical with His act of being it is nonsense to hold that He could do less than the best since that would entail that His action falls short of His action. (The question of whether or not it follows from this that our world is the best and only actualizable world God could create was addressed in Chapter 7.) So Morris's more moderate attempt to leave God morally significant options does not succeed, at least within the framework of perfect being theology. The intuition that a person is more praiseworthy when he has the option to choose between good and evil or between good and better is appropriate when directed towards rational creatures. When applied to God it means sacrificing most of the attributes ascribed to a perfect being. On the question of moral virtue, it is better to allow that God's goodness is different from our own in that He is the source which we merely reflect. This is why God alone is worthy not only of praise but also of worship.[15]

A related question has been raised in the contemporary literature, and that is whether or not God can be said to have obligations or duties. William Alston holds that 'the lack of any possibility of God's doing other than the best prevents the application of terms in the "ought" family to God'.[16] Morris holds that, as necessarily good, God cannot be said to have literal duties since 'duty' implies adherence to a standard which one could fail to meet. God can be said to have duties in the analogical sense that He will necessarily act *'in accordance with* those principles which would express duties for a moral agent in his relevant circumstances'.[17]

However we understand the meanings of the terms 'duty' or 'obligation', perfect being theology in the classic tradition is clear on the issues. God's activity is the best and the standard for all good and God 'cannot' fall short of that. My intuitions are with Alston that it seems something of an abuse of the language to say that God *ought* to do the best.[18] Nor does God adhere to any principles external to Himself. He 'must' love us, treat us well, desire our welfare and so on, but this 'must' is grounded in His nature. He does not have obligations towards us imposed from the outside, as it were, either through our deserving or through some extrinsic moral principles. God does not *owe* us anything, and yet we can trust with absolute certainty that He will 'do right' by us, not because of who *we* are, but because of who *He* is.

We have said repeatedly that God is the source of value, and that He does not adhere to any external moral principles. These points raise the perennial dilemma posed by Socrates in Plato's *Euthyphro*. The monotheist puts the question this way: Does God will something because it is good, or is something good because God wills it? ('Will' here can be taken to comprehend both commanding and loving.) The traditional answer among Christians for the 800 years from Augustine through Aquinas was a resounding 'Neither!' This is the only answer which can be squared with perfect being theology.

To say that God wills something because it is good implies that there is some standard of good, or set of true ethical propositions, outside God which He recognizes and to which He conforms His will. This view does have its defenders among contemporary philosophers of religion. Swinburne, for example, defends the first disjunct of the *Euthyphro* dilemma, when he holds that, while some actions are made obligatory or wrong by divine command, *'some* actions are obligatory or wrong independently of what anyone commands'.[19] Swinburne argues that no omniscient and perfectly free being could command us to do wrong, but the wrongness of the act does not derive from the fact that such a being could not command it. Apparently Swinburne believes that there are moral principles which exist independently of God. The adherent of perfect being theology cannot accept this. It conflicts with divine aseity. If God is good because He conforms to an external 'realm' of value or morality, then He could not be good were it not for the existence of this independent 'realm'. But since it is God's nature to be good necessarily and, given the doctrine of simplicity, God's goodness is identical with His being, on this view God's existence would depend upon something outside Himself and He would not be absolutely *a se*.

Moreover, on the view that God commands something because it's good, it is difficult to see just what role should be assigned to God in the moral scheme of things. Is He just a messenger who reports what the law already happens to be? But if the moral law exists independently of God, and ought to be obeyed in any case, why give a key role to the divine middleman? Swinburne addresses this issue when he argues that *some* actions are obligatory or wrong because God commands them. This is because God is our creator and sustainer and so ought to be obeyed as one ought to obey one's parents, and also because God has property rights over the inanimate universe since He has created it *ex nihilo*.[20]

This response does not seem adequate. True, parents and property owners do possess a certain authority, a right to be obeyed, when it comes to the behavior of their children and the disposition of their property. And yet it makes sense to ask whether or not a command issued by the parents or the property owner is a *good* command. Is it wise, beneficial, just? If so, then it should be obeyed, but that would be true without the addition of the parent's or property owner's command, though perhaps the authority of the parents or the property owner does provide even more reason for obedience. Alternatively, if the command is wrong then it might not be right to obey it. Thus whether or not the parent's or the property owner's command is really binding depends on whether it conforms to external moral principles. Perhaps the authority of the parent or the property owner really does create an obligation which would not otherwise exist in situations where what is commanded is intrinsically neutral morally. Swinburne offers the example of ordering bedtime for one time rather than another as a parental command which creates obligation simply because it is commanded by the parent. But this suggests a very weak connection between divine commands and human obligation; we ought to do what God commands so long as what is commanded is something that we ought to do even without God or it's something with no intrinsic moral value. Better just to reject the first disjunct of the *Euthyphro* dilemma. There is no value or set of moral principles outside God to which He conforms and which He reports to us.

Can we then say that something is good because God commands it? A

number of contemporary philosophers subscribe to various versions of
what is termed a 'divine command' theory, and sometimes this theory is
summed up by saying that the moral order comes from or is grounded in or
dependent upon the will of God. It is very important to be clear as to what
is meant here, and the difficulty in clarification is exacerbated by the fact
that contemporary philosophers sometimes associate their divine command theories with the voluntarism of Scotus and Ockham without fully
appreciating what was at stake in the later medieval debate over the
relationship of God to the moral order. It will prove useful to take a quick
look at the controversy as it appeared in the thirteenth and fourteenth
centuries.

The issue confronting the later middle ages was not precisely the
Euthyphro dilemma since nobody would have thought of advancing the
view that God conforms to a standard of value or a moral code which
exists outside Himself. What was at stake was the nature of the divine will.
Earlier Islamic thinkers like Avicenna and Averroes had subscribed to a
view of God which owed more to Aristotle and Plotinus than to the Koran
and which saw the Creator as Thought thinking Itself and as willing by
necessity rather than by choice, a far cry from the personal agent God of
revelation who takes an interest in and interacts with His creation. A
cluster of associated beliefs along these lines circulated in the universities of
the Latin West in the thirteenth century and were condemned by the Bishop
of Paris in 1277. Thus there was significant interest in defending the
freedom of the divine will. The question was roughly this: Can God will
anything logically possible? And when the focus was on God as the source
of value, the question became: Could God command us to do anything
logically (or physically) possible? No one doubted that the fundamental
ethical principle for human beings was to obey God. If God commands one
to do something, one has an obligation to do it. But is God's will so
unlimited that He can command us to do anything in our power, and hence
make any possible action obligatory? Or does God's willing in some way
flow from or reflect His other attributes, His wisdom and His love, in such
a way that His commands in our regard must conform to what He knows
to be best for us?

Aquinas subscribed to the latter view. A thing is what it is because it
reflects a divine understanding of a certain nature. The good for anything
is to fulfill its nature, to actualize its potential. This means that the divine
nature itself is the standard for all good in that it is perfectly actualized
being with no potential. When things strive towards fulfillment they are
imitating God. The good for human beings is to become the best examples
of humanness possible. According to Aquinas, the principles of ethics are

basically a guide for the promotion of the well-being of humans, hence Aquinas calls the rules by which God governs human beings the Natural Law. So, for example, we are by nature social animals. We cannot flourish except among others of our kind in properly functioning societies. When God commands that we do not murder or steal or covet, He is looking out for the well-being of the creatures He loves.

Though it is Aquinas who works out Natural Law ethics most systematically, it is clear that earlier Christian thinkers, well before the reintroduction of Aristotle to the Latin West, take it for granted that God commands what is for our good. In *On the Literal Meaning of Genesis* Augustine ponders why God forbade the eating of the fruit of the Tree of Knowledge. The reason it is puzzling is precisely because in this case it really does seem that the prohibition is without reason in the sense that the tree itself must have been good. It seems to be only God's forbidding it that makes eating its fruit wrong. But God does not issue commands without reason, and so Augustine suggests that the unique usefulness of the prohibition was to teach human beings the importance of obedience . . . a lesson which could be taught best when there was no obvious harm from the action itself so that one who obeys the command would do so only to be obedient. Augustine goes on to speculate that when someone obeys God without understanding the reason for the command 'perhaps by the merit of his obedience he will have grounds for seeing the reason of God's command'. He concludes that, 'we must not fear that He could command what is not for our good'.[21]

According to Aquinas even God cannot undo the Natural Law, that is, He cannot make it be the case that a basic principle of the Natural Law should cease to be operative. Stealing is wrong because it impedes human flourishing, and even God cannot, *ceteris paribus*, make it be the case that stealing is right. The *ceteris paribus* is important, of course, because life is very complicated and situations may arise in which one ought to steal (or at least do something which under ordinary circumstances would fall under the definition of 'stealing').[22] But as long as all other things are equal, if a certain sort of action is right or wrong, God cannot change its moral standing by divine fiat. He cannot will that we should do the wrong thereby making it right. But, in Aquinas' view, at least, none of this imposes undue restraints on the divine will. God cannot command just anything, but this is because His will follows from (or in fact is identical with) His wisdom and His goodness. If His will is 'limited' it is only by His own nature.

Scotus and Ockham disagree. With respect to what God can will in our regard, the laws of logic are the only limit. The rightness and wrongness of an act are separate from whether or not the act produces some benefit. If God commands that we do a thing, we *ought* to do it. Scotus frames the question very clearly:

> I ask whether, with all circumstances staying the same in the act of killing a man, with only the circumstance of prohibition and non-prohibition changing, could God make that act, which is prohibited at another time with such other circumstances, be permitted and not prohibited on another occasion?[23]

He responds that this must be possible for God. For one thing, He's actually done it, as in the case of Abraham and Isaac.[24] More importantly, if the moral laws were just true in themselves, then the divine intellect would necessarily know them as true, and 'then the divine will would necessarily agree with them as apprehended, or it would not be right'. But this would entail 'that the divine will is unconditionally necessarily determined with respect to something other than itself which is capable of being willed'. And that, in Scotus' view, places too severe a limitation on the divine will.[25]

Scotus is willing to qualify his voluntarism. Commands that have to do immediately with our behavior towards God are intrinsically necessary, since God Himself is a necessary being.[26] Ockham did not allow even this qualification. Apparently God could will that we should hate Him, and if that is what He commands, then that is what we should do.[27]

Clearly there is a heavy price to pay if we are to safeguard the absolute freedom of God's will in this way. (Note that these problems are analogous to those with the Cartesian view that God 'creates' necessary truths.) First, it renders the moral law arbitrary, with consequences that seem impossible to accept. If tomorrow God should command that we torture small children for no other reason than that He commands it then that will be the right thing to do. It is no good responding that since the divine will is eternal and immutable, the moral laws we actually have must always remain in force. God could eternally and immutably will that at the stroke of midnight (GMT) on 31 January 1999 the entire decalogue is to be negated. There is no reason for the moral law as it stands, and there is no reason that it could not change.

A related problem has to do with the nature of God Himself. We take it for granted that God is good, or even necessarily good. But if the moral order is completely arbitrary then the term 'good' seems to lose any positive content. Presumably we construct our concept of what is good as we experience good actions, good things and good people in this world. The voluntarist holds that God transcends our value categories in that He decides them by fiat and could have (and perhaps *has*) decided differently. In the final analysis 'good' just means 'what God wills' and God could will anything logically possible. So the God of the voluntarist is not 'good' in any meaningful sense. The desire to safeguard God's free will has resulted in a picture of God which is impossible to square with perfect being theology and the demands of actual religious practice. If this is what the second disjunct of the *Euthyphro* dilemma entails, then it, too, must be rejected. The most adequate solution seems to be that of the tradition; God neither conforms to nor 'creates' the moral order, but rather the rules of morality are a guide for how the human being might best imitate God. Sometimes God lays down the law directly, and sometimes we can figure out parts of it for ourselves, but whether we recognize it or not, when we do the right thing we are reflecting the divine nature.

A number of contemporary philosophers of religion have been impressed with the religious significance of seeing God as the absolute source of morality. They have spelled out various divine command theories of which the core is that right and wrong are dependent on the will of God. But contemporary thinkers are not willing to go the whole way with Scotus and Ockham, for the reasons given above. Robert Adams, for example, offers a 'modified divine command theory'. He begins with the intuition, which Scotus and Ockham would have rejected, that pointless cruelty would not be morally right even if God were to command it. Still, right and wrong are a function of what God commands, but only on the condition that 'God does not command cruelty for its own sake – or, more generally, that God loves his human creatures'.[28] While it is logically possible that God could command cruelty, it would be against His character which we can trust to remain loving. Thus we have a divine command theory which does not violate our moral intuitions.

Adams's God, who is not good necessarily, is not the God of perfect being theology, and so one might take issue with him on his description of God. But setting that aside, there are still problems. Adams's modified divine command theory abandons what Scotus and Ockham would have viewed as the key virtue of their voluntarism, that it safeguards the absolute freedom and authority of the will of God with respect to values and ethics. But it is not clear that Adams's theory solves either of the problems raised by voluntarism, that the theory violates our moral intuitions and that it entails that 'good' when attributed to God has no content.

First, Adams leaves it an open question whether it is metaphysically possible that God might act 'out of character'.[29] This does seem to be a crucial question, though. Adams holds that 'The believer's concept of ethical wrongness therefore breaks down if one tries to apply it to the unthinkable case in which God commands cruelty for its own sake.'[30] But if it is really (in some sense) possible that God should command pointless cruelty tomorrow, then, though perhaps pointless cruelty will not be obligatory, since the believer's ethical framework has been destroyed, it is not wrong. But it seems a serious violation of our moral intuitions to say that pointless cruelty might not be wrong tomorrow. And if Adams grants that we won't be obliged to obey God, should He command pointless cruelty, he has admitted that God is not the final authority in our universe. Alternatively, if Adams argues that God's character is immutable and so He cannot, in any real sense, command pointless cruelty, he has given up what was, at least traditionally, the motive behind divine command theory, which was to preserve the limitlessness of the divine will. If God's commands flow inevitably from His character then Adams seems to have modified the divine command theory so much that it begins to look much closer to the views of Aquinas than to those of Scotus and Ockham.

Nor has Adams disposed of the *Euthyphro* dilemma. In response to the criticism that if right and wrong are defined by God's will then God, considered in Himself, transcends the term 'good', Adams argues that God may be considered good in non-ethical senses: we are 'expressing a favorable emotional attitude' towards Him, He is kind, He possesses various virtues.[31] Adams's language leaves open the possibility that our ascription to God of the attribute of goodness is just a subjective judgement on our part: we like Him because He has been nice to us and possesses likable qualities. But this seems obviously inadequate, in that then God could be both good and not-good depending on differing subjective human attitudes towards Him. I will take it that Adams holds that God's character is objectively good, though not in a moral sense. But then the *Euthyphro* dilemma arises again, this time in connection with God's character. Is God good because He possesses certain good properties, or are His properties good because *He* possesses them? If the former then God is dependent upon extrinsic properties for His virtue and so He is not independent. And since it is His good character which constitutes the necessary condition for His authority over the moral order, the moral law is grounded ultimately not in God, but in these good qualities on which His good character depends. And if God's properties are good because He possesses them then if He had been an unloving divinity, as Adams holds to be possible at least logically, then being unloving would have been the 'good' characteristic, and so, again, 'good' when applied to God comes to mean just 'however God is' and loses all positive content. The *Euthyphro* problem is best solved by insisting that all value is grounded in the nature of God.

This is basically the move which a number of contemporary philosophers of religion make. William Alston, for example, offers 'Some suggestions for divine command theorists', in which he comes very close to what Aquinas would suggest. Alston defends the equation of human moral duties with whatever God commands, but denies the additional voluntarist premise that God can command anything logically possible. Instead he accepts the judgement of perfect being theology with respect to God's goodness: 'Since He is perfectly good by nature, it is impossible that God should command us to act in ways that are not for the best'.[32] But this does not imply that God's will must conform to external values. On the contrary, 'we can think of God Himself, the individual being, as the supreme standard of goodness'.[33] As the classic tradition insisted, God neither creates nor conforms to the standards of value: He *is* the standard.

Whether or not it is possible to construct a coherent account which takes God's nature to be the absolute standard of value including moral value along other than Thomist lines remains to be seen. The advantage of Aquinas' Natural Law Ethics is that it explains, in a systematic and metaphysically sophisticated way, how ethical precepts reflect the divine nature. My impression is that this ethic of self-fulfillment is viewed with suspicion by many contemporary philosophers of religion, and not only because it is associated with the Church of Rome. The ultimate goal, in Natural Law Ethics, is happiness for the individual, which, in Christian terms, means eternal happiness with God in heaven. This is not an egoistic ethic, since, being social animals, our own happiness is inextricably bound up with that of our family, friends and neighbors. It is our nature to love others, a nature which imitates God's and is recognizable even when corrupted by sin. In Kant's example of the misanthrope and the philanthropist, Aquinas would be deeply puzzled by Kant's judgement that it is the one who hates his neighbors but still does the right thing who is the truly virtuous human being.[34] Aquinas would undoubtedly hold that it is the man who gives free reign to his natural inclination to love his neighbors who is on the road to heaven.

In any case, those imbued with the Kantian ethic of duty are apt to find even the baptized Aristotle a bit of a hedonist. Time forbids a discussion of this issue here, but I ask the open-minded reader to consider the gospel message. I would argue that there is much there about love, and little if anything about duty. It is on *love* of God and of one's neighbor as oneself that the law and the prophets rest. And, though this may not be high-minded enough for Kant, Scripture has it that the purpose of our life is not that we should do the right thing just to do the right thing, but rather that we should come to final happiness in the Lord. The Natural Law Ethic which fits so nicely with perfect being theology accords very well with the message of the Gospels.

NOTES

1. Swinburne, *Coherence of Theism* (1993), p. 184.
2. Morris, 'Duty and divine goodness', p. 26.
3. Robert Brown, for example, accuses the 'Christian Platonists and Aristotelians' of equivocating between these two senses of good ('God's ability to will moral evil', p. 10). See also, Philip Quinn, 'Moral obligation, religious demand, and practical conflict', p. 205, and Bruce R. Reichenbach, *Evil and a Good God*, p. 138.
4. This is a very common assumption in medieval thought. One very nice expression of it is found in Augustine's *Confessions*, Book VII, Chapter 12, where he is proving that everything that *is* is good.
5. A. A. Howsepian, 'Is God necessarily good?'
6. Paul Helm, in comments on an earlier draft of this manuscript, suggests that this insistence on the *absolute* trustworthiness of God may entail commitment to 'an argument parallel to an unacceptable form of skeptical reasoning which says: unless there is no possibility of p being false I cannot know p'. By way of example he says, 'my reliance on the table that my computer is presently sitting on is totally unreserved even though it is logically possible that the table will disintegrate in 10 seconds'. I grant that for all practical purposes we can and must rely on the imperfectly trustworthy objects and people which constitute our created universe. Note, though, that in a theistic universe it is metaphysically possible that Prof. Helm's table may disintegrate in ten seconds due to an act of God. Further, I understand that on some analyses of the behavior of subatomic particles it is empirically possible that a presently sturdy table may disintegrate in ten seconds. My point is that an adequate object of worship which occupies the role of source of all being and value must be completely trustworthy in a way in which created things and people cannot be.
7. Reichenbach, *Evil and a Good God*, pp. 138–40.
8. This suggestion is made by Brown, 'God's ability to will moral evil', pp. 16–17.
9. With respect to the Amalekites, the tradition will insist that, difficult though it may be for us to see how, their destruction was morally justified.
10. Timothy Jackson, 'Is God just', see pp. 396–8.
11. I thank Sophia Rogers for this apt characterization.
12. As I mentioned in Chapter 7, though Augustine does emphasize the importance of free will, he is a compatibilist, and never suggests that in order to be good it must be genuinely possible for one to choose otherwise.
13. This is the conclusion of his dialogue, *On the Fall of Satan*. See my 'Anselm's indeterminism'.
14. Morris, 'Duty and divine goodness'.
15. I argue this at more length in 'Anselm on praising a necessarily perfect being'.
16. Alston, *Divine Nature and Human Language*. Eleonore Stump takes issue with Alston, but the dispute is about the meaning and usage of words more than about what God's necessary goodness actually entails (Stump, 'God's obligations').
17. Morris, 'Duty and divine goodness', p. 36.
18. Aquinas makes a similar point in ST I, Q.93, art.4.
19. Swinburne, *Coherence of Theism* (1993), p. 210.
20. Swinburne, *Coherence of Theism* (1993), pp. 213–14. See also Richard Swinburne, 'Duty and the will of God', especially p. 298.
21. Augustine, *On the Literal Meaning of Genesis*, Book VIII, Chapter 13. I am following the Taylor translation, vol. 42 in Ancient Christian Writers.
22. ST I, Q.94, arts. 4 and 5.
23. *Oxford Commentary*, Book III, Dist.37. I am following the translation by James J. Walsh in Arthur Hyman and James J. Walsh (eds), *Philosophy in the Middle Ages*, p. 644.
24. Augustine and Aquinas would hold that this is not a case where God has made a murder simply be good by divine fiat. There are cases where it is legitimate for one man to kill another, for example, as punishment for a crime, and God has the authority to order an execution. In the same way, when God commands the Israelites to take the valuables of the Egyptians He is not commanding them to steal. He is transferring His property from those who deserve to be punished by losing it to those who deserve to possess it and who need it to accomplish what He has in mind. See ST I, Q.100,

art.8, reply to obj.3. (Further, it does seem crucially important that God stopped Abraham from killing Isaac.)
25. *Oxford Commentary*, pp. 644–5.
26. *Oxford Commentary*, p. 645.
27. For an overview of the subject see Janine Idziak's introduction to Andrew of Neufchateau, OFM, *Questions on an Ethics of Divine Commands*, pp. xxv–xxxii.
28. Robert Adams, 'A modified divine command theory of ethical wrongness', see p. 102.
29. Adams, 'Modified divine command theory of ethical wrongness', p. 122, note 2.
30. Adams, 'Modified divine command theory of ethical wrongness', p. 107.
31. Adams, 'Modified divine command theory of ethical wrongness', pp. 113–16.
32. Alston, *Divine Nature and Human Language*, p. 266.
33. Alston, *Divine Nature and Human Language*, p. 268. William Mann, 'Modality, morality, and God', argues from divine simplicity that God's willing and His knowing are the same. He must will moral truths, but these truths do not exist independently of God. 'The necessary truths just are (part of) the expression of God's perfectly rational mental activity: they have no status independent of that activity' (p. 94). And Philip Quinn, 'The primacy of God's will in Christian ethics', offers a qualified endorsement of Alston's suggestion that 'God himself is the supreme criterion of moral goodness' (p. 498).
34. See *Kant's Theory of Ethics* (as T. K. Abbott's translation of Kant's ethical writings is entitled), Section 1, 'The nature of morality'; Subsection 2, 'A good will is alone unqualifiedly good'.

10

Evil

In this final chapter we turn from looking at God, to looking at the world. And we may well dislike what we see. The world is full of evil; the moral evil of wicked choices and the pain and suffering that follow from them, and the natural evil of all the harm produced by natural disasters, diseases and the everyday struggle for survival. Some philosophers have argued that the evil in our world is inconsistent with the existence of God, or at least that it renders God's existence highly improbable.[1] The theme of this book has been the nature of God, rather than proofs for His existence, and so this last chapter will be cast more as a theodicy than a defense. A defense tries to show that the existence of God is possible in spite of evil. A theodicy tries to offer some explanation for how or why a good God would permit evil. A number of contemporary philosophers argue that, given our epistemic position with respect to God, we should not expect to have a clue regarding why He allows evil.[2] I am sympathetic to this point. We cannot expect to comprehend fully the divine rationale for evil. Still, we can get a glimpse of some plausible reasons why God might permit it. Though it is not strictly necessary for spelling out the attributes of a perfect being, some efforts to construct a theodicy will provide a useful conclusion to this work, for a number of reasons.

First, it could be argued that perfect being theology is more vulnerable to the atheist case against God based on evil than are some other versions of theism. The perfect being theologian cannot reconcile God and evil by attributing some lack or weakness to God, or by insisting that there are forces at work in the universe outside God's control. Nor, as we saw in the previous chapter, can she allow that God Himself may have a momentary lapse into evil. God is the absolute source of all, and does not do evil. I have gone so far as to argue that, within perfect being theology, one ought to hold that ours is the best of all divinely actualizable worlds. As I noted in Chapter 8, the tradition of perfect being theology is divided on the question. The philosopher who holds that God could not create a best of all possible worlds can argue that in any world God produced the rational creatures could rightly suppose that He could have made a better. Thus the fact that an omnipotent being could have made a better world than ours is not evidence against the existence of God.[3] But I have argued that the most consistent position for the perfect being theologian is that God, being the best, does the best He can, and our world is it. If this is a plausible view, then does not the fact that in many ways our world seems to be quite a dreadful place cast special doubt on the existence of the God of perfect being theology? It is a fair question, and some attempt to explain how and why God permits evil will help to answer it.

A second reason for attempting a theodicy here is that throughout this work I have insisted upon the value of libertarian freedom, and that insistence has raised some serious difficulties for the project of a systematic perfect being theology. Are there choices which God's causal omniscience does not cause? Are there limited creatures which an omnipotent creator cannot control? Perhaps the most intractable problem arose in the discussion of the traditional doctrine of divine simplicity. I felt forced to conclude that human choices affect God's knowledge and actions. But if God's knowledge and actions are one and identical to His nature then human beings 'contribute' to the nature of God. And somehow God's unified act of knowing encompasses both the truths which depend on His eternal and immutable nature and will, and also the truths which depend upon human choices. This begins to seem like an exceedingly qualified version of perfect simplicity. If one could jettison libertarian freedom, replacing it with a compatibilist account, the system of perfect being theology would flow more smoothly. However, as I hope to show in this chapter, libertarianism allows for a more satisfactory theodicy than does compatibilism, and thus I will argue that the less than elegant philosophy of God required by belief in libertarian freedom is a price worth paying.

A third reason for attempting a theodicy here is that we have laid some of the foundation in earlier chapters and so we can appeal to already established points in assessing what moves will or will not further the project of justifying God's ways to man within a systematic and traditional perfect being theology. Finally, on the important question of why God allows so much natural evil, the classic tradition I have been defending throughout offers what I take to be a very powerful answer which rests upon points made earlier in this work, and which is almost ignored in the contemporary debate. It will be worthwhile to propose that answer in order to bring it into the modern discussion.

Our theodicy will offer three mutually consistent arguments. First, the possibility of moral evil is the necessary consequence of God's creating beings with significant freedom. Second, the laws of nature and the suffering which they produce play a beneficial role in the development of human beings. Third, and this is the traditional argument which has not found a place in the contemporary discussion, pain and suffering are an inevitable result of being an inhabitant of our physical universe, and it's better to exist and suffer than not to exist at all. The order of presentation is important here, because the third argument will seem more plausible when it is appreciated how much evil is the result of free will and how evil can contribute to 'soul-building'.

First, a few assumptions should be spelled out. In the earlier chapters of this book I have more or less tried to steer clear of specifically Christian assumptions. A number of contemporary philosophers of religion argue that when the question is how a good God could allow evil, the Christian theist cannot answer effectively in abstraction from the values and goods specific to Christianity.[4] I shall take this advice to heart and work from an admittedly Christian perspective.

In this discussion I shall assume what was argued for earlier in this book. For example, one premise which will prove extremely important was defended (albeit briefly) in Chapter 8 on the nature of creation: occasionalism is false. While it is the case that God sustains all things in being from moment to moment, He sustains them as objectively existing beings, independent of created minds, and possessing natures largely constituted by the role they play in the universal system of causes and effects. God sustains both the flame and the cotton with all of their properties, but nonetheless it is true that the flame burns the cotton. God could, and sometimes does, work miracles . . . that is, He circumvents one way or another the otherwise metaphysically necessary causal processes at work in the universe. By and large, though, He prefers to 'let nature take its course', since constant disruption of the system of cause and effect would mean the destruction of the objects involved.

A final presupposition: there will be no talk here of God's duties, obligations or rights. I noted in the last chapter that such language seems inappropriate for the being whose very nature it is to be the absolute source of all value and the perfect good of which all other goods are a dim reflection.

Why, then, does God permit evil? First we must distinguish between two kinds of evil . . . or better, two kinds of phenomena which, though very different, both raise the problem of how a good God could allow them. First there is 'moral evil' which I shall take to be morally bad choices and the pain and suffering which follows from them. This is a somewhat non-standard definition in that 'moral evil' in the contemporary literature is often taken to be the pain and suffering which results from any free choice, including the neutral or the good ones.[5] For example, I may freely choose to undergo chemotherapy as a cancer treatment. This may be a morally good choice, and yet pain and suffering will result. On the standard current definition such pain and suffering would be termed moral evils.

I have two reasons for preferring my non-standard analysis. First, this standard definition seems to imply that the only evil is the pain and suffering. The classic tradition finds sin a more deeply puzzling problem than pain, and takes it as self-evident that the greatest evil of the evil choice is the choice itself which distances one from God. A choice can be evil even if it does not end in pain and suffering, beyond the self-inflicted harm to the agent of being severed from the source of his being and value. Second, the answer to the question of why God permits the evil choice and its harmful consequences is significantly different from the answer to why God permits the neutral or good choice and the harmful consequences which may follow. I will argue below that the reason God (usually) permits evil choices is that the option to choose between good and evil is necessary for morally significant freedom which is a great good being prerequisite for us to become virtuous human beings. He (usually) allows the harmful consequences of the wicked choice because preventing them too often would undermine the seriousness of the option.

This 'free will theodicy' explains why God permits evil choices and the pain and suffering which follows from them, and it may explain the pain and suffering caused by neutral or good choices in some situations. But it does not work for all (or even for very many?) cases of neutral or good choices. Notice the differences. First, there is no question of why God would 'permit' the neutral or good choices themselves. He has no objection to the former and the latter are exactly what He hopes for from His creatures. But how can we explain the harmful consequences? If good or neutral choices never produced pain and suffering the live option between good and bad would not be undermined, and so the argument that the evil is justified as a requisite for morally significant freedom is not effective here. In the example above about chemotherapy our question is not, 'Why did God permit me to choose to fight my cancer and inflict pain on myself?' We know the answer to that one . . . it was, by hypothesis, the morally right choice to make. What puzzles us is why God permitted me to get cancer in the first place, and why He permits the cure to involve pain and suffering. Free will theodicy does not answer these questions. I take it that most if not all of the pain and suffering which results from morally neutral or good choices is properly discussed under natural evil (the possibility of counter examples does not vitiate the point), and so it is clearer not to lump together all the pain and suffering which results from free choices. I will argue below that 'moral evil', wicked choices and the harm they cause, really does make the universe a worse place. It really 'should not happen'. God permits it, and for good reason, but He does not cause it. The same is not true of natural evil.

Natural evil is, by and large, the pain and suffering caused by things other than the wicked choices of rational agents, things like natural disasters, diseases and the everyday struggle to survive. There is nothing evil at all about the tornado, the cancerous cell, or the tiger in itself. All are God's creatures. I will argue below that in the final analysis it is unreasonable to hold that the pain and suffering which these things cause 'should not have happened', and so natural 'evil' is very different from moral evil. The common ground between them is that both demand explanation in a universe authored by an omniscient, omnipotent, perfectly good being.

Let us look first at moral evil. God could have prevented Auschwitz. Why did He stand back? The traditional answer which is widely accepted today is that God permits moral evil because the possibility of its occurrence is a side-effect of creating beings with free will, and free will is an extremely valuable thing. Without freedom we might be very acceptable lower animals or automata, but we could not be good, rational creatures, and that is a much better thing to be. The problem is that the will can and does choose evil as well as good. Still, freedom is such a great good that it outweighs the evil of wicked choices.

Some contemporary philosophers of religion find this assessment implausible, arguing that, while freedom may be a good thing, there are exercises of free will which could not possibly be worth their cost in pain and suffering. The defender of free will theodicy within perfect being theology will respond that, for rational creatures, the ability to freely choose *for* God which entails the ability to choose against Him and do evil is the most important thing about us. Terrible as the price is, freedom is worth it. This does not commit the defender to holding that freedom would be worth *any* price, only that the actual freedom exercised in the actual world is worth the actual cost in pain and suffering. Nor is the defender committed to the view that God *never* steps in to negate a free choice or its consequences. He just doesn't do it often enough to vitiate our freedom.

Some critics argue that a good God would not permit the pain and suffering of the victim in the interests of allowing the freedom of the agent since that would be sacrificing one person for another.[6] The defender will respond that the rules that hold between creatures do not hold between creatures and God. We belong to God absolutely. We have no 'rights' against Him. Nonetheless it must be remembered that, on the Christian understanding, one's present life is merely a prelude to everlasting life, and God, not out of 'duty' but out of love, can see to it that however much one suffers in this world, that suffering is dwarfed and swallowed up in joy in the next. (There may be a qualification to this. See the 'Postscript on Hell' at the end of this chapter.)

But couldn't God have created free beings such that they would always choose the good? Augustine, being a compatibilist, says 'Yes'. We are drawn to choose what we choose through love, and God could see to it that everyone is always drawn towards the good. Though his *On Free Will*[7] provides the *locus classicus* for the position that free will has enormous value because without it the human being could not truly be virtuous, the text does not support the view that Augustine advanced a libertarian doctrine of freedom. What the text says is that we could not choose good or evil if we did not have free will, but it does not say that in order to make a free choice we must have genuinely open options. In his *Retractions* Augustine explains that those who saw in *On Free Will* a defense of a more radical human freedom misunderstood his point.[8] In his discussion of the fall of the bad angels in *The City of God,* and in his discussion of the fall of man in his last work *Unfinished Work against Julian* Augustine makes it clear that if the rational creature chooses the bad it is because it is drawn by desire for lesser things due to its having been made from nothing. If it chooses the good it is because it is drawn upwards by desire through the grace of God. In either case the will is free, but inevitably chooses what it most desires.[9] Thus Augustine cannot justify God's permission of moral evil by arguing that a genuinely open option to choose evil is necessary for the possibility of freely choosing the good.

Augustine, in *On the Literal Meaning of Genesis*, holds that God could have made only beings who freely choose only the good because they have no desire to choose otherwise. However, it is a better world which includes some of this sort of being (the good angels) and other good beings who freely choose the good *in spite of* temptation to do otherwise (holy men). But what of a third group of free beings, those who succumb to temptation and choose evil? Augustine grants that God could turn their wills to good. Why does He not do so? God only knows. We can say at least this: God uses the just punishment of the wicked for the instruction of the good. In fact, were it not for sinners, a whole class of beings could not exist, those who are led to the good through a consideration of the fate of evil-doers. Does God then *need* sin in order to accomplish His ends? Augustine will not go quite this far. The most we can say is that God could create free beings who would choose only the good, but He chooses to create beings who will sin because He withholds His grace, and He puts these sinners to good use.[10]

This compatibilist view has some aspects which recommend it to the perfect being theologian. With God in complete control there is no puzzle over omnipotence in a universe with free creatures. Compatibilist freedom conforms to the will of God. Nor does the compatibilist face the libertarian's problem with divine simplicity. For the libertarian the difficulty is how to make sense of the idea that God could know and do all He knows and does in one act, identical to his nature, which encompasses knowing both the eternal and immutable truths following from the divine nature and will and the contingent truths produced by creaturely free choice. The libertarian had the related difficulty of explaining how God's knowledge could be the cause of all things yet human choices be the sole source of sin. On the compatibilist view these problems do not arise. God is the only locus of power in the universe. The creaturely free choice could not be otherwise, and, like everything else in the universe, is eternally and immutably known and willed by God. This makes for an elegant perfect being theology, but difficulties arise when we try to construct a compatibilist theodicy.

God is in absolute control, yet there is evil. It is hard to imagine that the good purpose for which God uses the sinner, on Augustine's account, could not possibly be accomplished through some alternative. And could it really be worth the cost of all the wickedness, pain and suffering of moral evil? The compatibilist could argue that we have no way of assessing whether or not the good will outweigh the evil in the end, and so we can allow that it might. Moreover, God as absolute sovereign is under no obligation to balance the cosmic books. But both of these moves take us away from constructing a theodicy in the direction of holding that it is just not possible to justify God's ways to man.

Perhaps even more problematic, the Augustinian line seems to place the ultimate responsibility for moral evil with God Himself. Augustine argues that rational creatures, including Adam and Eve before the fall, cannot choose the good without grace, which is irresistible when offered. And it is up to God alone to decide whether or not they get it. Those who do evil cannot help themselves. They are inevitably drawn to it, since they lack the grace which God could give but chooses to withhold.[11] Augustine insists that creatures choose evil through their own wills, and this is quite true, but they could not will otherwise, and it is hard to see how their maker can escape the responsibility. Could the creator of a magnet justly blame it for being drawn towards the iron when the only thing that would prevent its being drawn is action on the part of the creator which the creator chooses not to take? Though I grant that libertarian freedom is hard to square with divine simplicity, it seems to me that compatibilist freedom is even harder to square with divine goodness.

As I noted in Chapter 7 on omnipotence, Anselm rejects Augustine's compatibilism arguing that God has given us indeterminist freedom so that we will make choices which genuinely originate with us. This is so that we may possess a trace of *aseity* and, though in a very limited way, by clinging to the good God has given us, contribute to our own creation. The option to choose evil, though not requisite for freedom *per se*, is a necessary condition for the *morally significant freedom* which allows the creature to become better by choosing good on its own. On Anselm's view, God cannot make it so that creatures always *freely* (with this morally significant freedom) choose the good any more than He can make a round square.

But granting that God could not control a free being once He has made it, couldn't He create only those rational beings whom He foreknows will freely choose only the good? This is a serious possibility on the Molinist understanding of divine foreknowledge discussed in Chapter 6. On that view God has middle knowledge of how any possible creature would freely choose in any possible situation and exercises control by choosing which situations and creatures to actualize. Plantinga offers the possibility of 'transworld depravity', (loosely) the notion that in all possible worlds all possible free creatures freely choose some evil, to defend the view that God could not ensure that free beings would avoid evil.[12] This view, while possible, does not seem very plausible, and in any case will not concern us since Molinism is intrinsically problematic and cannot be squared with perfect being theology for the reasons discussed in Chapter 6. I argued that God's knowledge is direct. If a choice really does originate with a creature, God knows it from the creature's making it, and only from that. Thus He cannot know what a creature will freely choose 'until' (in a logical, not a temporal sense) He has made the creature and it has chosen.

Granted that God could not decide beforehand to create only those who would choose the good, couldn't He at least step in and prevent the consequences of bad choices? As the murderer is strangling the five year-old couldn't God cause him to faint, saving the child's life? No. As Eleonore Stump expresses the point, 'If God immediately removed or prevented the consequences of any free choice eventuating in major evil, his creatures would not have that significant exercise of free will and would thus not be persons'.[13] I would not hold that it is necessarily the case that God 'stands back' in every instance. Perhaps He does miraculously interfere between the free choice and its effect from time to time. (If the murderer were about to faint in any case because of physical causes already at work, then there is no question of God stepping in or standing back. If God introduces a new cause, not part of the previously existing system of secondary causes, then He works a miracle.) That the Nazis' 'Thousand Year Reich' lasted less than two decades may be in part due to divine intervention. God only knows. But presumably He cannot prevent the consequences of evil choices too often without impairing the human capacity for significant freedom. Thus a perfectly good God permits moral evil because the possibility of evil choices is a requisite for the morally significant freedom without which we cannot become the good creatures He wants us to be. The actuality of evil choices is our doing, and God permits their consequences, since a constant divine eradication of the effects of evil choices would make those choices no longer viable options.

Why, though, is there so very much moral evil? The traditional Christian explanation is that the original human beings, created good by God, chose evil, destroyed their relationship with their creator, and in so doing plunged themselves and succeeding generations into the misery and ignorance which has been the story of mankind.[14] (One might express this by saying that pain and suffering are God's *punishment* for sin, so long as it is clear that, at least on the natural law ethics I have been espousing, to sin is to do that which must necessarily destroy one's happiness. It is not as if God steps in with some extra punishment, not organically flowing from the sin.) I take it that a cursory glance at history will render plausible the view that something has gone very wrong with humanity from the beginning. The person who can look at our past and judge that we are doing about as well as can be expected is a pessimist indeed! In answer to Hume's point that a good God would have made human existence more palatable by making us just a bit better, perhaps a little less lazy, for example,[15] the tradition responds that God did make us better. The shortcomings in human nature are the result of human choices. Why did God permit the consequences of those original sins to affect the rest of the race? Because, again, significant freedom requires that evil choices be allowed to produce their results. If the Christian view is right, though, there is a cure. God, by becoming incarnate, has miraculously intervened to mitigate and even reverse the consequences of the first fall.

It is important to note that if one allows this free will theodicy then one has successfully explained why it is that God permits a great deal of what might at first glance look like purely natural evil. I explained natural evil above as the pain and suffering produced, not by wicked moral choices, but by natural phenomena (with perhaps neutral or good choices also involved). This is a bit too simple, in that there is pain and suffering which is immediately caused by natural phenomena, but which would not have occurred without bad moral choices having been made, and which is in the final analysis attributable to the moral choices. If I die of thirst in the desert, the immediate cause may be the parching sun. But if it is you who took me into the desert and left me there with no water the fault is yours. And note that the sun shining is not evil in any sense at all. It is my pain and suffering which can be considered evil. The sun is just doing its job. It is you who have put me in harm's way. When a drought occurs in some parts of Africa, thousands die. When a drought occurs in North America, the price of lettuce goes up. The problem then is not the lack of rain or natural scarcity but the national and international systems of human relations which prevent people from getting the resources they need. And these systems are the products of moral choices, some of which are bad. The list of apparently natural evil which is really caused or at least wildly exacerbated by moral evil could go on and on.

Given the doctrine of the fall, most, if not all, apparently natural evil suffered by human beings can be traced ultimately to free will. One might hold that when humanity was properly related to God we possessed the power and knowledge to avoid natural evils, and we lost it in the original sin.[16] Even if one does not attribute such almost superhuman abilities to pre-lapsarian humanity one could hold that, though the earliest human beings might have faced a great deal of purely natural evil, if they had not sinned succeeding generations would have had far less evil to deal with. If, from the beginning, humans had been more interested in helping everybody lead the good and happy life and less interested in power and stuff who knows where we would be now? The cure for cancer might have been discovered a millennium ago. We might now be able to predict the hurricane with great accuracy a month in advance and whisk everyone out of harm's way with who knows what non-polluting methods of transportation. (My students invariably point out that many of our most significant technological achievements have been the result of warfare, to which I respond that in an unfallen world, at least possibly, we'd be just as motivated to make the technological progress and wouldn't have the wars.) Thus a great deal, if not all, of the pain and suffering which natural phenomena cause human beings can be attributed, at least in part, to moral evil.

In an effort to render the existence of evil consistent with that of God

Plantinga has extended the scope of moral evil to cover *all* natural evils, including the pain and suffering of animals. (It should be noted that Plantinga is giving a defense, not a theodicy. He claims only to show that evil and God are compossible, not to offer a satisfying, or even plausible, analysis of why God permits evil.) Possibly there are non-human creatures (fallen angels, perhaps) to whom all natural evil is due.[17] Now, I do not automatically rule out the existence of demons, however the role Plantinga has assigned to them seems at odds with the classic tradition's commitment to the idea that it is God who sustains all things in being.[18]

Augustine, in *The City of God,* having just finished a disquisition on the goodness of fleas, writes, 'For there is nothing in nature, even among the last and least of the little creatures, which is not brought into being by [God] . . .'[19] And a few chapters later, 'there are three questions to be asked in respect of any created being: "Who made it?", "How?", and "Why?". I put forward the answers: "God", "Through his word", "Because it is good." '[20] Plantinga's suggestion seems to entail that while God made the lamb, the parakeet and the brachiosaur, Satan made the lion, the hawk and the Tyrannosaurus Rex. That is to give predators far too little credit and Satan far too much. While a plausible theodicy can assign the responsibility for a great deal of apparently natural evil to free will, I do not think all natural evil can be justified in this way. We need to look at additional explanations for why God permits evil.

Why does God permit the pain and suffering which is not the consequence of free will? In the contemporary literature a host of suggestions are offered for the benefits human beings receive, either from the existence of a consistent natural order of which pain and suffering are an ineradicable result, or directly from pain and suffering themselves. Each of these suggestions has a certain plausibility and, since none are mutually exclusive, taken together they make a good case that it is better for us that we live in a universe in which there is pain and suffering rather than in one in which we go from comfort to comfort.

One connecting theme in these theodicies is that it is a mistake to believe that a good human life consists in unalloyed pleasure. The good human life is one in which good moral choices can be made and virtues developed. For this purpose a physical universe ordered through natural laws and containing pain and suffering may be a necessity. John Hick holds that

> The divine purpose behind the world is one of soul-making . . . The kind of goodness which . . . God desires in his creatures could not in fact be created except through a long process of creaturely experience in response to challenges and disciplines of various kinds.[21]

It can be argued that human beings could not be moral agents at all except in a world which operates by natural laws. Natural evils are the unavoidable consequences of these laws.[22] The divine option of running the world according to a series of miraculous interventions would make moral activity impossible for human agents because they would not know what sorts of consequences would follow from their actions. Swinburne argues that in order to be moral beings we must understand the good and harm that we can do, and that knowledge comes through a universe in which pain and suffering occur naturally. 'So if God is to give us the strong true beliefs we need to make our serious choices, he must give us in general *knowledge* of the effects of our actions . . .' And it is better that this knowledge comes through our interactions with the world, so that we can have 'well-justified knowledge, and the opportunity to learn from experience and to choose to seek new knowledge'.[23]

One might respond to these points by arguing that the soul-building and the knowledge required for it could occur just as well in a universe in which there is no purely natural evil. Perhaps there is a possible world in which all the pain and suffering necessary to fulfill the divine purposes are traceable to free will. If so the natural evil in our world seems gratuitous and is evidence for atheism.[24] The problem with this argument is that it depends on being able to describe this happy possible world in such a way as to convince the skeptic that it really *is* possible, and that is a difficult, perhaps impossibly difficult, task.[25] I will have more to say below on the subject of other supposedly possible worlds, supposedly better than ours.

The above theodicies focus on the importance of a natural order in general for the possibility of morally serious choices for human agents. A somewhat different approach is taken by Eleonore Stump, who focuses, not on the natural order and the human species in general, but on the particular pain and suffering of particular individuals. Unlike Hick, she does not hold that a resistant physical world is naturally necessary for soul-building. Rather, she accepts the doctrine of the fall of humanity, and concludes that pain and suffering are necessary to bring about a 'cure' for the diseased condition in which we presently find ourselves.

> The fixing of a defective free will by a person's freely willing that God fix his will is, I think, the foundation of a Christian solution to the problem of evil . . . So things that contribute to a person's humbling, to his awareness of his own evil, and to his unhappiness with his present state contribute to his willing God's help.

The pain and suffering caused by both free choices and natural phenomena are required to achieve this cure.[26]

It is crucial to Stump's argument that the good to be achieved by the cure outweigh the pain and suffering. The goods realizable in this life would certainly be insufficient, and so Stump is careful to insist that the reason the will needs to be 'fixed' is so that the human agent can enjoy a future of everlasting beatitude with God. The good which awaits will far outweigh any evil our world has to offer.

Stump takes one step beyond this point to a principle which strikes me as problematic. She is talking about the pain and suffering which results from free will, but I take it that she would accept a similar principle with respect to purely natural 'evil'. She writes,

> It seems to me nonetheless that a perfectly good entity who was also omniscient and omnipotent must govern the evil resulting from the misuse of that significant freedom in such a way that the sufferings of any particular person are outweighed by the good which the suffering produces *for that person* . . .[27]

Thus there is a correlation between a particular future good and a particular instance of suffering such that if that suffering had not occurred the future good would not have either. This specific instance of suffering was necessary to produce the good.

The theoretical motivation here is clear. It seems wrong that the victim himself should not be compensated for the specific harm, even if it is allowed that that harm was necessary for some overall good. I think the problem arises when we try to translate this *prima facie* principle of fairness to the real world. Take the example of a five year-old beaten, raped and strangled by her mother's boyfriend. Any Christian can agree that God can bless that child with an everlasting future of happiness which will render the past pain nothing by comparison. But Stump's view is that the pain itself was necessary for some good *for the child*, and this seems to me to entail such a violation of our intuition that it cannot be right. This child suffered as few children do. Stump holds that there was a reason for it, beyond the necessity of allowing the consequences of free will. What sort of reason? Was this child so unusually stained with original sin that the cure in her case had to be so extreme? Is that what we shall tell every grieving parent whose child undergoes hideous suffering? Impossible. Is there some special good that can only be achieved through this sort of suffering, and God has singled out this child for such a blessing? Lucky murder victim! Should other parents regret that it wasn't *their* child beaten, raped and strangled? Again, impossible. The murderer has done something unqualifiedly horrible. That God has not stepped in with a miraculous intervention may be justifiable. And certainly, those involved may respond to the murder in a way which makes them better human beings. But the idea that the child *needed* to be murdered to achieve a future good is too hard.[28]

All of the above arguments focus on pain and suffering in connection to some value for human beings. The rest of the sentient universe has received short shrift. What of animal pain? Let us allow that God is good in permitting various natural 'evils' for the benefit of mankind. Still, even in our own small corner of the universe, there seems to be an enormous amount of pain and suffering which has little if anything to do with human beings. What of those eons before the appearance of *homo sapiens*? S. Paul Schilling writes of the 'pain and travail of evolution; the waste and cruelty of the struggle for survival of individuals and species . . .' and sees this as evidence that if there is a god he is not omnipotent.[29] Upon hearing two animals fighting in the forest Quentin Smith records,

> It seemed to me self-evident that the natural law that *animals must savagely kill and devour each other in order to survive* was an evil natural law and that the obtaining of the law was sufficient evidence that God did not exist.[30]

He defends the intuition by arguing that things did not have to be this way. Were there a God He could have made a better world. Instead of the actual world He could have made W in which, 'For each predator that exists in the actual world, there is a vegetarian counterpart in W.' A counterpart is something which 'looks just like [the original] . . . but which has different DNA . . .' so that it is programmed to behave differently. W would include counterpart humans, as well. 'The Florence Nightingale counterpart performs her medical deeds and the Beethoven counterpart composes his symphonies, but they eat soybeans instead of pork.'[31] Wouldn't W be a better world than ours? And then there is the fawn burning slowly to death after the forest fire in the famous article by William Rowe.[32] Why in the world does God permit all the carnage?

First it should be noted that much animal pain has been a great good for human beings in that it has been at least part of the causal system of evolution that has produced the human species. As van Inwagen says, 'for all we know, the amount of pain that organisms have experienced in the actual world, or some amount morally equivalent to that amount, is necessary for the natural evolution of conscious animals'.[33] The critic will ask why God didn't just make human beings by *fiat* without all the painful rigmarole of evolution. The response is that apparently God prefers to work with secondary causes. (This does not rule out miracles, but suggests that they will be few and far between. Too many divine interventions between cause and effect would destroy the connection.) Van Inwagen holds that we have no trustworthy modal intuitions on the question of whether or not a massively irregular world is preferable to a world with animal suffering, and that is enough to defend belief in the existence of God from the evidential argument from evil.[34] I would go one step beyond this and argue, as I did in Chapter 8, that there are good reasons to deny occasionalism. (A massively irregular world, if not quite occasionalist, would be close enough to succumb to the same criticisms.) Assuming the importance of natural causes, and given that we are the product of evolution and have no reason to believe that any other system of natural causes could possibly have produced us, prehuman animal pain is justified by its role in bringing us into being.

The critic may suggest that God could have accomplished our creation through natural causes but without animal suffering by making prehuman animals behave as they have behaved by replacing the motivation of pain with some equally effective motivator.[35] (If He directly causes their behavior without a secondary cause we are falling back into occasionalism.) The response is that we have absolutely no reason to believe that there is some equally effective motivator for sentient beings.[36] And if the critic should insist that God, being omnipotent, could come up with something, the answer is that God cannot do the impossible.[37]

But what of all the animal suffering which lies outside of the causal system which has produced and sustained human beings? How can that be justified? The classic tradition has an answer which, to my knowledge, has not surfaced in the contemporary debate. The medieval Christian philosophers, at least from Augustine through Aquinas, answered unanimously that corruptible things will inevitably fall apart one way or another. When they do, if they are sentient, they will probably hurt. Then why did God make them? Because, in the words of Augustine, 'each single thing is good and collectively they are very good, for our God made his whole creation *very good*'.[38] It is a corollary of perfect being theology, in which God is simultaneously pure act and the perfect standard for good, that everything that exists in the created universe reflects the divine nature and is good. Things may be good for human beings, but they are also good in themselves. Human beings are the most important of God's corporeal creatures. There is even a sense in which all lesser creatures were made for us. Being made in God's image as rational beings we are the only ones who can appreciate their value. Nonetheless all things have an intrinsic value irrespective of their value for us.

Augustine writes,

it is the nature of things considered in itself, without regard to our convenience or inconvenience, that gives glory to the Creator . . . so all nature's substances are good, because they exist and therefore have their own mode and kind of being, and , in their fashion, a peace and harmony among themselves . . . Those which have not been given an eternal existence obey the laws of the Creator in changing for the better or the worse in accordance with the lines of development he has laid down for them in the scheme of things; and all tend, in God's plan, to that end which is included in the whole design for the government of the universe. But it is ensured that the process of destruction, which results in the disappearance of mutable and mortal natures, brings what existed to non-existence in such a way as to allow the consequent production of what is destined to come into being.[39]

As Augustine sees things, it is good that all things exist, predator and prey, galactic cluster and sub-atomic particle. But to exist is to exist as a certain kind of thing which behaves in a certain way. To wish that the tiger did not hunt or the fire did not burn is to wish that they did not exist. Quentin Smith's suggestion of a possible world with no predators but only predator 'counterparts' is absurd. Aquinas notes the suggestion that, in Paradise, 'those animals which now are fierce and kill others would, in that state, have been tame, not only in regard to man, but also in regard to other animals'. He responds,

But this is quite unreasonable. For the nature of animals was not changed by man's sin, as if those whose nature now it is to devour the flesh of others, as the lion and falcon, would then have lived on herbs.[40]

It is the nature of the lion and the falcon to hunt and kill. And the lion and the falcon are intrinsically good things. It would be unreasonable to prefer, as Smith does, that they had never existed in the interests of ensuring a painless life for the rabbit. It is especially unreasonable given the theory of evolution, for it is clear that the rabbit has evolved as he has because of his role as prey. So Smith would do away not only with the predators but with the prey.

If Smith should respond that God, being omnipotent, could create the rabbit without the evolutionary causal history of rabbits in the actual world, then we are back with occasionalism . . . God just bringing things into being without secondary causes. Assuming the value of secondary causality, if you remove the predators you get a radically different world from ours with radically different inhabitants. (The same point applies with respect to Rowe's fawn. If you do away with the properties of the fire and the fawn such that the latter does not feel pain from having been in contact with the former you have really done away with the fire and fawn altogether.) Augustine and the classic tradition hold that it is better for the rabbit or the fawn to exist, even if it will die a painful death, than not to exist at all. I suspect, based on introspection and analogy, that if, *per impossibile*, the rabbit or the fawn could express an opinion on the question they would agree.[41] Smith may be willing to grant that his 'counterpart' possible world is not really possible after all and still maintain that he can imagine *some* possible world in which there are no predators, and it is a better world than ours, but I am skeptical. The classic tradition holds that, even setting aside human beings and their interests, our universe with its myriad inhabitants is a very good place. It is produced by God through secondary causes, and if you wish away a part of the system here and a part there you destroy the whole.

A great deal of this world's evil can be attributed, directly or indirectly, to free will. Moral evil should not happen, and the world would have been better if we rational creatures had chosen to make it so. The pain and suffering which comes from purely natural events, though, is just a necessary consequence of the system of causes which constitutes the physical world. You cannot erase it without erasing the ordered cosmos. Stay out of the tiger's path if at all possible, but do not wish him never to have been created. He is an ineradicable part of the whole which has produced us and, like everything that comes from God, is intrinsically good.

POSTSCRIPT ON HELL

In a discussion of the problem of evil one feels compelled to say a word about Hell. It has been a hot topic among contemporary philosophers of religion, some arguing that a good God could not permit the dispropor- tionate suffering which eternal damnation implies, others holding that God will allow us to live the eternity we choose even if we choose eternal misery.[42] Philosophically speaking, I am not sure we have sufficient information to decide beyond a shadow of a doubt. From the perspective of perfect being theology it is enough to say this: the existence of Hell is negotiable, the goodness of God is not. If the existence of Hell is inconsistent with the perfection of God, there is no ultimate and eternal damnation. If it is consistent, then there may be. Luckily for each of us there is only one soul over which *we* have any final say, and it is perfectly clear that we should keep that soul turned to God, whatever lies in the opposite direction.

NOTES

1. The modern *locus classicus* for the position that the existence of God is logically impossible given the evil in the world is J. L. Mackie's 'Evil and omnipotence'. For the position that the existence of God is unlikely, the 'evidential' argument from evil, the seminal article is William Rowe's, 'The problem of evil and some varieties of atheism'. The consensus among contemporary philosophers of religion is that the logical problem of evil can be defeated, but a number of philosophers support the evidential argument. See Daniel Howard-Snyder (ed.), *The Evidential Argument from Evil*.

2. See, for example: William Alston, 'The inductive argument from evil and the human cognitive condition'; Alvin Plantinga, 'Epistemic probability and evil'; Peter van Inwagen, 'The problem of evil, the problem of air, and the problem of silence'; and Stephen J. Wykstra, 'The Humean obstacle to evidential arguments from suffering: On avoiding the evils of "appearance"'.

3. George N. Schlesinger offers a version of this argument in *New Perspectives on Old-Time Religion*, Chapter 2. David O'Connor attempts, successfully in my view, to defeat Schlesinger's argument in *God and Inscrutable Evil*, Chapter 7.

4. See for example, Marilyn McCord Adams, 'Problems of evil: More advice to Christian philosophers'.

5. I am indebted to my colleague Jeffrey Jordan for calling this to my attention.

6. Russell, 'Persistent problem of evil'.

7. *On Free Will*, Book 2, xviii, 48.

8. *Retractions*, Book I, Chapter 9, 4–6. A common interpretation of Augustine reads him as originally an indeterminist who became a compatibilist under the pressure of attempting to answer the Pelagians, who believed that God's grace was not the necessary first cause of the salvation of the human being. My own view is that there is nothing in the earlier Augustinian texts which demands an indeterminist reading.

9. *The City of God*, Book XII, Chapter 9; *Unfinished Work against Julian*, Book 5, Chapter 57.

10. *On the Literal Meaning of Genesis*, Book 11, Chapters 7–11.

11. See my 'Irrelevance of original sin in Augustine's doctrine of the will'.

12. Plantinga, *Nature of Necessity*, p. 186.

13. Eleonore Stump, 'The problem of evil', p. 405.

14. For a contemporary exposition of this view see Peter van Inwagen, 'The magnitude, duration, and distribution of evil'.

15. David Hume, *Dialogues Concerning Natural Religion*, Part XI.

16. van Inwagen, 'Magnitude, duration, and distribution of evil'.

17. Plantinga, *Nature of Necessity*, p. 192.

18. Robert Adams, 'Plantinga on the problem of evil', p. 246.

19. *City of God* XI, 15.

20. *City of God* XI, 23.

21. John Hick, *Evil and the God of Love*, p. 344.

22. Reichenbach, *Evil and a Good God*, p. 101–4.

23. Swinburne, *Providence and the Problem of Evil*, p. 177.

24. O'Connor, *God and Inscrutable Evil*, pp. 93–111.

25. See my review of O'Connor, *God and Inscrutable Evil*, in *Religious Studies*, 35, pp. 231–6.

26. Stump, 'Problem of evil', pp. 408–9. See also Stump,'Providence and Evil' and 'Aquinas on the sufferings of Job'.

27. Stump, 'Problem of evil', p. 411.

28. van Inwagen makes a similar point, 'Magnitude, duration, and distribution of evil', p. 119.

29. S. Paul Schilling, *God and Human Anguish*, p. 243.

30. Quentin Smith, 'An atheological argument from evil natural laws', p. 159.

31. Smith, 'Atheological argument from evil natural laws', pp. 164–5.

32. Rowe, 'Problem of evil and some varieties of atheism'.

33. van Inwagen, 'Problem of evil, the problem of air, and the problem of silence', p. 147.

34. van Inwagen, 'Problem of evil, the problem of air, and the problem of silence', pp. 148–52.

35. Peter Harrison, 'Theodicy and animal pain', argues that we do not have sufficient evidence to believe that animals do indeed feel pain. I find this implausible, but it should certainly be noted that we really do not have an accurate way of assessing the extent of animal suffering.

36. Hume suggests that the absence of pleasure would do the job as well (*Dialogues Concerning*

Natural Religion XI) but we have no evidence for that position, and I must say that introspection leads me to conclude otherwise.

37. That some state of affairs is perhaps in some minimal sense 'imaginable' does not entail that it is possible. See George Seddon, 'Logical possibility'.
38. *Confessions* VII, 12.
39. *City of God* XII, 4–5.
40. ST I, Q.96, art.1.
41. It is interesting that whereas the contemporary philosopher seems mainly concerned about pain, the medieval was mainly concerned about extinction. Augustine's question in the chapters from *The City of God* cited above is really why God made things which are corruptible, rather than why he made things that would feel pain. Augustine and Anselm and Aquinas consistently hold that it's better to exist, even if you are suffering, than not to exist at all. The tone of much of the contemporary discussion seems to imply that it is better not to exist. Perhaps (though I make this suggestion only very tentatively) pain was a much more pervasive part of the life of the medieval person than it is of the modern Westerner, and so it seemed more 'manageable' and less in need of explaining.
42. See, for example: Marilyn McCord Adams, 'The problem of hell: A problem of evil for Christians'; Jonathan Kvanvig, *The Problem of Hell*; Jerry Walls, *Hell: The Logic of Damnation*.

Bibliography

Adams, Marilyn McCord (1988), 'Problems of evil: More advice to Christian philosophers', *Faith and Philosophy*, 5, pp. 121–43.

Adams, Marilyn McCord (1993), 'The problem of hell: A problem of evil for Christians', in Stump (ed.), *Reasoned Faith*, pp. 301–27.

Adams, Robert (1977), 'Middle knowledge and the problem of evil', *American Philosophical Quarterly*, 14, pp. 109–17.

Adams, Robert (1985), 'Plantinga on the problem of evil', in Tomberlin and van Inwagen (eds), *Alvin Plantinga*, pp. 225–55.

Adams, Robert (1987), 'A modified divine command theory of ethical wrongness', in Adams, *The Virtue of Faith*, New York: Oxford University Press, pp. 97–122.

Algazali, *The Incoherence of the Philosophers*, the section 'Concerning the Natural Sciences', in Hyman and Walsh, *Philosophy in the Middle Ages*, pp. 283–91.

Alston, William (1987), 'Does God have beliefs?', *Religious Studies*, 22, pp. 287–306.

Alston, William (1989), *Divine Nature and Human Language*, Ithaca, NY: Cornell University Press.

Alston, William (1991), 'The inductive argument from evil and the human cognitive condition', in Tomberlin, *Philosophical Perspectives 5*, pp. 29–67.

Alston, William (1993), 'Aquinas on theological predication', in Stump, *Reasoned Faith*, pp. 145–78.

Anselm, *Opera Omnia*, ed. F. S. Schmitt, vols 1–6, Edinburgh: Thomas Nelson and Sons, 1940–68.

Aquinas, Thomas, *Basic Writings of Saint Thomas Aquinas*, trans. Anton C. Pegis, New York: Random House, 1945.

Aquinas, Thomas, *Summa Contra Gentiles*, trans. Anton C. Pegis, Notre Dame, IN: University of Notre Dame Press, 1975.

Averroes, *Tahafut al-Tahafut*, vol. 1, trans. Simon Van Den Bergh, London: Luzac and Co., 1954.

Blumenfeld, David (1978), 'On the compossibility of the divine attributes', *Philosophical Studies*, 34, pp. 91–103, reprinted in Morris, *Concept of God*, pp. 201–15.

Brown, Robert (1991), 'God's ability to will moral evil', *Faith and Philosophy*, 8, pp. 3–20.

Burns, Peter, SJ (1993), 'The status and function of divine simpleness in *Summa Theologiae* Ia, qq. 2–13', *The Thomist*, 57, pp. 1–26.

Chisholm, Roderick (1976), *Person and Object*, LaSalle, IL: Open Court Publishing.

Clarke, W. Norris (1973), 'A new look at the immutability of God', in Robert Roth (ed.), *God Knowable and Unknowable*, New York: Fordham University Press, pp. 43–72; reprinted in Clarke, *Explorations in Metaphysics*, pp. 183–210.

Clarke, W. Norris (1976), 'Analogy and the meaningfulness of language about God', *The Thomist*, 40, pp. 61–95.

Clarke, W. Norris (1994), *Explorations in Metaphysics*, Notre Dame, IN: University of Notre Dame Press.

Conee, Earl (1991), 'The possibility of power beyond possibility', in Tomberlin, *Philosophical Perspectives 5*, pp. 447–73.

Craig, William Lane (1990), 'Aquinas on God's knowledge of future contingents', *The Thomist*, 54, pp. 33–79.

Craig, William Lane (1990), 'God and real time', *Religious Studies*, 26, pp. 335–47.

Craig, William Lane (1991), *Divine Foreknowledge and Human Freedom*, Leiden: E. J. Brill.

Craig, William Lane (1994), 'The Special theory of relativity and theories of divine eternity', *Faith and Philosophy*, 11, pp. 19–37.

Craig, William Lane and Quentin Smith (1993), *Theism, Atheism, and Big Bang Cosmology*, Oxford: Clarendon Press.

Creel, Richard (1986), *Divine Impassibility*, Cambridge: Cambridge University Press.

Descartes, René (1955), *The Philosophical Works of Descartes*, trans Elizabeth S. Haldane and G. R. T. Ross, vol. 2, New York: Dover Publication.

Duns Scotus, John, *The Oxford Commentary on the Four Books of the Sentences*, in Hyman and Walsh, *Philosophy in the Middle Ages*, pp. 602–46.

Durrant, Michael (1992), 'The meaning of "God" – I', in Warner, *Religion and Philosophy*, pp. 71–84.

Eadmer (1962), *The Life of Saint Anselm Archbishop of Canterbury*, edited with introduction, notes and translation by R. W. Southern, London: Thomas Nelson and Sons.

Evans, Gillian (ed.) (1984), *A Concordance to the Works of St. Anselm*, Millwood, NY: Kraus International Publications.

Findlay, J. N. (1948), 'Can God's existence be disproved?', *Mind*, 57, pp. 176–83.

Fischer, John Martin (ed.) (1989), *God, Foreknowledge, and Freedom*, Stanford: Stanford University Press.

Flint, Thomas and Alfred J. Freddoso (1983), 'Maximal power', in Alfred J. Freddoso (ed.), *The Existence and Nature of God*, Notre Dame, IN: University of Notre Dame Press; reprinted in Morris, *Concept of God*, pp. 134–67.

Foster, John and Howard Robinson (eds)(1985), *Essays on Berkeley: A Tercentennial Celebration*, Oxford: Clarendon Press.

Frankfurt, Harry (1977), 'Descartes on the creation of the eternal truths', *Philosophical Review*, 86, pp. 36–57.

Franklin, Melissa (1993), 'The indispensability of the single-divine-attribute doctrine', *Religious Studies*, 29, pp. 433–42.

Freddoso, Alfred J. (1988), 'Medieval Aristotelianism and the case against secondary causation in nature', in Morris, *Divine and Human Action*, pp. 74–118.

Freddoso, Alfred J. (1988), *On Divine Foreknowledge* (translation with Introduction to Luis de Molina, *Liberi Arbitrii cum Gratiae Donis, Divina Praescientia, Providentia, Pradestinatione et Reprobatione Concordia*, Part IV), Ithaca, NY: Cornell University Press.

Freddoso, Alfred J. (1994), 'God's general concurrence with secondary causes: Pitfalls and prospects', *American Catholic Philosophical Quarterly*, 68, pp. 131–56.

Gale, Richard (1991), *On the Nature and Existence of God*, Cambridge: Cambridge University Press.

Gale, Richard (1993), 'Reply to Helm', *Religious Studies*, 29, pp. 257–63.

Garcia, Laura (1992), 'Divine freedom and creation', *Philosophical Quarterly*, 42, pp. 191–213.

Geach, Peter (1973), 'Omnipotence', *Philosophy*, pp. 7–20.

Geach, Peter (1992), 'The meaning of "God" – II', in Warner (ed.), *Religion and Philosophy*, pp. 85–90.

Gilson, Etienne (1956), *The Christian Philosophy of St. Thomas Aquinas*, trans. L. K. Shook, New York: Random House.

Glannon, Walter (1994), 'Omnipotence and the transfer of power', *International Journal for Philosophy of Religion*, 36, pp. 81–103.

Harris, James F. (1987), 'An empirical understanding of eternality', *International Journal for Philosophy of Religion*, 22, pp. 165–83.

Harrison, Peter (1989), 'Theodicy and animal pain', *Philosophy*, 64, pp. 79–92.

Hartshorne, Charles (1941), *Man's Vision of God*, New York: Harper and Row.

Hartshorne, Charles (1971), *Reality as Social Process*, New York: Hafner.

Hartshorne, Charles (1982), 'Grounds for believing in God's existence', in Leroy S. Rounder (ed.), *Meaning, Truth and God*, Notre Dame, IN: University of Notre Dame Press, pp. 17–33.

Hasker, William (1988), 'Hard facts and theological fatalism', *Nous*, 22, pp. 419–36; reprinted in Fischer, *God, Foreknowledge, and Freedom*, pp. 159–177.

Hasker, William (1988), 'Yes, God has beliefs!', *Religious Studies*, 24, pp. 385–9.

Hasker, William (1989), *God, Time and Knowledge*, Ithaca, NY: Cornell University Press.

Hasker, William (1993), 'How good/bad is middle knowledge? A reply to Basinger', *International Journal for Philosophy of Religion*, 33, pp. 111–18.

Helm, Paul (1975), 'Timelessness and foreknowledge', *Mind*, 84, pp. 516–27.

Helm, Paul (1988), *Eternal God*, Oxford: Clarendon Press.

Helm, Paul (1989), 'Omniscience and eternity', *Proceedings of the Aristotelian Society; Supplementary Volume*, 63, pp. 75–87.

Hick, John (1966), *Evil and the God of Love*, Glasgow: Collins.

Howard-Snyder, Daniel (ed.)(1996), *The Evidential Argument from Evil*, Bloomington, IN: Indiana University Press.

Howsepian, A. A. (1991), 'Is God necessarily good?', *Religious Studies*, 27, pp. 473–84.

Hughes, Christopher (1989), *On a Complex Theory of a Simple God*, Ithaca, NY: Cornell University Press.

Hyman, Arthur and James J. Walsh (eds) (1973), *Philosophy in the Middle Ages*, 2nd edn, Indianapolis, IN: Hackett Publishing Co.

Idziak, Janine (1997), Introduction to Andrew of Neufchateau, OFM, *Questions on an Ethics of Divine Commands*, Notre Dame, IN: University of Notre Dame Press.

Jackson, Timothy (1995), 'Is God just', *Faith and Philosophy*, pp. 393–408.

Kapitan, Tomis (1990), 'Action, uncertainty and divine impotence', *Analysis*, 50, pp. 127–33.

Kenney, Anthony (1979), *The God of the Philosophers*, Oxford: Oxford University Press.

Kirwan, Christopher (1989), *Augustine*, New York: Routledge.

Kondoleon, Theodore (1992), 'God's knowledge of future contingent singulars: A reply', *The Thomist*, 56, pp. 117–39.

Kretzmann, Norman (1991), 'A general problem of creation', in MacDonald, *Being and Goodness*, pp. 208–28.

Kretzmann, Norman (1991), 'A Particular Problem of Creation', in MacDonald, *Being and Goodness*, pp. 229–49.

Kretzmann, Norman (1997), *The Metaphysics of Theism*, Oxford: Clarendon Press.

Kvanvig, Jonathan L. (1986), *The Possibility of an All-Knowing God*, New York: St. Martin's Press.

Kvanvig, Jonathan L. (1993), *The Problem of Hell*, New York: Oxford University Press.

Kvanvig, Jonathan L. and Hugh J. McCann (1988), 'Divine conservation and the persistence of the world', in Morris, *Divine and Human Action*, pp. 13–49.

Kvanvig, Jonathan L. and Hugh J. McCann (1991), 'The occasionalist proselytizer', in Tomberlin, *Philosophical Perspectives 5*, pp. 587–615.

Lackey, Douglas (1974), 'A new disproof of the compatibility of foreknowledge and free choice', *Religious Studies*, 10, pp. 313–18.

LaCroix, Richard (1975), 'Swinburne on omnipotence', *International Journal for Philosophy of Religion*, 6, pp. 251–5.

LaCroix, Richard (1977), 'Augustine on the simplicity of God', *The New Scholasticism*, 51, 4, pp. 453–68.

LaCroix, Richard (1984), 'Descartes on God's ability to do the logically impossible', *Canadian Journal of Philosophy*, 14, pp. 455–75; reprinted in LaCroix (1993), *What Is God?* Buffalo, NY: Prometheus Books, pp. 152–73.

Leftow, Brian (1990), 'Is God an abstract object?', *Nous*, 24, 4, pp. 581–98.

Leftow, Brian (1991), *Time and Eternity*, Ithaca, NY: Cornell University Press.

Lewis, Delmas (1986), 'Persons, morality and tenselessness', *Philosophy and Phenomenological Research*, 47, pp. 305–9.

Lewis, Delmas (1988), 'Eternity, time and tenselessness', *Faith and Philosophy*, 5, pp. 72–86.

Lucas, J. R. (1989), *The Future: An Essay on God, Temporality and Truth*, Oxford: Basil Blackwell.

MacDonald, Scott (ed.) (1991), *Being and Goodness*, Ithaca, NY: Cornell University Press.

McInerny, Ralph (1968), *Studies in Analogy*, The Hague: Martinus Nijhoff.

Mackie, J. L. (1955), 'Evil and omnipotence', *Mind*, 64, pp. 200–12.

McTaggert, J. M. E. (1908), 'The unreality of time', *Mind*, 17, pp. 454–74; revised in *The Nature of Existence*, vol. 2 (Cambridge: Cambridge University Press, 1927), ch. 33; reprinted in Richard Gale (ed.)(1993), *The Philosophy of Time*, Garden City: Anchor Books, pp. 86–97.

Mann, William (1982), 'Divine simplicity', *Religious Studies*, 18, pp. 451–71.

Mann, William (1983), 'Simplicity and immutability in God', *International Philosophical Quarterly*, 23, pp. 267–76.

Mann, William (1986), 'Simplicity and properties: A reply to Morris's "On God and Mann: A view of divine simplicity"', *Religious Studies*, 22, pp. 343–53.

Mann, William (1989), 'Modality, morality, and God', *Nous*, 23, pp. 83–9.

Miller, Barry (1996), *A Most Unlikely God*, Notre Dame, IN: University of Notre Dame Press.

Morris, Thomas V. (1984), 'Duty and divine goodness', *American Philosophical Quarterly*, 21, pp. 261–8; reprinted in *Anselmian Explorations*, Notre Dame, IN: University of Notre Dame Press, 1987, pp. 26–41.

Morris, Thomas V. (1984), 'Properties, modalities, and God', *The Philosophical Review*, 93, pp. 35–55.

Morris, Thomas V. (1985), 'On God and Mann: A view of divine simplicity', *Religious Studies*, 21, pp. 299–318.

Morris, Thomas V. (1987), 'Perfect being theology', *Nous*, 21, March, pp. 19–30.

Morris, Thomas V. (1991), *Our Idea of God*, Notre Dame, IN: University of Notre Dame Press.

Morris, Thomas V. (ed.)(1987), *The Concept of God*, Oxford: Oxford University Press.

Morris, Thomas V. (ed.)(1988), *Divine and Human Action*, Ithaca, NY: Cornell University Press, pp. 74–118.

Nielsen, Kai (1989), *God, Scepticism and Modernity*, Ottawa: University of Ottawa Press.

O'Connor, David (1998), *God and Inscrutable Evil*, Lanham, MD: Rowman and Littlefield.

Oakes, Robert (1996), 'God and cosmos: Can the "mystery of mysteries" be solved?', *American Philosophical Quarterly*, 33, pp. 315–23.

Ockham, William (1969), *Treatise on Predestination and on the Foreknowledge of God and of Future Contingents*, in Marilyn McCord Adams and Norman Kretzmann (trans and eds), *Predestination, God's Foreknowledge, and Future Contingents*, New York: Meredith Corporation, pp. 34–79.

Oppy, Graham (1995), *Ontological Arguments and Belief in God*, Cambridge: Cambridge University Press.

Padgett, Alan (1993), 'Eternity and the special theory of relativity', *International Philosophical Quarterly*, 33, pp. 219–23.

Pike, Nelson (1965), 'Divine omniscience and voluntary action', *The Philosophical Review*, 74, pp. 27–46.

Pike, Nelson (1970), *God and Timelessness*, New York: Schocken.

Plantinga, Alvin (1967), *God and Other Minds*, Ithaca, NY: Cornell University Press.

Plantinga, Alvin (1974), *The Nature of Necessity*, Oxford: Clarendon Press.

Plantinga, Alvin (1980), *Does God Have a Nature?*, Milwaukee: Marquette University Press.

Plantinga, Alvin (1992), 'Epistemic probability and evil', in Kelly James Clark (ed.), *Our Knowledge of God*, Dordrecht: Kluwer Academic Publishers, pp. 39–63.

Prior, A. N. (1962), 'The formalities of omniscience', *Philosophy*, 37, pp. 114–29; reprinted in Prior (1968), *Papers on Time and Tense*, Oxford: Clarendon Press.

Quinn, Philip (1979), 'Divine conservation and Spinozistic pantheism', *Religious Studies*, 15, pp. 289–302.

Quinn, Philip (1986), 'Moral obligation, religious demand, and practical conflict', in Quinn, *Rationality, Religious Belief, and Moral Commitment*, Ithaca, NY: Cornell University Press, pp. 195–212.

Quinn, Philip (1992), 'The primacy of God's will in Christian ethics', in Tomberlin, *Philosophical Perspectives* 6, pp. 493–513.

Reichenbach, Bruce R. (1982), *Evil and a Good God*, New York: Fordham University Press.

Robinson, Michael D. (1995), *Eternity and Freedom*, Lanham: University Press of America.

Rogers, Katherin A. (1993), 'Anselm on praising a necessarily perfect being', *International Journal for Philosophy of Religion*, 34, pp. 41–52; reprinted in Rogers, *Anselmian Approach to God and Creation*, pp. 61–75.

Rogers, Katherin A. (1993), 'The medieval approach to aardvarks, escalators and God', *Journal of Value Inquiry*, 27, pp. 63–8.

Rogers, Katherin A. (1994), 'Eternity has no duration', *Religious Studies*, 30, pp. 1–16.

Rogers, Katherin A. (1996), 'Omniscience, eternity, and freedom', *International Philosophical Quarterly*, 36, pp. 399–412.

Rogers, Katherin A. (1996), 'St. Augustine on time and eternity', *American Catholic Philosophical Quarterly*, 70, pp. 207–23.

Rogers, Katherin A. (1996), 'The traditional doctrine of divine simplicity', *Religious Studies*, 32, pp. 165–86; reprinted in Rogers, *Anselmian Approach to God and Creation*, ch. 2.

Rogers, Katherin A. (1997), 'Anselm's Indeterminism', in Rogers, *Anselmian Approach to God and Creation*, pp. 91–101.

Rogers, Katherin A. (1997), *The Anselmian Approach to God and Creation*, Lewiston, NY: The Edwin Mellen Press.

Rogers, Katherin A. (1997), 'Eriugena and Anselm on God's causal omniscience', in Rogers, *Anselmian Approach to God and Creation*, pp. 121–9.

Rogers, Katherin A. (1997), 'How a perfect being creates: Anselm's theistic idealism', in Rogers, *Anselmian Approach to God and Creation*, pp. 223–61.

Rogers, Katherin A. (1997), 'The irrelevance of original sin in Augustine's doctrine of the will', in Rogers, *Anselmian Approach to God and Creation*, pp. 85–9.

Rogers, Katherin A. (1997), 'Middle knowledge versus knowledge of vision', in Rogers, *Anselmian Approach to God and Creation*, pp. 175–97.

Rogers, Katherin A. (1997), *The Neoplatonic Metaphysics and Epistemology of Anselm of Canterbury*, Lewiston, NY: The Edwin Mellen Press.

Ross, James (1961), 'Analogy as a rule of meaning for religious language', *International Philosophical Quarterly*, 1, pp. 468–502.

Ross, James (1969), *Philosophical Theology*, New York: The Bobbs–Merrill Company.

Ross, James (1981), *Portraying Analogy*, Cambridge: Cambridge University Press.

Rowe, William (1979), 'The problem of evil and some varieties of atheism', *American Philosophical Quarterly*, 16, pp. 335–41.

Rowe, William (1993), 'The problem of divine perfection and freedom', in Stump, *Reasoned Faith*, pp. 223–33.

Russell, Bruce (1989), 'The persistent problem of evil', *Faith and Philosophy*, 6, pp. 121–39.

Schilling, S. Paul (1977), *God and Human Anguish*, Nashville: Abingdon.

Schlesinger, George N. (1985), 'Divine perfection', *Religious Studies*, 21, 2, pp. 144–58.

Schlesinger, George N. (1988), *New Perspectives on Old-Time Religion*, Oxford: Clarendon Press.

Schrader, David (1991), 'The antinomy of divine necessity', *International Journal for Philosophy of Religion*, 30, pp. 45–59.

Seddon, George (1972), 'Logical possibility', *Mind*, 81, pp. 481–94.

Smith, Quentin (1991), 'An atheological argument from evil natural laws', *International Journal for Philosophy of Religion*, 29, pp. 159–74.

Stump, Eleonore (1985), 'The problem of evil', *Faith and Philosophy*, 2, pp. 392–423.

Stump, Eleonore (1990), 'Providence and evil', in Thomas Flint (ed.), *Christian Philosophy*, Notre Dame, IN: University of Notre Dame Press, pp. 51–91.

Stump, Eleonore (1992), 'God's obligations', in Tomberlin, *Philosophical Perspectives 6*, pp. 475–91.

Stump, Eleonore (1993), 'Aquinas on the sufferings of Job', in Stump, *Reasoned Faith*, pp. 328–57.

Stump, Eleonore (ed.)(1993), *Reasoned Faith*, Ithaca, NY: Cornell University Press.

Stump, Eleonore and Norman Kretzmann (1981), 'Eternity', *The Journal of Philosophy*, 78, pp. 429–58.

Stump, Eleonore and Norman Kretzmann (1985), 'Absolute simplicity', *Faith and Philosophy*, 2, pp. 353–82.

Stump, Eleonore and Norman Kretzmann (1987), 'Atemporal duration: A reply to Fitzgerald', *The Journal of Philosophy*, 84, pp. 214–19.

Stump, Eleonore and Norman Kretzmann (1991), 'Prophecy, past truth, and eternity', in Tomberlin, *Philosophical Perspectives 5*, pp. 395–424.

Sweeney, Leo (1992), *Divine Infinity in Greek and Medieval Thought*, New York: Peter Lang.

Swinburne, Richard (1973), 'Omnipotence', *American Philosophical Quarterly*, 10, pp. 231–7.

Swinburne, Richard (1977), *The Coherence of Theism*, Oxford: Clarendon Press.

Swinburne, Richard (1979), 'Duty and the will of God', in Janine Marie Idziak (ed.), *Divine Command Morality: Historical and Contemporary Readings*, New York: The Edwin Mellen Press, pp. 287–304.

Swinburne, Richard (1993), *The Coherence of Theism*, rev. edn, Oxford: Clarendon Press.

Swinburne, Richard (1996), *Is There a God?*, Oxford: Oxford University Press.

Swinburne, Richard (1998), *Providence and the Problem of Evil*, Oxford: Clarendon Press.

Tomberlin, James E. (ed.)(1991), *Philosophical Perspectives 5, Philosophy of Religion 1991*, Atascadero, CA: Ridgeview Publishing.

Tomberlin, James E. (ed.)(1992), *Philosophical Perspectives 6, Ethics 1992*, Atascadero, CA: Ridgeview Publishing Company.

Tomberlin, James E. and Peter van Inwagen (eds)(1985), *Alvin Plantinga*, Dordrecht: D. Reidel.

Vallicella, William (1992), 'Divine simplicity: A new defense', *Faith and Philosophy*, 9, pp. 508–25.

Vallicella, William (1996), 'Concurrentism or occasionalism?', *American Catholic Philosophical Quarterly*, 70, pp. 339–59.

van Inwagen, Peter (1988), 'The magnitude, duration, and distribution of evil', *Philosophical Topics*, 16, pp. 161–87; reprinted in van Inwagen (1995), *God, Knowledge, and Mystery*, Ithaca, NY: Cornell University Press, pp. 96–122.

van Inwagen, Peter (1991), 'The problem of Evil, the problem of air, and the problem of silence', in Tomberlin, *Philosophical Perspectives 5*, pp. 135–65; reprinted in van Inwagen, *God, Knowledge and Mystery*, pp. 66–95.

van Inwagen, Peter (1993), 'Genesis and evolution', in Stump, *Reasoned Faith*, pp. 93–127.

Walls, Jerry (1992), *Hell: The Logic of Damnation*, Notre Dame, IN: University of Notre Dame Press.

Warner, Martin (ed.)(1992), *Religion and Philosophy*, Supplement to *Philosophy*, 31, Cambridge: Cambridge University Press.

Westberg, Daniel (1996), 'Emotion and God: A reply to Marcel Sarot', *The Thomist*, 60, pp. 109–21.

Wierenga, Edward (1989), *The Nature of God*, Ithaca, NY: Cornell University Press.

Wippel, John F. (1987), 'Thomas Aquinas and participation', in Wippel (ed.), *Studies in Medieval Philosophy*, Washington, D.C.: Catholic University of America Press, pp. 117–58.

Wippel, John F. (1992), 'Thomas Aquinas on what philosophers can know about God', *American Catholic Philosophical Quarterly*, 66, pp. 279–98.

Wolterstorff, Nicholas (1975), 'God everlasting', in C. Orlebeke and D. L. Smedes (eds), *God and the Good: Essays in Honor of Henry Stob*, Grand Rapids, MI: Eerdmans, reprinted in Steven Cahn and David Shatz (eds)(1982), *Contemporary Philosophy of Religion*, New York: Oxford University Press, pp. 77–98.

Wolterstorff, Nicholas (1991), 'Divine simplicity', in Tomberlin, *Philosophical Perspectives 5*, pp. 531–52.

Wykstra, Stephen (1984), 'The Humean obstacle to evidential arguments from suffering: On avoiding the evils of "appearance"', *International Journal for Philosophy of Religion*, 16, pp. 73–93.

Zagzebski, Linda (1991), *The Dilemma of Freedom and Foreknowledge*, New York: Oxford University Press.

Index